STUDIES IN ENGLISH LITERATURES

Edited by Koray Melikoğlu

Naghmeh Varghaiyan

THE RHETORIC OF WOMEN'S HUMOUR IN BARBARA PYM'S FICTION

With a Preface by Orna Raz

For my daughters, Nihal and Nilay, who made me laugh and thus helped me to survive. May the free-spirited women who struggle to survive find similar humour.

Naghmeh Varghaiyan

THE RHETORIC OF WOMEN'S HUMOUR IN BARBARA PYM'S FICTION

With a Preface by Orna Raz

Bibliografische Information der Deutschen Nationalbibliothek
Die Deutsche Nationalbibliothek verzeichnet diese Publikation in der Deutschen Nationalbibliografie; detaillierte bibliografische Daten sind im Internet über http://dnb.d-nb.de abrufbar.

Bibliographic information published by the Deutsche Nationalbibliothek
Die Deutsche Nationalbibliothek lists this publication in the Deutsche Nationalbibliografie; detailed bibliographic data are available in the Internet at http://dnb.d-nb.de.

Cover image: *Portrait of a Woman in a Black Tie* by Amedeo Modigliani.
                          Source: WikiArt. Public Domain.

ISBN-13: 978-3-8382-1503-7
© *ibidem*-Verlag, Stuttgart 2021
Alle Rechte vorbehalten

Das Werk einschließlich aller seiner Teile ist urheberrechtlich geschützt. Jede Verwertung außerhalb der engen Grenzen des Urheberrechtsgesetzes ist ohne Zustimmung des Verlages unzulässig und strafbar. Dies gilt insbesondere für Vervielfältigungen, Übersetzungen, Mikroverfilmungen und elektronische Speicherformen sowie die Einspeicherung und Verarbeitung in elektronischen Systemen.

All rights reserved. No part of this publication may be reproduced, stored in or introduced into a retrieval system, or transmitted, in any form, or by any means (electronical, mechanical, photocopying, recording or otherwise) without the prior written permission of the publisher. Any person who does any unauthorized act in relation to this publication may be liable to criminal prosecution and civil claims for damages.

Printed in the EU

Contents

Acknowledgements	v
Abbreviations	vi
Preface by Orna Raz	vii
Introduction	1
1 Characteristics of Women's Humour	13
1.1 Myth of Women's Lack of a Sense of Humour	13
1.2 Undermining Women's Wit	14
1.3 Women's Language and *écriture féminine*	17
1.4 Difference between Irony and Humour	30
1.5 Necessity of a Humour of One's Own	34
1.6 Humour: A Female Device?	36
1.7 Misreading Women's Humour and Images of Women	38
1.8 Lack of Ending in the Works of Women Writers	40
1.9 Differences between Conventional Humour and Women's Humour	42
1.10 Women's Humour and Socio-Cultural Restraints	47
1.11 Ideology of Domesticity and Domestic Comedy	49
1.12 Characteristics of Women's Humour	52
1.13 Major Areas and Tactics of Female Humour	57
1.14 Self-Irony	59
1.15 Women Writers' Humour in the Nineteenth Century	60
1.16 Humour as a Device of Sympathy	61
1.17 Female Humour and Narrative Structure	65
1.18 Rhetoric of Humour in Pym's Novels	66
2 *Some Tame Gazelle*: Construction of Women's Veiled Humour	69
2.1 Role of Rhetorical Strategies in the Construction of Women's Humour in *STG*	70
2.1.1 Subversion of the Romantic Plot and the Discourse of Trivia	71
2.1.2 Belinda's Double Text Discourse	90
2.1.3 Function of Gossip in the Construction of Humorous Narrative	100
2.1.4 Understatement and Self-Deprecation	103

    2.1.5 Sympathetic Bond between Narrator and
          Heroine and among Characters   111
  2.2 Function of Themes and Motifs in the Construction of
      Humorous Plot   117
    2.2.1 Subversion of Female Stereotypes   117
    2.2.2 Subversion of Male Images   127
  2.3 Women's Humour as Social Critique: Undermining
      the Institution of Church and Clergymen   134
3 *Excellent Women*: Humour of Mildred Regarded
  as an Excellent Woman   141
  3.1 Rhetorical Strategies in the Construction of Women's
      Humour   142
    3.1.1 Understatement and Self-deprecation   143
    3.1.2 Mildred's Double-Voiced Discourse   152
  3.2 Themes and Motifs in the Construction of Humorous
      Plot   161
    3.2.1 Subversion of the Stereotype of Excellent Woman   161
    3.2.2 Subversion of Male Images   176
4 *Jane and Prudence*: Unconventional Wife and Satisfied
  Spinster   181
  4.1 Jane's Subversion of the Image of Conventional
      Clergyman's Wife   182
    4.1.1 Jane's Creation of a Fantastic World   182
    4.1.2 Jane's Reversal of the Serving Female   192
    4.1.3 Jane's and Prudence's Use of Double-Voiced
          Discourse   194
  4.2 Subversion of the Image of the Spinster and Prudence's
      Creation of a Romantic World   195
  4.3 Subversion of the Male Image by Exposure of Men's
      Indolence and Self-Indulgence   202
Conclusion   209
Works Cited   215

Acknowledgements

I began this study seven years ago in an environment in which neither women nor women's humour were considered important by official culture. Nobody knew Barbara Pym or was concerned with women's writing and humour. I began reading Pym's *Some Tame Gazelle* for the funny reason that I liked her name. What stuck in my memory was Pym's unique and specific humour. I decided to write my PhD dissertation on women's humour in her novels. The path was thorny and long since there was no study on women's humour at that time. However, I was lucky enough to have the support of my dear parents and friends, including my thesis advisor Assoc. Prof. Dr. Mustafa Zeki Çıraklı. I appreciate his help. I am also deeply thankful to Barbara Pym scholar Dr. Orna Raz for her invaluable encouragement, help and friendship.

Years later, with the encouragement of my husband, I decided to rework my dissertation into a book. Orna Raz kindly accepted to write the preface. I am also grateful to Rose Little and Deirdre Bryan-Brown for providing me with Barbara Pym's books from England. I thank Susan Mednick Bramson for sharing her views on Barbara Pym. The greatest thanks of all go to Assoc. Prof. Dr. Kerem Nayebpour, my husband, for his valuable comments, constant support, and kindness. He helped me to pursue my dream of a PhD and did all he could to provide a peaceful environment, so that I could study and write my dissertation. He also contributed much to the revision of the manuscript. This book could not be published without his contribution and support. I also appreciate and thank our dear friend, a painter himself, Buyuk Budagi, for his excellent suggestion for the front cover of this book.

May the world one day acknowledge the importance of women's literature and humour.

Abbreviations

EW   *Excellent Women*
JP   *Jane and Prudence*
STG *Some Tame Gazelle*

Preface by Orna Raz

Ever since the 1950s, when her books first emerged on the literary scene, Barbara Pym has been roundly praised for her brilliant sense of humor. Her original audience appreciated her satirically incisive depictions of everyday life and her many slyly topical references, and contemporary readers continue to enjoy her sparkling wit and gently ironic social critique. Pym's humor has also been the subject of much praise by other writers: Alexander McCall Smith has maintained that *"Excellent Women* is one of the 20th century's most endearing and amusing novels," while Jilly Cooper discloses that "even an umpteenth reading [of *Jane and Prudence*] this weekend was punctuated by gasps of joy, laughter and wonder that this lovely book should remain so fresh, funny and true to life."

While Pym's wit is generally acknowledged, very little specific research has been conducted about her employment of comic elements as a device. We might surmise that Pym's humor has often been considered a merely decorative aspect of her novels, rather than an integral aspect of her craft, one that shaped her characterizations and plots, and formed an integral part of her protagonists' engagements with – and the coping devices for navigating – the world depicted in her novels.

It is thus a particular pleasure to introduce a new book which constitutes a significant contribution to Pym scholarship, one that centers on the subject of humor in her novels. Naghmeh Varghaiyan's *The Rhetoric of Women's Humour in Barbara Pym's Fiction* is an important and insightful study of three early novels of Barbara Pym: *Some Tame Gazelle* (1950), *Excellent Women* (1952) and *Jane and Prudence* (1953). As Varghaiyan shows, Sevda Caliskan's claim that traditionally "women and humor [have been regarded as] quite incompatible categories" (49) remains unfortunately relevant to this day. By focusing her investigation on Pym, Varghaiyan makes a convincing case for a specifically female sense of humor, countering the centuries-long tradition of mistakenly regarding such "writings related to comedy and humor […] as serious works since they differed from the established conventions of comic writings."

Following a comprehensive opening survey of attitudes towards the humorous works produced by female writers, Varghaiyan devotes the rest of her book to Pym's early novels, of which at least two – *Excellent Women* and *Jane and Prudence* – are set in the post war era (the dating of the events in *Some Tame Gazelle*, which Pym began writing in the 1930s and revised after the second World War, is unclear). While Pym's female characters are not overtly rebellious, they grow discontent with the patriarchal reality of their day, and their wry and often comic observations come to represent a mode of coping with the world. As Varghaiyan astutely notes, a good sense of humor can be both a matter of personal survival as well as a weapon. But although Pym's female characters turn to humor to cope with various distressing realities of their day – indignities ranging from the mundane (a shared bathroom in *Excellent Women*) to the existential (the loneliness of a young unmarried woman in *Jane and Prudence*) – they are never cruel, and their humor is not used to humiliate or belittle fellow human beings. In that regard, Varghaiyan argues, female humor in Pym's work is different from conventional humor: it allows her heroines to undermine the authoritative power of the dominant male culture around them.

Writing this preface in the summer of 2020 amid the global COVID-19 pandemic affords a fresh and unexpected perspective from which to view Pym's novels of the 1950s. Rereading *Excellent Women*, I feel like I better understand the crucial importance of comic moments in ameliorating the various hardships the characters encounter as they navigate their new postwar reality. On social media, members of the "Barbara Pym Fan Club" on Facebook report that her novels are a constant source of consolation. Just the other day, one member shared how rereading *Some Tame Gazelle* helped her get over her grumpiness about having to postpone her vacation this year, and another reader wrote that he kept returning to her books because they were "wickedly funny."[1]

During a recent spate of correspondence with Varghaiyan, in which we checked in on each other during the pandemic, we found ourselves chatting, as usual, about Pym, the reason why we first became friends several years ago. The humorist and academic Regina Barreca claims that humor (or comedy) is the least universal textual territory. But perhaps the case of my friendship with Varghaiyan proves that Pym's humor transcends "age, race, ethnic background, and class." After all, Varghaiyan and I are probably as distant a readership as Pym could have ever imagined: two women

---

[1] <https://www.facebook.com/groups/5250054113/?epa=SEARCH_BOX>

living in the Middle East: a Muslim and a Jew bound in friendship through our mutual admiration for her novels, with their humorous depictions of wry spinsters and bumbling curates; jumble sales and the ritual and hierarchy of tea pouring. If a stronger argument exists for the importance of appreciating female humor, I am eager to hear it.

Introduction

This book explores the basic characteristics and functions of women's humour in British novelist Barbara Pym's *Some Tame Gazelle* (*STG*), *Excellent Women* (*EW*) and *Jane and Prudence* (*JP*). The heroines featured in these novels manage to survive in a patriarchal culture through their personalities and humour. Guided by Pym's structural and thematic strategies, their subversive humour undermines the authoritative power of the dominating culture. Although this study focuses on subjects, themes, and topics that are relevant to women, Pym did not have an openly feminist agenda. But since, as Michael Cotsell points out, "any study of Pym must keep in mind that its subject is a woman author, exploring one phase of women's experience" (7), feminist concerns have to be considered in an analysis of her work.

Although theories of humour have undergone fundamental changes, they have mostly remained under the influence of the standards set by the dominant patriarchal perspectives. Accordingly, the classical theory of humour has failed to provide an adequate set of terminology, or effective technical tools with which to analyse the specific sense of humour of female writers.

This study is based on terminologies offered by forerunners of the theory of women's writing such as Eileen Gillooly, Regina Barreca, and Nancy Walker. Dismissing conventional theories of humour in female writing, this study aims to offer an alternative approach to such humour as instantiated by Pym's novels.

Barreca highlights the inadequacy of conventional theories of humour in relation to female comical writing. According to her study, comedy has been traditionally defined in these ways: as a "celebration of fertility and regeneration," as "the vulgar and exaggerated presentation of the familiar," as "catharsis of desire and frustration," as a "social safety valve," as a "carnival," as an "unconscious, psychological reaction to personal and social instabilities," and as a "happy ending, joyous celebration, and reestablishment of order" (introduction 8). Such definitions, as Barreca understands, do not exemplify women's comic writing, which primarily "has to do with power and its systematic misappropriation." In spite of its undermining power, traditional humour substantiates the dominant cultural values, mostly patriarchal. Judith Curlee also emphasises this point, stating that traditional and conventional comic discourse supports the patriarchal order since it "generally maintains the status quo in society by failing to problematize the kinds of inequity that it often reveals" (35). Thus, the traditional comic discourse has covertly and invariably been in the service of the dominating patriarchal culture.

According to Barreca, numerous events and details in life determine, and have an impact on, "the way we create and respond to" (*Untamed* 12) the humorous and humour. Thus, the theoretical discussions on humour and comedy, as one of the artistic mediums of humour, had long existed before the commencement of any structural analysis in literary studies. In the canonised sense of the term, humour can be described as something which causes one to smile and/or to laugh. This concept has been a relatively recent phenomenon, although the concept of comedy has always existed in literary texts.[2] "*Comedy,*" according to Alleen and Don Nilsen, "is a term that literary scholars 'owned' long before the popular culture gave it today's more generalized meaning of something that brings smiles and laughter" (246). The definition of the term 'comedy,' however, has undergone enormous changes throughout time. For instance, as Alleen and Don Nilsen point out, in medieval times it "was applied to literary works that were not necessarily created for the purpose of arousing laughter, however, it had happier endings and less exalted styles than tragedies." In the Middle Ages it was categorised into different parts such as "*High Comedy* (what we now refer to as *smart comedy* or *literary comedy*) relied for its humour on wit and sophistication, while *low comedy* relied on burlesque, crude jokes, and buffoonery" (246). As Barreca highlights, the lack of a universal

---

[2] Theorists of humour have defined three types of humour on the basis of superiority theories, repression/release theories, and incongruity theories. Superiority theory suggests that laughter is rooted in the glorification of the self, mostly at the expense of others. Thomas Hobbes argued that we laugh at others' limitations because it makes us feel superior. "Sigmund Freud believed that aggressive and sexual drives, necessary for survival, are repressed in their socially unacceptable form by the ego. "Humor thus provides a socially acceptable and pleasurable form of release of this repressed psychic energy" (Naranjo-Huebl 12). Incongruity theories focus on similarity and dissimilarity and how, in the presence of certain other factors such as surprise or suddenness and a perception of harmlessness, they elicit laughter. "Humor occurs, according to most incongruity theorists, when two distinct logic patterns or models of thought unexpectedly collide" (12).

definition for comedy is due to the fact that "out of all the textual territories explored," it is "the least universal" (12). The reason is that comedy appears to be fundamentally subjective in nature so that its production as well as its reception is contextually gender-based since "age, race, ethnic background, and class are all significant factors in the production and reception of humor" (Barreca 12).

Theorists and humourists throughout history, however, have only paid attention to men's humour. This intellectual subordination of women was mostly due to the fact that, as Virginia Woolf states in *A Room of One's Own* "nothing could be expected of women intellectually" (55) since numerous intellectuals believed in "the mental, moral and physical inferiority of women" (31). Likewise, as Regina Gagnier suggests, despite the fact that some recent works address the effects of gender on humour, "historically theorists of humour have been men, and they have seldom considered the role of gender in humor" (136). Barreca also asserts that male theorists such as Freud and others before him misinterpreted the specificity of women's humor as humourlessness: "What early theorists like Freud failed to understand is that women do not lack a sense of humour; they just find different things funny" (qtd. in Bennett 37).

There has been a long-standing claim against feminists' lack of a sense of humour. As Barreca argues, the belief that women lack a sense of humour is specific to men only, since "women typically have hidden this trait from men in order to appear traditionally 'feminine.'" Accordingly, she emphasises that "it is no secret to women that women have a sense of humor" (*Snow White* 103). Thus, a theory of women's humour is indeed necessary to analyse the true nature of the humour in the works of female writers and to prevent misinterpretations of such texts. As Gail Finney sums up, in addition to Judy Little's work, the works of Walker, Barreca, Gillooly, Sochen, and Zita Dresner have "effectively exploded the myth that women have no sense of humour" (1).

The comedy present in Pym's work holds a special place in literature and can be classified as high comedy.[3] Mason Cooley names "realism and comedy" amongst the most significant ingredients of her fiction ("Barbara"

---

[3] Lord David Cecil praises Pym's novels as "the finest examples of high comedy to have appeared in England during the past seventy-five years" (qtd. in Long 221).

384). Her specific type of comedy is mostly marked by indirectness and subtlety. While mainly rendering the lives and traditions of middle-class ordinary people, Pym depicts them and the human condition as "shot through with the antic spirit of comedy" (Cooley "Barbara" 384). By experience, Pym was entirely familiar with the conventions and traditions of the middle classes. Her awareness of the nature of middle-class culture and mentality significantly contributed to her detailed descriptions of middle-class life and people. Moreover, the Pyms were closely associated with the church and the vicarage, or "the vicar and curates" (Long 3).[4]

Pym's novels *STG, EW*, and *JP* were published in 1950, 1952 and 1953, respectively, by Jonathan Cape. Following the publication of her sixth novel *No Fond Return of Love,* a prolonged period of negative critical responses to Pym's novels began with the publication of her novel *An Unsuitable Attachment*. This period lasted for fourteen years. Despite suffering from depression and a lack of self-assurance, Pym continued writing several novels including an unpublished academic novel, and *The Sweet Dove Died*. Pym's unpublished works were only published after Lord David Cecil and Phillip Larkin in the *Times Literary Supplement* in 1977 "named her one of the nation's most underrated novelists" (Bentley et al. 286). Since then, various articles, books and dissertations have been written about her novels.[5]

Published in 1950, *STG* was Pym's first novel. Her first experience as a novelist was generally favoured by critics and the critical reviews were mostly approving. Some critics connect this novel with the English sense of humour and traditional comedy. Being narrated from an omniscient point of view, the novel, in Long's words, is "modestly voiced yet sharply

---

[4] Pym began studying English literature at Oxford in 1931 and graduated in 1934. During World War II, she worked as a censor in the Postal and Telegraph Censorship in Bristol. In 1943 she joined the Wrens (Women's Royal Naval Service). Later, she worked as an editorial assistant at the International Institute of African Languages and Culture in London where she continued to work until 1974.

[5] Pym enjoyed relative popularity afterwards. According to Long, she "reacted to this sudden fame unpretentiously, and her habits of living did not change" (23). Within some years, her health began to deteriorate and she became gravely ill by January 1980. Chemotherapy was unsuccessful and she died on January 11, 1980, and was buried in Finstock.

focused" (14). *STG* is mostly considered as one of the most humorous novels of Pym. According to Long, it comprises Pym's "characteristic ironies, ambivalences, and sense of the ridiculous," displaying a humour coloured with "gentle malice" (Long 15). Her wit was considered to be subtle and indirect. Long argues that after *STG,* Pym began to "focus [on] her comic vision" (8). According to Cooley, the novel helped to establish Pym as a successful writer of comedy whose domain extends from "farce to the rarefied mental acrobatics of high comedy" ("Barbara" 367). Pym's thoughtful employment of wit, as well as the attentive application of comic tactics and strategies contributes to the reversal and parodying of "literary convention" ("Barbara" 367). Critics generally agree that this novel subverts the romantic plot. Cooley, who studied Pym's comic vision, suggests that this novel "both celebrates and mocks romantic comedy" ("Barbara" 367). Reversing conventional literary structure and subject matter, Pym's subtle and gentle humour in *STG* undermines the long-held values of the prevailing patriarchal culture.

Critics also classify Pym's second novel *EW* (1952) as a comic work. Here Pym satirises the figure of spinster and the Church of England (Long 15). According to Long, the critical reviews of this novel were exceedingly favourable as they stressed the novel's brilliant comedy instead of its partial tone of "isolation and loneliness" (15). Cooley argues that Pym in this work effectively surmounts the hard task of accomplishing "comic effects" without breaking up the "realistic surface" ("Barbara" 367).

The first-person narration recounts the story of Mildred Lathbury, a country clergyman's daughter, who is living alone in a shabby apartment in London. Mildred "establishes the character type of the 'excellent woman,' who is at the center of most of Pym's fiction" (Cooley, "Barbara" 368). However, Marina Mackay suggests that although Pym appears to deride these excellent women, she is in fact "sympathetic" (161) towards them.

JP, Pym's third novel chosen for this study, is narrated by an omniscient narrator and is mainly about two friends, Jane and Prudence. The mood and setting of this novel, in Long's words, is "lighthearted yet extremely knowing, and the institution of marriage is examined from within and without." The novel subverts the romantic plot and is in stark contrast to the "quest for romantic love" (16). According to Cooley, it is "one of

Pym's most purely funny novels. It handles the theme of appearance and reality, convention and fact, in a light and playful way" ("Barbara" 372). Moreover, it "is more obviously 'literary' in its inspiration and more explicitly comic" (370). It covers unexampled subjects such as inefficient wives and clergymen, unemotional mothers and egoist male characters.

Pym wrote a number of novels after *JP*; some of these were published during her lifetime, others posthumously. The experience of working as an editor in an anthropology institute helped her in shaping the subject matter and the characters of *Less Than Angels*, published in 1955, which primarily deals with the lives of anthropologists.

According to Cooley, most of Pym's novels written during this era are "in an entirely modern world, postreligious and fragmented." Human relations are "noncommittal and in flux" ("Barbara" 372). Although *Less Than Angels* appears to be much gloomier than Pym's earlier novels, Long asserts that one reviewer's note on it – a "humorous treatment of the anthropologists" – reminds us of Austen's "extracting comedy from the dull or pompous'" (16).

Pym's next novel, *A Glass of Blessings* (1958), is extensively praised for its singular and mighty comedy. Cooley considers this novel as "the most elegant and gossamer of Barbara Pym's comedies" ("Barbara" 378). According to Long, Pym with her "faultlessly wry, deadpan humor that is typical of the understated quality of the work," created one of the most appreciated comic novels. *A Glass of Blessings* is generally praised by reviewers, in particular for its "brilliant characterisation" and its "sparkling feminine malice" (Long 17).

Comic vision and techniques are noticeable in Pym's subsequent novels as well. In her sixth novel, *No Fond Return of Love* (1961), Pym, applies "the most delicately comic scenes as well as broad comedy" (Long 17). The reviewers' critique of the novel was also favourable and pointed to Pym's sharp, tricky and devious wit (17). Pym's next novel, *An Unsuitable Attachment,* which was rejected numerous times, was finally published posthumously in 1982. Ackley here finds "serious flaws in unity, focus, and credibility." For instance, "there are too many characters given equal attention" (7). Pym's next posthumous novel, *The Sweet Dove Died*, published in 1987, deals with the subject of homosexuality. In Long's words, the novel became a "study in feminine wounding and isolation" (20). In *An Academic Question*, published in 1986, Pym practises a "different style" (Ackley 7). Although she failed, Pym tried to modernise her work. According to Ackley, the novel has "a few purely Pym characters and scenes" (8).

Quartet in Autumn (1977) is Pym's only Booker Prize finalist novel. It differs considerably from her other works and can be described as a "study in urban isolation" (Long 21). It is much bleaker than her earlier novels and an extreme instance of "dark irony" (Cooley, "Barbara" 380). It is generally considered as a turning point, after which "Pym turned away from comedy to write tragedy or at least a very dark and sad realism" (380). However, as Pym stated in an interview in the BBC program *Finding a Voice*, it appears that her purpose in writing this novel was to present the novel not as tragic, but "as fundamentally comic" (Cooley, "Barbara" 380). Thus, traces of Pym's wry style of humour are evident even in this seemingly bleak novel. Humour is a basic narrative element in Pym's next two novels. *A Few Green Leaves* (1980) can be regarded as a typical Pym novel containing "small or ordinary lives, love of eccentricity, and attraction to vicars and spinsters" (Long 23). *Crampton Hodnet* (1985) can also be considered amongst Pym's most humorous works. As Cooley states, by presenting "British respectability," an indication of a secure and unchanging society, Pym both "burlesques and glorifies" the small group of common people who engage in daily activities of "love affairs and gossip" free from evils such as "war, disease, ageing, poverty, and more imperious passions" ("Barbara" 364). All in all, humour is a continuing aspect of Pym's entire canon.

Women have been considered as being humourless over centuries, and their comedic and humorous writings have been ignored or misunderstood as serious works since they differed from the established conventions of comic literature. However, a more recent view of women's writing proposes that, in Showalter's words: "Women writing are not [...] *inside* and *outside* of the male tradition; they are inside two traditions simultaneously" (202; emphasis original). Women's writing is a "double-voiced discourse" (204) containing the inscriptions of both the dominant male culture and the oppressed, muted female one. The two discourses are not segregated but interwoven and simultaneous. In addition to its relation to general culture and literature, women's literature treats matters relating to women's lives and experiences. In this respect, women's humour differs from mainstream humour.

The operation of the two-fold discourse is detectable in the novels treated here. While at the surface level it is the orthodox discourse which controls the narration, at the undercurrent level a resistant or an already oppressed but disrupting discourse lies at the centre of the textual orientation. This disruption is achieved mainly by humour in the selected narratives, in which the humorous voice largely operates as a strategy to *resist* and *survive* within the general culture. Therefore, it is arguable that Pym's narratives contribute to the construction of women's culture through a (re)description of conventionalised issues from the female perspective.

Pym's humorous style seems to spring from her character. Her sense of humour would attract everybody during her lifetime. One person who in particular recognised Pym's sense of humour was Robert Liddell. He appreciates Pym's "original and quaint sense of humour – which she freely employed against herself. [...] Like myself" (qtd. in Long 5). Pym's self-irony and her self-effacing humour primarily originated from her experiences in life and her temper. Her artistic vision involves creating a humorous situation out of tragic circumstances and distressing conditions. As Ackley rightly points out, "Pym implies that seeing the comic in things helps keep a balanced perspective on the sad and indefinite" (12). Pym was able to deal with "her characters and their experiences with humour and detachment" irrespective of "how serious her subject matter [was] – with illness, aging, decay, and death" (Ackley 3). In Pym's comedy, Long finds "a special and distinctive charm." At the same time, he thinks that Pym's comedy includes a certain kind of sorrow. For example, most of her characters seek satisfaction in relationships that, "elusively, are only just out of reach of realization" (24).

Pym's effective use of humour has been compared to Jane Austen's, although Pym was embarrassed by such a tribute given to her. Ackley holds that "Pym's style reminds one of Austen's command of the humorous scene and her detached observations" (12). Pym's central characters also portray her own "witty and wry sense of humour" (Ackley 21). Pym's genuine talent and her skill lie in detecting humour in relation to "just about every character and event" (Ackley 16). Her concern for the affairs of the "domestic life such as food and clothing" is coherent with her belief "in the importance of small details" (16). For instance, the descriptions of preparing food, eating, and drinking are represented as having a significant role in the construction of Pym's narratives. They also have a huge impact on the lives of the involved characters. Likewise, details of the characters' clothing are employed for a humorous narrative. "Pym," according to Cooley, "learned to combine humour with a delight in ordinary experience in order to rise up from the black depths to the saving surface of existence. She thus personified the very spirit of comedy by laughing away her sorrows" (*Comic* 6). Ackley finds Pym's manner of handling misfortunate and pitiful conditions are "gentle, subtle and understated, seldom acrylic" (20).

Spinsters are considered to be Pym's most mirthful and comic characters. However, avoiding stereotypes, she does not use her humour to humiliate. There are many reasons why Pym selected spinsters as her main characters. Having an undefined role in society, unmarried women are able to turn their hardships into humour since they are capable of creating satisfaction "despite unrequited love, solitude, and tedious work" (Cooley 4). Rather than denigrating her spinster characters, Pym uses her humour to sympathetically take a stand for victimised women in an oppressing patriarchal culture. The target of his kind of humour is the prevailing authoritarian system, not its victims. Pym's ridicule extends beyond the individual level; by deriding male characters, she also criticises the dominant culture which creates hypocritical, absurd individuals.

Despite recognition of the comic as "the shaping spirit" (Long 3) of Pym's work, Cooley's comprehensive study of her comedy and her comic vision, for instance, is limited to the textual analysis of ironical humour. Cooley does not establish a particular theoretical basis. As Wyatt-Brown proposes, it is time to "examine the unexpected subsoil from which Pym's comedy emerged" (xiii).

Pym's humour reflects the socio-cultural and historical circumstances of 1950s England. In her exploration of this relationship, Orna Raz holds that Pym "limits her criticism to what she knows and often likes best" (6). Raz's claim arises out of Pym's own statement: "I suppose I criticize and mock at the clergy and the C. of E. [the Church of England] because I am fond of them" (qtd. in Raz 7). Therefore, the relatively subdued quality of Pym's criticism is partially due to "the affection she has for her characters and her milieu" (7).

According to Anne M. Wyatt-Brown, there is a close connection between Pym's life and her fictional works. Conducting a biographical study, she argues that Pym's novels represent events of her own life: Pym "shared the perspective of marginal women, women of her generation, who, despite education and cultivation, felt they had no recognizable role left in the modern world," because "social changes had undermined [women's] inherited status" (2). Pym accompanies this estrangement with "comic good humour."

Cotsell argues that Pym's female point of view records and unveils seemingly insignificant matters in the lives of the characters. In agreement with other critics, Cotsell also contends that Pym considers humour to be an essential tactic in order to defy "disappointments" by means of maintaining "a humorous and hopeful engagement with life" (5).

Pym's novels are measured against the novel of manners. As Annette Weld states, the novel of manners is interwoven with comedy and its roots "lie deeply buried in the comic mode" (8). Pym's novels appear to be "creating a female, post-war perspective on a world where manners and social behavior are more often bypassed by popular writers in favor of the graphically violent or sexually explicit" (15). It should be noted that Pym's notion of manners deviates from the traditional nineteenth-century notion. While presenting so-called proper manners, respectability, suitability, and conventionality are criticised and ridiculed as merely the traditional set of rules and norms.

Pym's female characters mostly seek romance and love. Pym presents either the absence of love or failure in love in all its forms, transforming failure into comedy. In some way, she is able to *relieve* failure. Diana Benet attests to Pym's "development from the comic to the tragic and from a feminine to a universal vision" (3). Exploring the function of gender in Pym's novels, Janice Rossen argues that Pym "was a feminist writer in the 1950s before feminism became fashionable" (2). Laura L. Doan elaborates the role and function of the spinster in society and in Pym's fiction. She argues that by applying a "dual-voiced narrative" (152), Pym presents two opposing viewpoints in relation to the spinster: "the voice of the patriarchy and the voice challenging that authority" (152). Relying on her own experience as a spinster and by expressing the experiences of being treated in the margins of society, Pym is able to break down the stereotype usually , surrounding the spinster.

According to Ellen M. Tsagaris, Pym through the discourse of trivia effectively undermines the "discourse of the romance novel" (9), stressing the "trivial," as well as focusing on "the woman's point of view" (29). As an established expert on Woolf, Pym, and Brook-Rose, Judy Little argues that the voices existent in women's discourse are "appositional" and related to each other rather than being "oppositional" or subversive (2). In a similar vein, this book tries to show how Pym creates an appositional discourse and produces a significant discourse out of a seemingly insignificant one through what Little refers to as positioning "the discourse of the trivial" within "the ordinary and the everyday" (76).

Chapter 1, The History and Characteristics of Women's Humour, explores the reasons behind the myth of women's humourlessness and shows how the presuppositions and prejudgments of the dominant culture have affected women's manifestation of humour. The humour specific to women is discussed in its deviation from conventional humour. The chapter in the process explores different theories of women's humour.

Chapter 2 examines the function of humour in *STG*. The narrative voice in this novel mocks and criticises the hypocrisies and absurdities of respectable community. Belinda Bede's critique of her community, in a covert and oblique manner, subverts the power of religious authoritarian institutions such as the church and the clergy. The humorous tone and the trivial discourse in the narrative undermine the dominant male discourse. The narrative subverts both the conventional romantic plot and the so-called happy ending by eliminating the possible marriage of the two protagonists at the end of the novel.

Chapter 3 examines *EW*. The main focus is on the central character Mildred Lathbury's ironic and comic account of her community and society during post-war England. Being on the verge of spinsterhood, Mildred narrates humorously the conventions, conducts and manners of the people surrounding her. Her paradoxical status, as both an unrelated single woman and an active member of the community, allows her to identify the deficiencies and hypocrisies in the individuals connected to the power structure, such as men in critical positions and clergymen. In a similar way to *STG*, *EW* presents spinsters not as sacrificial and selfless women, but independent individuals capable of loving and being loved and who, in fact, detest being regarded as men's helpmates.

Chapter 4, which examines *JP*, focuses on the two protagonists', Jane's and Prudence's, lives in their search for false myths and stereotypes. The main sources of humour here are how Jane as the inefficient wife of a clergyman subverts the presuppositions about women as helpmates of the clergy and the mocking of Prudence's incessant seeking of romance.

This study contends that, unlike conventional humour, Pym's humour neither humiliates nor ridicules the female characters at its centre; on the contrary, it creates a sympathetic bond between the heroine and the reader, as well as between the female characters themselves through demonstrating their victimisation by patriarchal culture. Pym's humour hits hard on images and stereotypes such as the spinster and the Byronic hero by undermining the values and presuppositions associated with them. The female characters' understatement and self-deprecation are not meant to humiliate them; rather, the characters are empowered by positioning themselves in the place of the oppressors, thus preventing further oppression. Pym artfully employs the double-voiced discourse such that it neither threatens nor endangers the dominant order but helps initiate reforms within that order. Pym also reverses the romantic love plot through the discourse of trivia, and by creating the significant out of the insignificant, and making gossip function as a shaping force of the narrative.

1 Characteristics of Women's Humour

> Comedy is dangerous. Humor is a weapon. Laughter is refusal and triumph. (Barreca, *Untamed* 30)

This study examines women's humour as a subcategory of women's writing. This humour, therefore, requires a different quality of reading and a different type of knowledge than male humour. The view of women's humour[6] as an aberration from the male norm will be engaged.

The possibility of a distinct women's writing has always been a controversial subject among feminist critics. Elaine Showalter considers women's writing as an achievable end within the dominant trend. Similarly, Sandra Gilbert and Susan Gubar believe that women writers can inscribe their own character in the dominant language they write and speak. Eileen Gillooly, Nancy Walker, and Regina Barreca also argue that women's humour must be considered as a distinct type. Thus, major feminist critics acknowledge the existence of a distinct women's humour through which a woman writer can imprint her unique character, voice, and culture in the canon.

1.1 Myth of Women's Lack of a Sense of Humour

Literary theorists and critics have rarely associated women with humour. Their sense of humour has mostly been discredited, even negated. As one reason for this Walker suggests that comedy, considered to be "boisterous

---

[6] As Franzini (811-12) states, theorists also refer to this type as 'female humour' and 'feminine humour.' 'Women's humour,' however, is the term proposed by current scholarship. Gillooly, Walker, and Barreca use the terms 'female,' 'feminine,' and 'feminist' in connection with humour interchangeably. Gillooly mostly has 'feminine humor' while Walker prefers 'women's humour' and Barreca often uses 'feminist humor.' Gloria Kaufman, however, distinguishes between 'female' humour and 'feminist' humour. She sharply distinguishes female humour as a "humour of hopelessness" from feminist humour or "humour of hope" (qtd. in Franzini 811). Walker also suggests that female humour is more "self-deprecatory" and more disguised" than feminist humour. In addition, female humour "refers to humor about or by women without necessarily implying any affiliation with feminist philosophy. Such humor may ridicule a person or social system without implying any demands for change" (Franzini 811). Jay Gallvin defines feminist humour as a kind of "humor which reveals and ridicules the absurdity of gender stereotypes and gender based inequality" (qtd. in Franzini 812).

and aggressive," was "temperamentally unsuited to women": Women should remain "lady-like and angel-like" because aggression was "improper" to them (94). According to Gillooly, women writers, particularly those who wrote comedies, crossed the established gender borders and, therefore, regarded as "not only 'scandalous' scribblers but, given the *double entendre* of female publication (public woman = prostitute), suspiciously whorish as well" (*Smile* 4; emphasis original).

In order to highlight the limitation of women's humour, critics generally refer to women's roles in comedies. According to Walker, comedies do not represent women truly because they "are restricted to some stereotypes, being unlike women's real selves." She argues that "Female roles in comedy are limited and limiting, and are often misinterpreted as evidence of the limitations of female humour" (*Disobedient* 94).

Another formidable challenge that kept women from participating in comedic writings and performances was that sexual themes were considered necessary for comedy and comedic performances, but considered inappropriate for women. A woman who is an object in the sexual marketplace cannot participate in the joke-telling tradition or write in a comic mode; otherwise, as Barreca rightly points out, she might be regarded as "sexually promiscuous." This is because of the assumption "that it takes a certain 'fallen' knowledge to make a joke"; thus, "only old women – or women who are somehow outside the sexual marketplace – are permitted to make lewd remarks" (qtd. in Stott 94). They are thus entitled to participate in the joke-telling and comic-writing tradition. As a spinster, to whom these criteria apply, Pym used her entitlement, but in a patriarchal society it was neither easy nor a pleasant task for her. Consequently, her humour is subtle and indirect.

1.2 Undermining Women's Wit

Women's exclusion from writing, according to Walker, has had a considerable influence on their creation of a literature and humour of their own: "The exclusion of women from language and the authority it confers has become a common trope in women's writing itself" (*Disobedient* 2). Historically, women have often been forbidden from telling jokes. In explanation, the sociologist Paul McGhee states that "women are neither expected, nor trained, to joke in this culture. [...] it seems reasonable to propose that attempting a witty remark is often an intrusive, disturbing and aggressive act, and within this culture, probably unacceptable for a female" (qtd. in Barreca, introduction 5). McGhee finds a close connection between the controlling socio-cultural power and the successful use of humour: According to him, the initiation of humour has culturally become associated with males rather than with females because males hold the power (Bunkers 162).

Moreover, women's talent in writing has been ascribed to the potential power of the genre itself rather than to female authors (Walker, *Very* 94). Walker also holds that men's insufficient or distorted understanding of a woman's thoughts and desires stands in the way of their appreciation of female humour (*Very* 94). In order to be able to identify with women's humour, men must step down from the state of being originators of the law and standards and sympathise with marginalised female writers. A common example of misunderstanding is the misreading of

> women's protest against a male-dominated culture that is embedded in women's humor. To find such humor amusing requires that the reader assents to the political proposition it contains, and just as women find uncomfortable the negative images of themselves found in male literature, so men find it difficult to appreciate accusations that they occupy the role of oppressor. (Walker, *Very* 72)

Writings on ethics, conduct, and social etiquettes have exerted a profound effect on women's humorous styles, often silencing women's voices. Even though wit is typically considered a virtue, John Gregory, for example, warns women against exercising their wit:

> Wit is the most dangerous talent you can possess. It must be guarded with great discretion and good nature, otherwise it will create you many enemies. [...] Wit is perfectly consistent with softness and delicacy; yet they are seldom found united. Wit is so flattering to vanity, that they who possess it

become intoxicated, and lose all self-command. (Qtd. in Walker, *Disobedient* 93)

Some conduct books advised women how best to serve selflessly in the roles ascribed to them. A series of conduct books by Sarah Stikney Ellis, for instance, and similar publications, "gave specific, detailed directions on how to most selflessly serve in the domestic roles available to women" Gillooly, *Smile* 248). Ellis's advice is grounded "on her belief that female self interest lies in selflessness." If women carry out the labours related with their roles as "wife, mother, unmarried daughter most fully and self-lessly the women will best be appreciated and therefore be financially provided for" (qtd. in *Smile* 248).

Wit is considered the most significant factor in comic writing. Walker differentiates wit from sentimentality:

> If sentimentality in literature is a result of powerlessness, wit may be seen as its opposite: an expression of confidence and power. The word remains closely associated with its Old English origin in *wita*, "one who knows." Long before it acquired the connotation of amusement, wit was connected with knowledge, understanding, perception. Sentimentality exerts a passive, often subversive power; wit, on the other hand, is a direct and open expression of perceptions, taking for granted a position of strength and insight. ("Wit" 6)

Wit is a mental state as well as a strategy for writers to prevent their fall into the pit of sentimentality. While wit has mostly been considered an integral part of men's writings, it is seen as a dangerous weapon in women's hands. However, Pym's rational use of it makes the total body of her work unsentimental as well as witty. According to the conventional ideology of domesticity and the proper female, women are exclusively a source of comfort to their husbands. A witty woman, as conduct writer James Fordyce has it, is "a permanent nuisance for the comfort and ease of the husband since she always criticizes him" (qtd. in Bilger 22-23). Therefore,

Fordyce does not approve of women exercising wit as it goes along with criticism.

Audrey Bilger asserts that since "middle-class women had few outside forums in which to register their discontent with their place within the domestic sphere" (23), conduct books and their advice to refrain from criticising men can interpreted as upholding the whole patriarchal system rather than just the domestic domain. Similarly, Walker proposes that:

> by the mid-nineteenth century [...] the 'cult of domesticity' was so firmly entrenched that womanly wit had difficulty maneuvering around the image of ideal womanhood – an image that denigrated woman's intellect in favor of her emotional and intuitive nature. (*Very* 27)

1.3 Women's Language and *écriture féminine*

Critical theories have often emphasised the different functions of language in men's and women's speech acts. In the patriarchal tradition, women have often been secluded and marginalised from the unifying power of linguistic conventions. The foundation of women's language," according to Robin Lakoff, is her marginality from the "serious concerns of life" (48), which are the domain of men.

The expression of a woman's thoughts is restrained: "In appropriate women's speech, strong expression of feeling is avoided, expression of uncertainty is favored, and means of expression in regard to subject-matter deemed 'trivial' to the 'real' world are elaborated" (Lakoff 48). Women are considered objects whose "sexual nature" and "social roles" require them to use euphemism and be "derivative and dependent in relation to men" (45). Women have usually been regarded as dependent beings or powerless sexual objects. Therefore, women's language is "restricted in use to women and [...] descriptive of women alone" (Lakoff 45). It systematically withholds power from women.

Women writers, however, have made efforts to overcome the linguistic barriers by following certain stylistic strategies in their works. Therefore, men's and women's relations to power differ considerably because of their differences in using language. Pym's self-censorship, self-effacement, and use of indirect, subtle language are considered to be the most significant linguistic features of her works. In addition to being an unmarried woman-writer and living on the periphery of her society, Pym had no direct access to the power structures. Thus, her conservative and indirect use of language in her writings is due to her peculiar socio-cultural position as a woman-writer, living in the margins of society.

The concept of women's writing has long been a controversial issue among feminist theorists. Anglo-American and French feminist critics such as Virginia Woolf, Hélène Cixous, Luce Irigaray, Showalter, and Gilbert and Gubar have theorised about the boundaries, possibilities, content, and structure of such writing. There is a controversy among scholars concerning the labelling of different types of women's humour. The comedian Kate Clinton, according to Linda Pershing, makes a distinction between "feminist humor" and "mainstream male and female humor" (qtd. in Pershing, 223-24). In her description, rather than being "covert," feminist humour is "overt." Instead of being passive, it is "active," and in contrast to conventional female humour's anti-revolutionary strategies, feminist humour is grounded "on the possibility of change." Rather than escapist, feminist humour is transformational: it "transforms painful expression." Thus, it surpasses the duality which considers that "serious is more real. Serious is truth. Humorous is less than real, trivial, trifling." Moreover, feminist humour "does not ridicule or humiliate, instead, it is thoughtful."

Nancy A. Walker also differentiates feminist humour from women's humour. According to her, "the collective consciousness of women as an identifiable group with common problems and interests leads ultimately to a feminist humor" (*Very* 13). Based on this tradition, feminist humour has two forms. The most frequent type of feminist humour "makes use of a double text to pose a subtle challenge to the stereotype or the circumstance that the writer appears superficially merely to describe." The other sort of feminist humour "stresses discrimination, and has tended to emerge during the periods of organized agitation for women's rights. This type of feminist humor may parody anti-suffrage arguments, or may, by the use of fantasy, posit a society in which women are powerful" (*Very* 13). Walker argues that although women's humour differs from feminist humour, "it has a feminist consciousness or stance than has been acknowledged" (*Very* 142).

By recalling Naomi Weisstein's view on feminist humour, Walker argues that in women's condition there exists "an absurdity that they should use for their own purposes" (*Very* 143). According to Weisstein, it is a success "to turn what is defined as a ridiculous state of being into your own definition of the ridiculous, to take control of the quality of the absurdity, [and] to turn it away from yourself." A humorous writer, according to Weisstein, must demonstrate that "nobody is either WOMAN or 'lady,' and that all this is very funny indeed" (qtd. in Walker, *Very* 143).

Feminist humour, therefore, has the capability to redefine conventional views about women, thus proving that it is the male-centred culture that is ridiculous – not women. Walker draws on Gloria Kaufman in order to show their shared emphasis on the role of social system in feminist humour. According to Kaufman, social revolution is the desired purpose inherent in feminist humour. Women's aim in ridiculing the system is to transform it. Female humour, as Kaufman says, "may ridicule a person or a system from an accepting point of view ('that's life'), while the *nonacceptance* of oppression characterizes feminist humor and satire" (qtd. in Walker, *Very* 143; emphasis original). Kaufman concludes that while on the one hand female humour is normally less biting than feminist humour, on the other hand, it is "humor of hope" since it rejects oppression and refuses to submit to the existent conditions. In other words, feminist humour does not ridicule the action itself, since deriding the absurd action is to make it appear unimportant. Rather, as Walker says, it derides the ideology of gender inequality in order to depict this inequality as "absurd and powerless." Similarly, the author of the female humour "is not merely 'accepting' the status quo, but is in fact calling attention to gender inequality, in ways designed to lead to its ultimate rejection" (*Very* 145).

Theorists of feminist humour have unanimously proposed that an effective way of resisting the dominant patriarchal order for women writers is through using a particular type of humour. It can enable them to enter their muted voice into the dominant general culture based on male standards. Central to their discussion is the point that since texts written by women are encoded by their particular biology, psyche, language use, culture, and unique experience, the decoding of such texts requires quite a different kind of approach which should take into account the fundamental characteristics of women's writing as a whole. In other words, any study on women's humour, including the present one, presupposes the existence of women's writing as a distinct type of writing that needs to be investigated based on a different approach. The main reason for such a presupposition is the fact that women writers explore female experiences in non-conventional, non-canonised ways.

Virginia Woolf advises women writers to create their own tradition of writing. Although women might learn "a few tricks" from male writers, they cannot generally benefit from the dominant male tradition. When a woman writer began writing in the past, "Perhaps the first thing she would find [...] was that there was no common sentence ready for her use" (*Room* 79). And such a "lack of tradition, such a scarcity and inadequacy of tools" spared the woman author "freedom and fullness of expression" (80). To create such a tradition, not only the female, but also the male writer's mind should function androgynously: "woman-manly and man-womanly," because it is "when this fusion takes place that the mind is fully fertilized and uses all its faculties" (102). A woman writer can find her own tradition if the female part of her brain functions cooperatively with the male part, or if she can use all faculties of her brain simultaneously. Thus, Woolf's emphasis lies mainly on the role of the author's psyche in the creation of a different kind of tradition. Besides that, Woolf condemns the social conditions for restricting women's creativity since the psyches of women writers are basically the by-products of social conditions.[7]

Furthermore, by referring to the "angel in the house" as an ideal of womanhood, Woolf highlights the socio-historical connotation of the concept as an "influential Victorian ideal of deferential, sportive and domestic womanhood" (Parsons 85). This ideal woman was thought to be "intensely sympathetic. She was immensely charming. She was utterly unselfish. She excelled in the difficult arts of family life. She sacrificed herself daily. [...] She was so constituted that she never had a mind or a wish of her own, but preferred to sympathize always with the minds and wishes of others. [...] Her purity was supposed to be her chief beauty – her blushes, her great

---

[7] In other words, "Woolf's strategy enables her to recover a history of women's writing at the same time condemning social conditions that made direct literary channels (pamphlets, broadsheets, books) closed to women" (Fernald 112).

grace" (Woolf, *Death*). As Woolf suggests, women themselves have unconsciously strengthened such a cultural myth by internalising it over the years. Thus, Woolf considers "Killing the Angel in the House" a significant task of the woman writer. In her own writings, Woolf struggled to dispose of the established image since, as she argues, "had I not killed her she would have killed me. She would have plucked the heart out of my writing" (*Death*).

Pym's fiction includes such angels – Belinda Bede, Mildred Lathbury, and Jane Cleveland are among them. At least, society expects them to be angels. Although they may appear to be helpmates, their thoughts show how they dislike being considered as such. The socio-cultural expectations towards women prevent them from expressing their true selves and from revealing their experiences in their writing. In the case of her characters' traits and their life accounts, Pym ironically criticises the existing socio-cultural conditions which act as invisible obstacles preventing their private and social contributions. Pym's criticism was about the cultural realities of her time. As Gillooly states, "in the globalizing middle-class culture of the late twentieth-century," a culture which was financially and mentally based on the satisfaction of "self-interest." it was not an easy task for female virtues such as "self-sacrifice and eager sympathy" to seem "ludicrous" (*Smile* 208).

According to American feminist and literary critic Elaine Showalter's argument in her *A Literature of Her Own*,[8] women's specific condition in the patriarchal society should be taken as the most important factor in encouraging them to create a different kind of literature – their own literature. She coined the term "gynocriticism" in order to pose the significant issue of "difference." Her main purpose was to "constitute women as a distinct literary group" and to recognise and analyse the "difference of women's writing" (15), which is why women's writing should be rediscovered and extended. In developing her theory on the direct relationship between

---

[8] Showalter developed the idea of *A Literature of Their Own* with reference to Woolf's argument in *A Room of One's Own*. In a manner similar to Woolf's, she raises another issue of Woolf's "flight into androgyny." According to Toril Moi, Showalter sees Woolf's insistence on the androgynous nature of the great writer as "a flight away from feminism." Yet, the idea of "a tradition of their own" is provoking enough to draw attention to women's literature, or "a literature of their own" (282).

women's writing and women's culture, Showalter critically reviews existing theories about the relationship between a woman's text and her body, psyche, and language. According to this discussion, the shift from "an androcentric to a gynocentric" criticism is owed to Patricia Meyer Spacks's studies. Showalter emphasises the importance of Spacks's analysis of "how women's writing had been different, and how womanhood itself shaped women's creative expression" (15).

Showalter regards the concept of *écriture féminine*, which was proposed by Hélène Cixous,[9] as possibly the most significant contribution to the issue of women's writing. Showalter considers it "the inscription of the female body and female difference in language and text." *Écriture feminine* signifies a "Utopian possibility rather than a literary practice" (15) since showing the defining differences in women's writing is a challenging task. Showalter also argues that there is no agreement among critics whether women's writing is be considered a stylistic or a generic matter, or a subject related to experience, or "produced by the reading process, as some textual critics would maintain" (16). Critics in general believe that the difference in women's writing is affected by all these factors. That is, women writers' style, the experience they convey, and the themes and subjects they write about differ to a great extent from what is common in mainstream literature. According to critics such as Judith Fetterley and Jonathan Culler, women's reading process differs from that of men.

While discussing differences, theorists of women's writing generally take into account four factors – biology, language, psychoanalysis, and culture. Although feminist criticism resists the patriarchal attribution of lower biological status to women, it takes into account the metaphorical signifi-

---

[9] In her essay "The Laugh of the Medusa," Cixous urges women writers to "look at the Medusa straight on to see her. And she's not deadly. She's beautiful and she's laughing" (2048). This statement, according to Walker, calls women writers to "break the bonds of cultural conditioning and write in their own voices" (*Very* 86). Such triumphant laugh, as Cixous argues, emerges whenever a woman uses her true voice; "writing is *the very possibility of change*, the space that can serve as a springboard for subversive thought, the precursory movement of a transformation of social and cultural structures" (2043; emphasis original). According to Irigaray, one way for women's affirmation in the dominant culture is "to laugh among themselves. Laughter, according to Irigaray, is an indication of sexual rebellion and a means of transcending the phallic power that oppresses women" (Bennett 57).

cance of female biological difference in women's own writings and the writings about them. In *The Madwoman in the Attic*, for instance, Gilbert and Gubar construct their explanation of women's writing around metaphors of literary paternity. As Gilbert and Gubar understand, a woman writer undergoes anxiety of authorship caused by "socio-economic oppression and intellectual inferiorization as they have been considered to necessarily lack the instrument of generative power" (*Madwoman* 293). Hence, women writers' anxiety is greatly felt "through the words they have produced and their anxiety of authorship is not only due to their status as mere 'writers,' but also due to their status as 'women writers.' The term refers to the 'conscious fears of [writing] authority' of a woman writer who conceives of the act of writing as 'inappropriate to her sex'" (293). Gilbert and Gubar also cite socio-historical and cultural reasons for women's absence from canonical literature. According to them, internalised cultural beliefs keep women away from reading and writing by restricting their self-awareness. Gilbert and Gubar propose that

> women's intellectual capabilities were overlooked, and they were given little chance to express themselves through literature. Only men could refer to themselves as the creators of artistic works in the colonial puritan society. Women almost always felt that they committed sin when they happened to put something in ink. Indeed, reading and writing were considered rather dangerous for women. (293)

In Showalter's discussion of the rhetorical history of women's writing in Anglo-American and French Feminism, Showalter highlights the defining importance of language from their perspectives. According to Nelly Furman, for instance, "It is through the medium of language that we define and categorize areas of difference and similarity, which in turn allow us to comprehend the world around us" (qtd. in Showalter 20). Male-centred categorisations predominate American English and "subtly shape our understanding and perception of reality; this is why attention is increasingly directed to the inherently oppressive aspects for women of a male-constructed language system." Annie Leclerc proposes that women writers, in the first place, should "invent a language that is not oppressive, a language that does not leave speechless but that loosens the tongue" (qtd. in Showalter 21). In this way, through the gradual disruption of established patriarchal language, women writers can enter the appropriate language of their own into the existing discourse.

Showalter argues that women writers have long been accused of disrupting male discourse even before the rise of such discussions, mostly in the French tradition of feminist criticism. She emphasises that "the concept of a women's language is not original with feminist criticism; it is very ancient and appears frequently in folklore and myth. In such myths, the essence of women's language is its secrecy; what is really being described is the male fantasy of the enigmatic nature of the feminine" (21). Such a traditional view of women's language is a misidentified recognition based on male illusion. Comparing the invention of a new language particular to women to the selection of a language in a decolonised society, Showalter argues that some women, by using the existing male language, endeavour to deliver their own experience through it. They gradually disrupt the established language in order to make their own voices heard and inscribe their style in the general writing tradition. In contrast, other critics believe that women writers should establish a fundamentally new language. As Showalter puts it, "The language issue in feminist criticism has emerged, in a sense, after our revolution, and it reveals the tensions in the women's movement between those who would stay outside the academic establishments and the institutions of criticism and those who would enter and even conquer them" (22). Showalter acknowledges that "the concept of the women's language is riddled with difficulties" because "there is no mother tongue, no genderlect spoken by the female population in a society, which differs significantly from the dominant language" (22). Moreover, the possibility of women's language, its feasibility, as Showalter states, is not certain from the linguistic perspective either:

> English and American linguists agree that "there is absolutely no evidence that would suggest the sexes are pre-programmed to develop structurally different linguistic systems." Furthermore, the many specific differences in male

> and female speech, intonation, and language use that have been identified cannot be explained in terms of "two separate sex-specific languages" [McConnell-Ginet] but need to be considered instead in terms of styles, strategies, and contexts of linguistic performance. (22-23)

Showalter does not advocate a specific language for women as distinct from the male tradition. Instead, she holds that a new women's language should be extracted from the dominant language. Her suggestion to feminist criticism

> is to concentrate on women's access to language, on the available lexical range from which words can be selected, on the ideological and cultural determinants of expression. The problem is not that language is insufficient to express women's consciousness but that women have been denied the full resources of language and have been forced into silence, euphemism, or circumlocution. (23)

Therefore, women writers should primarily employ all the capacities of the existing language to be heard in that discourse because "women's literature is still haunted by the ghosts of repressed language, and until we have exorcised those ghosts, it ought not to be in language that we base our theory of difference" (23).

Showalter's understanding of women's writing is in line with Gilbert and Gubar's argument that "the female subject is not necessarily alienated from the words she writes and speaks" ("Sexual" 516). They argue that by using the existing discourse a woman writer can enter "not just female *jouissance* but female *puissance*" or her own *identity* into the dominant culture. In this way and "in spite of the feminist doubt and masculinist dread," Gilbert and Gubar confirm that "woman has not been sentenced to transcribe male penmanship; rather, she commands sentences which inscribe her own powerful character" ("Sexual" 516; emphasis original). Gilbert and Gubar, therefore, do not advocate a totally new female writing tradition; instead, according to them, "there has always been an '*écriture féminine*;' it has just been overlooked" (Berg 10). They hold that in order to express their particular experiences, women have "come to terms with the urgent need for female literary authority through fantasies about the possession of a mother tongue" (qtd. in Berg 10). The so-called "mother tongue," according to Berg, is considered to be "primordial, passionate, powerful, [and] private." It also includes "new words, a new language to express what has never been expressed before, [and] the woman's experience." This new type of language is "a subversive language powerful enough to subvert patriarchal power" (Berg 11).

As with women's writing, feminist critics also disagree about the existence of a distinct women's culture. The relationship between women's culture and general culture based on the patriarchal values is by no means straightforward. To define women's culture, some basic models have been proposed by critics, historians and anthropologists. Some critics point out the existence of a totally separate sphere as a necessity for the possibility of a separate female culture. In contrast, Edwin Ardener proposes a diagram on the relationship between the dominant and the muted group, maintaining that a great deal of the two spheres overlap, while there is still a "wild zone" which belongs to the muted group, and stands outside the male domain (qtd. in Showalter 200):

> If we think of the wild zone metaphysically, or in terms of consciousness, it has no corresponding male space since all of male consciousness is within the circle of the dominant structure and thus accessible to or structured by language. In this sense, the 'wild' is always imaginary; from the male point of view, it may simply be the projection of the unconscious. In terms of cultural anthropology, women know what the male crescent is like, even if they have never seen it, because it becomes the subject of legend (like the wilderness). But men do not know what is in the wild. (Showalter 200)

Criticising those who think that it is possible for female writers to write only in the wild zone extracted from the dominant sphere, Showalter asserts that, "we must also understand that there can be no writing or criticism totally outside of the dominant structure" since the publication industry totally depends on the "economic and political pressures of the male-dominated society." Therefore, "the concept of a woman's text in the wild zone is a playful abstraction." Showalter believes that "women's writing is a 'double-voiced discourse' that always embodies the social, literary, and cultural heritages of both the muted and the dominant." Thus, women's writing cannot be considered as "*inside* and *outside* of the male tradition;" rather, it is "inside two traditions simultaneously" and reflects the characteristics of both traditions (201-02; emphasis original). Moreover, some critics have tried to explain the production and interpretation of the women- authored texts by the theory of double-text[10].

Showalter, then, believes in a two-fold relationship between the general, dominant culture and women's muted culture: "One of the great advantages of the women's-culture model is that it shows how the female tradition can be a positive source of strength and solidarity as well as a negative source of powerlessness; it can generate its own experiences and symbols which are not simply the obverse of the male tradition" (204). Showalter highlights the importance of such cultural models in the reading of women's fiction, proposing that:

> Women's fiction can be read as a double-voiced discourse, containing a "dominant" and a "muted" story [...] I have described it elsewhere as an object/field problem in which we must keep two alternative oscillating texts simultaneously in view: "In the purest feminist literary criticism we are [...] presented with a radical alteration of our vision, a demand that we see meaning in what has previously been empty space. The orthodox plot recedes, and another plot, hitherto

---

[10] Based on the American humourist Frances M. Whitcher's idea, Walker explains that humour is contradictory to the "conventional definition of ideal womanhood" since women are generally considered to be "passive" and "inferior" while humour is "aggressive" and "occupies a position of superiority" (*Very* 12). Thus, Whitcher developed "a text that functions on two levels." The first layer of the text seems to certify "popular stereotypes of women," and the second layer indicates the sources of these stereotypes in a "culture that defines women in terms of their relationships with men."

submerged in the anonymity of the background, stands out in bold relief like a thumbprint. (204)

Pym's texts can also be considered as a double-voiced discourse in Showalter's sense. The first part of this is the dominant patriarchal discourse. The second part is the humorous discourse of the woman writer which, standing outside the power relations, ridicules the dominant discourse as well as the values and the ideology related to it.

Acting within the limitations of the existent dominant culture, the exploration of women's culture can be regarded as the most important part of the search for a theory of women's writing. The appearance of such culture can help to redefine conventionally established female roles, functions, activities, tastes and behaviours from a woman's perspective based on her real life experiences. By the same token, Pym's novels represent women's lives as a distinct way of life differing from the dominant one.

STG, for instance, depicts the lives of two middle-class, middle-aged, unmarried sisters. The narrative mostly focuses on their disjointed viewpoints which subtly disrupt dominant cultural values. Similarly, *EW* displays Mildred's unique values, beliefs and behaviours which oppose the dominant post-WW II culture of 1950s England. Likewise, the lives of Jane and Prudence in *JP* show their disconnected cultures and perspectives and their centrifugal drive away from the prevalent stream of patriarchal culture. Pym in these narratives attempts to redefine fundamental concepts from the women's perspective.

Although feminist critics and theorists disagree over the existence of a separate kind of writing called women's writing, nonetheless, they commonly accept that female experiences in women's writings may vary from male experiences due to differences in their biology, history, language, and culture. Thus, women are seen capable of finding a way of expression to disrupt the deep structure of the patriarchal tradition. Thus, by working within the existing male tradition, women writers include in their writing some subtleties which are related to their own being and existence in order to imprint their voice or biological, historical, linguistic, and cultural concerns in the literary canon. In order to understand such texts, readers should also take into account the historical concerns of the woman author who mostly imagine their implied readers be aware of the woman writer's conditions as a whole.

Female humour is generally considered to be one of the techniques female authors use in order to have their own voices heard and also to criticise the existing patriarchal tradition. Besides, women's humour is addressed to a particular group of readers since only some well-informed readers can interpret and decode the strategies women use in their writings in order to neutralise the masculine obstacles. Related to this, Gillooly argues that since "the production and content of the humour are gender-marked," thus, the readers for such humour are also probably "gender-marked" (*Smile* xx). Moreover, the relation between the writer of the humour and her/his addressee is a significant issue. The traditional and conventional forms of humour call for an extremely rigid "emotional distance" between the writer and his addressee whom Gillooly calls his "victim" (*Smile* 12). In contrast, women writers' humour comforts the "suffering self ... soliciting readerly empathy for her in the process" (*Smile* 12). Referring to the problem-novels, such as Jane Austen's, Gillooly states that "Curiously, the narrator's relation to the heroine in the problem novels is at once less distant and less stable than in the others" (*Smile* 80). The relation between the heroine and the narrator is, however, of a compromising nature and, thus at some point, the narrator makes some alterations in the relationship. As Gillooly proposes, what has usually been labelled as Jane Austen's "irony," severely settles "the quality of all her narrator-heroine relationships" (*Smile* 80). The narrator sometimes distances herself from her heroine, while at other times intimately connects and wordplays with her.

Pym's works, as are the case with Austen's novels, raise a significant question of the prevalent mode – are they mostly ironic or humours? This study considers Pym's writings as humorous, rather than ironic. Similarly, Jane Austen's texts are of consideration in terms of the recurrent mistaking women's humour as irony, and have symptomatic value in this context. As Gillooly points out, theorists of women's humour suggest that Austen should not be considered as an "ironist" but rather a humourist, because of the "affective closeness she sustains between her narrator and heroine, even when the latter is the object of narrative amusement" (*Smile* 80).

Gillooly, furthermore, asserts that a certain emotional distance that exists between "the ironist and the ironized," however, can either be "experienced by the reader abstractly (in the disjunction between the ideal and real) or immediately (in the disproportionate knowledge of reader and character)." In contrast, there exists a "necessary emotional distance" in feminine humour. This emotive intimacy inscribed in the "narrator-heroine bond" (*Smile* 80) ends in Austen's texts as being instances of female humour rather than irony, as has been considered until now. Accordingly, the woman writer's bond to the source based on which she constructs her own sense of humour is not authoritative and mastering; rather, it is sympathetic and respectful owing to the particular socio-cultural experiences encountered by women. Gillooly further argues that female humour in this way can work "as a tactic of cultural as well as textual resistance" (*Smile* xx). This statement shows that female humour is not only a textual device, but also a cultural and ethnical resistance and can benefit from women's individual lives. In a similar manner to Austen's, Pym's works have mostly been considered by scholars and critics as ironical works. However, the present study considers Pym's writings as humorous, rather than ironic.

1.4. Difference between Irony and Humour

Women writers have not only used humour in their writings, they have reflected on it as well. According to Gillooly, George Eliot, for example, studied the different kinds of humour and the nature of the ludicrous. Eliot differentiates three main groups of humour. The first type, related to the illiterate and uncultivated, is "barbaric" humour. This kind of humour is associated with ludicrous events or situations, and the pleasure is evoked through "its 'flavor' in 'triumphant egoism or intolerance,' and its origins in 'the cruel mockery of a savage at the writhings of a suffering enemy.'" This type is totally aggressive in dealing with its victims since its pleasure comes from the farcical deriding of an individual and laughing at its pain in the hands of its victimisers. The second type of humour, "wit" in Eliot's classification, is based on the mental faculty and its significant features are "ingenuity, condensation, and instantaneousness." This "wit" is not different from "reasoning raised to a higher power."

Eliot suggests that "both barbaric humor and 'wit' are troped as masculine strategies." The latter is close to what other theorists refer to as irony. Although it is not as rough and aggressive as the first type, it lacks the shaping element of women's humour. It solely deals with reason, intellect and wordplay. This type also displays "hostility toward the Other."

The third type of humour, according to Eliot, is "sympathetic humor," which is closer to women's humour. She describes this type as "a refined, 'higher form' of humor, which 'in proportion as it associates itself with the sympathetic emotions,' with the 'sympathetic presentation of incongruous elements in human nature and life,' [and] frequently attains the status of 'poetry.'" It has much in common with women's humour in many respects. First of all, it creates a sense of sympathy that accompanies the exchange of discourse caught up in a continuum of further suggestions. Patriarchal wit, by contrast, comes out as a weapon directed against a certain addressee while sympathetic humour, according to Gillooly, "is not simply feminine but preoedipally maternal." Moreover, Eliot proposes that "in being 'poetic' and imaginative, it [sympathetic humor] is 'of earlier growth than Wit,' and thus prior to reason and the Law." As Eliot adds, "'maternal' feelings belong solely to women" and woman novelists "have a precious specialty, lying quite apart from masculine aptitudes and experience." Eliot states that "'chastened delicate humor'," in addition to being metaphorically maternal, is "the chief aim and measure of female writing as well" (qtd. in Gilloolly, *Smile* 165-66).

Modern critics have frequently defined and evaluated irony and humour based on a pattern of dual oppositions. For instance, by contrasting their relationship with law, Deleuze argues that "The first way of overturning the law is ironic, where irony appears as an art of principles, of ascent towards the principles and of overturning principles. The second is humour, which is an art of consequences and descents, of suspensions and falls" (qtd. in Colebrook 129). While irony "ascends" the existing context, the "descending" humour functions inside the existing context focusing on the "bodies, particularities, noises and disruptions that are in excess of the system and law of speech" (Colebrook 129).

According to Candace D. Lang's distinction of irony from humour, which highlights the ideological potential inherent in each, the two linguistically different phenomena have mistakenly been marked as "irony" despite their diametrically different meanings. The function of an ironic text is to present "a preexistent idea or concept like any sincere statement in language" (Lang 5). The purpose of irony is limitation and suppression of meaning addressed to a specific addressee. Humour, by contrast, avoids addressing meaning to a particular addressee by employing linguistic ambiguities and connotative resonances. The ironist is often in distress because of the inadequacy of language for self-expression, while for the humourist language plays a constitutive role for both thought ego. The ironist needs to twist the function of language and his/her aim is the expression of meaning, whereas the humourist needs to exert language elements and his/her purpose is the production of meaning. The ironist has a certain intention or message in advance while the humourist has little idea what will emerge in the process. The humorous text does not express meaning in the "traditional, etymological sense of exteriorizing what was interior to the authorial psyche;" but it brings together linguistic elements and arranges them "into systems offering a variety of potential meanings to be actualized by the reader" (Lang 7). In an ironic text, the intended meaning of the author/intender prevails over the reader/addressee's. In other words, with an implication that s/he has a complete identity or message, the author tries to control the meaning of the text. But "the author" in the humorous text is of secondary importance. The humourist, unlike the ironist, creates potential meaning(s) to be actualized by "the reader." For the humourist, the discourse/text is central and the potential meaning(s) are liberated. The liberated humourist text, therefore, contributes to the consolidation of the very presence of the utterer. As Lang argues, "The humourist critic focuses on the functioning of the text at the level of the signifier, rather than seeking to somehow 'see through' the language to its referent or authorial source" (7). Consequently, the reader of humorous texts is relatively free to read and interpret such texts. Thus, irony can be interpreted or translated while humour can be commented or rewritten. If a statement can be negated in an ironic statement, then we can achieve a signifier-signified match. In other words, "when the signifier coincides with the signified," we can assume that "irony becomes serious" (Lang 41-42).

Considering Lang's discussion, Gillooly argues that Hegelian or romantic irony is "based upon a logic of binary oppositions (like ideal/real, meaning/expression, subject/object, male/female, master/slave)" ("Women" 446-77). Moreover, romantic irony refers to the "notion that the word itself is but an envelope for the idea." This type of irony functions based on negation and the assertion that there is "a primary and originary intention" behind written words (Lang 2-3), even though these words fail to express it adequately. Thus, it is the inequality "between the idea and the word that constitutes the 'irony'" (Gillooly, "Women" 477). On the other hand, Socratic irony, or what Lang labels as humour, keeps away from the "simple splitting or duplication" (115) of meaning. This is the most important feature of Hegelian irony which "limit[s] one's reading to the extraction of a coherent message" (Lang 193). In opposition to irony, which seeks "truth," humour is understood "only as a divergence from truth, with no subsequent moment of convergence" (Lang 42). Humour disseminates signification through challenging "the traditional concept of meaning as a transcendental signified" (Lang 194). As Colebrook, based on Deleuze's understanding of the concept, argues:

> Humour falls or collapses: 'down' from meaning and intentions to the singularities of life that have no order, no high and low, no before and after. Humour can reverse or pervert logic, disrupt moral categories or dissolve the body into parts without any governing intention. Humour is not the reversal of cause and effect but the abandonment of the 'before and after' relations – the very line of time – that allow us to think in terms of causes and intentions, of grounds and consequents. (134; emphasis original)

Gillooly similarly argues that humour not only rejects the "'truth' of a master discourse or interpretation" ("Women" 477) but also endangers its basis.[11] Therefore, in contrast to irony, which is an outcome of binary log-

---

[11] Moreover, Gillooly, as Stimpson points out, differentiates feminine humour from irony. According to Gillooly, there has been a tendency to associate "irony with masculinity" for a number of reasons (xix).

ic, humour produces "multiple, often conflicting, interpretive possibilities" in language and, consequently, subverts the potency of the prescribed language. Thus seen, while irony functions as "a principle of antithesis, humour operates as a principle of subversion." Considering the fact that "the *rire* of irony corresponds to the *derire* of humor" (Lang 186; emphasis original), it can be argued that the ridiculing and mocking of the official and the law, as well as its "dialectic discourse" (Gillooly, "Women" 477), may function as a technique for domination. The user of irony tends to master the other(s), and since irony operates as a "momentary or sustained recognition of existential dissonance," it also includes, among others, "sarcasm and satire as well as a host of otherwise unspecified and not necessarily funny incongruities in life and representation" (*Smile* xxi). Moreover, the most elemental constituent of irony is "The disparity between the idea and the word (or between normative and individual action)" (*Smile* xxii). Being a masculine trope, "in its comic incarnation, irony presumes not only an *alazon* but an *eiron* or figure of disguised authority." This figure is "an awkward posture for the feminine to maintain in almost any existent culture" (*Smile* xxii).

1.5 Necessity of a Humour of One's Own

One of the most controversial issues among critics is whether women's humour is different from male humour. In her *A Room of One's Own*, Woolf differentiates between conventional humour and women's humour as related to women's experience. Woolf foregrounds women's humour concentrating on their distinct experiences. Thus, as Judy Little argues, comedy "written by women may be different from comedy written by men" (*Comedy* ix) since, according to Woolf, men's and women's "values" are to some extent different although the prevailing values are masculine. She maintains that "the values of women differ very often from the values which have been made by the other sex." Woolf considers this difference very "natural" and unquestionable: "this is so" (*Room* 76). However, she sidelines the constraints imposed by the existing male standards prevailing over the context in which women writers produce literature. She adds:

> Speaking crudely, football and sport are 'important'; the worship of fashion, the buying of clothes 'trivial'. And these values are inevitably transferred from life to fiction. This is an important book, the critic assumes, because it deals with war. This is an insignificant book because it deals with the feelings of women in a drawing room. A scene in a battlefield is more important than a scene in a shop - everywhere and much more subtly the difference of value persists. (*Room* 77)

Woolf, nevertheless, recommends women to draw on their particular experiences, caused by their particular condition, as an advantage in order to write their own peculiar humour through which they can see and laugh at men's absurdities and hypocrisies: "learn to laugh, without bitterness, at the vanities – say rather at the peculiarities, for it is a less offensive word – of the other sex" (*Room* 94). Thus, Woolf prepares the basis for women's humour and encourages them to express themselves humorously.

Exploring and questioning the conventional theories related with humour, theory of women's humour has recently appeared as an outstanding strategy of reading women's fiction. By considering the rise and development of the theories of humour and their application, a comprehensive theoretical study of women's humour necessarily puts into question the traditional claim that since women do not have a sense of humour, or at best a particular or distinct one, humour is primarily considered to be a male dominion. Some of the twentieth century thinkers, such as Schopenhauer, Bergson, and Freud declared that "women had no sense of humor" (Sochen 9). Thus, it is no surprise that women's humour has been ignored and misread since the patriarchal ideology did not recognise women's sense of humour as a separate and specific type of humour in its own right. As June Sochen observes, "the conservative point of view dominated, and the rebellious one, albeit a powerful one, was looked at suspiciously by all lovers of the status quo, it took a long time to overthrow the long-held notions about women's alleged lack of capacity to laugh and to create laughter" (10). Consequently, it was a challenging task for the dominating male system to grant recognition to this type of humour for women's use and to provide the required conditions to broaden and theorise about it.

According to the theorists who essentially consider humour as a male art, any theorising about women's humour is invalid. Referring to this situation, Kate Sanborn, as the first woman who published an influential book on women's humour, proposes that "While the wit of men, as a subject for admiration and discussion, is now threadbare, the wit of women has been almost utterly ignored and unrecognized" (1). Theorists of women's humour thus tend to highlight it as a separate *ignored* and *unrecognized* category of humour, particular to women. The theory that women do indeed possess a humour of their own initiated further investigation of their particular style of humour and its difference from the conventional male humour. For instance, in the introduction to her anthology, Sanborn admits that her decision to collect women's humour is largely due to the myth that women do not have a sense of humour. Her purpose in collecting the humorous writings of women is an attempt to prove the falsity of the general belief, as put by Richard Grant White, that comedy is the "rarest of qualities in woman" (qtd. in Sanborn 13). Sanborn, moreover, describes her desire to publish such a book by stating that "it roused such a host of brilliant recollections that it was a temptation to try to materialize the ghosts that were haunting me; to lay forever the suspicion that they did not exist" (13). Although Sanborn does not theorise about women's humour in her book, she collects English women's humorous writings and claims that "there were many literary Englishwomen who had undoubted humour" (15). Accordingly, women's humour is generally believed to have appeared in women's texts as a remarkable rhetorical device.

1.6 Humour: A Female Device?

The kind and function of humour in women's writing have always been under debate. For example, by referring to the problematic history of the theory of women's humour, Gillooly states that Lang's discussion contributed a lot to the study of women's humour her personal lack of interest in women's use of humour. As Gillooly says, Lang "suggests why 'humor' as opposed to irony, comedy, or another formulation is the most appropriate general term by which to refer to what is amusing in women's writing"

("Women" 477). She further proposes that the peculiar characteristics inherent in women's humour including, for instance, "the characteristic subtlety, the intercategorical nature, of female humor ... conforms more fully to a reading attuned to polyvalence than to the strict either/or dualism associated with Hegelian irony" ("Women" 477). Moreover, dissimilar to irony that attempts "to dominate signification" in order to remove other 'trivial' and insignificant meanings, women's humour is in fact "adversarial and oppositional to the dominant discourse" without threatening or endangering the foundations of the dominant order. Therefore, humour, as Gillooly asserts, "like female utterance, is unauthorized discourse," "It is not a sharply contrasted principle enforcing the law by negation, instead, it is beyond the law and thus "dangerously subversive of its hegemony" ("Women" 477-78).

In her attempt to theorise about female irony, Gillooly argues that, in comparison to the "reinforcement of ego characteristic of irony," female ego is fabricated as "dispersed, relational, passive, and renunciative." Thus, as Gillooly states, the female writer benefits more from humour because it provides her more "sympathetic relation to self" (*Smile* xxii). Walker also points out "women's quite different relationship to authority" (*Very* 12) while at the same time demonstrating women's alienation from the dominant order. Agreeing with Walker, Gillooly asserts that if irony is a "masculine" device, which is a "direct negative response to the Law," then "feminine irony," obstructed by the women's peculiar position in society, is only expressed as "silence" (*Smile* xxii). Moreover, Walker proposes that language, as being the most essential constituent of women's writing, is applied in two different styles. The first group of women writers resist and challenge "the male-dominated language, either by appropriating male discourse for women's purposes or by altering or subverting it." This is the strategy that women comic writers employ in their writings. They resist and challenge the "dominant discourse" by the application of comic strategies such as "irony." The second group of women writers stress "women's exclusion from language – their silence." These writers, according to Walker, mostly tend towards modes such as fantasy as another accompanying narrative strategy (*Feminist* 44). Those women writers, who chose to challenge the male-centred language by various strategies, must realise that "the initial step in negating the hegemony of oppressive language is to question its authority by making fun of it." (Walker, *Feminist* 44) Pym applies this tactic effectively in her fiction. For example, although she accepts religion as her ideology, yet, she challenges it in a peculiar humorous tone. Thus, in Walker's words, by employing humour that contradicts "the power of hegemonic discourse," by her refusal "to take that power seriously," and by "pointing to the absurdity of the official language of a culture," the woman comic writer can build up resistance against the dominance of the male-centred language (*Feminist* 44).

Pym's ridiculing tone regarding patriarchal discourse is observable in her dealing with the very topics and themes which are regarded as insignificant by male critics and writers. Barreca also points out the disregard of the literary and cultural critics for women's humour, "When it *can* be seen, comedy written by women is perceived as trivial, silly and unworthy of serious attention." (*Untamed* 20). Thus, since women writers mostly write outside the domain of "power and authority," many critics consider women's writing activities less significant than those of men: "by writing comedy, in which the unofficial nature of the world is explored (to paraphrase Bakhtin), women are damned to insignificant twice over" since "traditional arguments posit that women's comedy, as in women's gossip, the unimportant discuss the unofficial" (Barreca, *Untamed* 20). Thus, it is possible to regard women writers' humour as generally unimportant through evaluating the subjects they write about as insignificant.

1.7 Misreading Women's Humour and Images of Women

Misreading and misunderstanding women's humorous writing is the most problematic subject in women's writing. Women comic writers have often been victims of the misreading and misunderstandings of the critics. In this regard, Barreca states that "Women's humor has not so much been ignored as it has been unrecognized, passed over, or misread as tragic" (*Untamed* 17). Furthermore, as Gillooly refers to it, women's comic writings are often valued according to the *universal* standards: "Because readers have historically been taught to identify and appreciate the presence of humour according to 'universal' standards and to privilege certain of these over others, they frequently ignore or misread humour produced by women whenever it refuses to conform to the established standards" (*Women* 475). Barreca also underlines the role of *universal* standards by proposing that the important problem in reading and recognizing women's humour has been measuring their humour against the so-called universals (*Untamed* 45).

According to critics such as Woolf, the fact that many woman writers choose to write about the so-called small details of life (e.g. birth, death, marriage, and sex) implies that women cannot master the universal subjects (e.g. sports, finance, and academics) (*Room* 77). Woolf highlights the inefficiency of the literary critical tradition to "recognize and read women's humour" rather than the "inability of women to produce comedy that accounts for the absence of critical material on the subject" (*Room* 20). By the same token, while some critics and scholars misread Pym's humour as *serious* and *sober*, they misrecognise her subtle and covert style of humour.

As it is true about the existing images and stereotypes for women, classification of women into types and groups, rather than considering them as individuals, has been one of the significant factors in misreading their humour through the years. As long as the conventionalised stereotypes for women ignore their individualities, working against their particular private and social states, and as long as a woman is viewed merely as "helpmate, sex object, and domestic servant, she cannot at the same time be allowed the capacity for humour, with its implication of superiority and its fundamental critique of social reality" (Walker, *Very* 98). Therefore, in order to read women's humour without the prejudices and presuppositions, and to understand it, first of all the negative stereotypes related with women must be wiped out. Understanding women's historical, cultural and social states is obligatory for reading and understanding their particular type of humour. Further, what in fact differentiates women's humorous writing from those of men, originates from differences in the way women relate to culture, as well as from the lack of a balance between the authorised and the unauthorised, and the workings of the power between them. The authorised and the dominant are not always powerful and the unauthorised and marginal are not always powerless.

The balance between the power of the authorised and the unauthorised may sometimes turn counter-wise. Walker proposes that the "delicate balance between power and powerlessness" shapes the "themes and forms of women's humorous writing." She also adds that women's literature "has described myriad aspects of women's lives, employing familiar stereotypes about women for the purpose of mocking those stereotypes and showing their absurdity and even their danger" (*Very* 10). Pym employs these stereotypes in her writing in order to display the absurd and subordinating view of the patriarchal culture in relation to these stereotypes. Likewise, Walker states that, "It is for this reason that women's humor so often seems to turn on and perpetuate traditional stereotypes of women: the gossipy spinster, the nagging wife, the inept housekeeper, the lovelorn woman, the dumb blonde. These are some of the roles in which women have been cast by men and male institutions, and as such they have, until quite recently, seemed fixed" (*Very* 11). Similarly, Pym's novels are full of spinsters, unloved women, and tactless housewives. She depicts these women not primarily to exhibit their ineffectiveness, but to display the shortcomings of the male-centred culture in dealing with them. Walker also observes that: "What female humorists have done with these stereotypes, however, is to subvert them. The housewives who cannot reach perfection ... are in this situation because the standards for their performance are impossibly high; the lovelorn women ... are victims of male indifference and the double standard" (*Very* 11). Pym likewise resists and undermines the dominant order by ridiculing the standards set for women by the prevailing culture. In addition to subverting the standards prescribed for women, women's humour also criticises the institutions and individuals who are in some manner associated with the power structures.

1.8 Lack of Ending in the Works of Women Writers

One significant difference that theorists of women's humour point out is that between the endings of novels written by female and male humorous writers. Barreca considers women's humour a specific type of humour stating that comedies by female writers have no "happy endings" (introduction 8). Instead, "The endings of comic works by women writers," as Barreca states, "do not, ultimately, reproduce the expected hierarchies, or if they do there is often an attendant sense of dislocation even with the happiest ending" (*Untamed* 23).[12] Following that, Little considers "lack of closure" or "lack of resolution" as the fundamental characteristic of the feminist comedy (qtd. in *Untamed* 29). However, despite their non-comedic endings, women's humorous writings "can indeed be classified as comedies" (Barreca, introduction 8). Similarly, the narrative endings in Pym's selected novels do not conform to the established norms of comedy; for instance, the endings of Pym's novels differ from the endings of the traditional plots. Although marriage and union are obtained at the end of some of her novels, they cannot be considered a great change in the fate of the characters. In fact, marriages and unions are reversed as unfortunate destinies of the characters. In many of Pym's novels, nothing in particular happens at the end, and everything goes on as before.

Thus, the endings of women's comedy differ sharply, and considerably, from the male's traditional perspective of the term comedy. This particular type of comedy does, as Barreca emphasises, destroy social order without establishing a new and different one. Moreover, it revolts against the norms and the values of the patriarchal system which have already penetrated into the socio-cultural deep structure. Barreca, moreover, proposes that women's comedic writings "may contain very little joyous celebration" and in contrast to the comedies produced as "a safety valve," they are produced as "an inflammatory device." The result of this type of humour "is not to purge desire and frustration" but "to transform it into action" (*Untamed* 18). Similarly, Walker argues that women's writings lack a definite ending. It implies that the text does not allow for a closure. As she observes: "A feminine textual body is recognized by the fact that it is always endless, without ending: there's no closure, it doesn't stop." She suggests that there exists in women's texts the tone of being interminable, "A feminine text starts on all sides, all at once, starts twenty times, thirty times, over (*Feminist* 11). Accordingly, as Stott argues, even though women wrote comedies, which they in fact did, they were criticised for being restricted in themes compared to men's comedies which deal with *important*

---

[12] Similar to Jane Austen, who, according to Barreca, "refuses to provide the final satisfaction of a romance achieved through routes other than the path dictated by the textual necessity of a happy ending" (*Untamed* 24), Pym in her novels barely does "provide the final satisfaction" caused by the final reunion.

aspects of life: "Female comedians only discuss 'women's' themes – relationships, shopping, and menstruation, for example – whereas male topics are thought to be unbounded and therefore to have universal appeal" (94).

Pym's novels are mostly inconclusive. In other words, no satisfactory conclusion may be drawn after reading them. The three selected novels in this stury are open-ended and the reader can imagine dozens of possible endings for them. It is for the purpose of comedy that Pym deliberately keeps her novels open-ended. For instance, the ending of *EW* gives only some hints that Everard might ask Mildred to marry him. Through the narrator's report of her inner thoughts, Mildred is reported as imagining herself at Everard's "sink peeling potatoes and washing up;" doing Everard's indexing and proofreading for a "nice change" (*EW* 255). Moreover, the endings of *STG* and *JP* suggest implicitly that they are in fact *non-endings*. For example, it is possible to imagine that Belinda and Harriet Bede, despite having suitors, will stay unmarried; Belinda will remain in love with Henry; Harriet will go on flirting with the young curates; and/or Jane will seek worthy suitors for Prudence Bates, while Prudence will fall in and out of love with imaginary lovers! This sharp contrast between the endings of the women's and men's writings makes possible the other differences between the more conventional humour and women's specific humour.

1.9 Differences between Conventional Humour and Women's Humour

Feminist critics and theorists of humour claim that women have a humour peculiar to themselves that differs widely from men's conventional humour. According to Gail Finne, women's humour is different from men's and is particular to themselves: "The gender of the creator of comedy makes a difference in the kind of comedy produced" (1). Reading and encoding this humour calls for a particular type of historical, social, and political knowledge about women's condition since according to Walker, "women's relation to language, literature, education and cultural traditions has been made problematic and complex by centuries of unequal access to power and agency within these systems" (*Disobedient* 2). Gillooly also "demarcates" women's humour from men's and proposes to investigate the peculiar techniques: "Those narrative, rhetorical, and affective tactics that – because of their passivity, indirection, and self-effacement – have been gendered feminine in nineteenth-century British culture" (*Smile* xix). Hence, on account of women's unequal relation to language and power, women are obliged to apply different tactics and strategies so that they might overcome the dominating patriarchal language. Consequently, this results in their producing a different kind of humour.

The writer' gender, therefore, has a determining effect on the kind of humour present in his/her writings. For example, Finney observes that "the gender of the creator of comedy can make a difference in the kind of comedy produced" (1). Theorists also argue that the socio-cultural conditions have operated against women's manifestation of humour. Based on Walker's opinion, the main cause of women's limitation in expressing their humour is that they "have lacked opportunities for free expression of their humour due to the cultural expectations regarding their status and behaviour." However, women have always struggled to reject this opposition. Hence, to resist this lack, as Walker puts it, "women have typically masked their humorous utterance with a pose of anxious adherence to cultural norms" (*Very* 86). Consequently, women's humour lacks the direct and aggressive nature of men's humour. Since women live in a patriarchal society, they have to adapt their humour to the realities of the society wherein they live. As a result, women's resistance to the patriarchal order occurs in a particular context where they have to survive and their humour takes the form of indirect resistance to power. Moreover, according to Walker, the paradoxical beliefs about women and their position and status in society, such as the general culture's belief in their sinfulness and at the same time the simultaneous admiration "for their purity," are some of the reasons for women's use of subversive forms of humour. Women have always resisted against such patriarchal beliefs "by means of a subversive laughter" (*Very* 86).

Some critics argue that women's humour mostly supports the oppressed and the powerless, rather than supporting the oppressors and the powerful. For instance, Barbara Bennett suggests that a significant difference between male and female humour is what Emily Toth in her article "Female Wits" has termed as the "humane humor rule." Toth argues that women, in contrast to men, "target the powerful rather than the powerless and rarely ridicule an aspect of a person or society that cannot be changed." She then gives the example of the "physically handicapped, choosing instead to attack those who hold narrow-minded attitudes and adhere to cultural stereotypes" (qtd. in Bennett 13). Likewise, Barreca observes that "Women are more likely to make fun of those in high and seemingly invulnerable positions than their male counterparts." To put the same thought differently, women's humour, according to Barreca, "is power-sensitive" or it is "often anarchic and apocalyptic; the unsolicited laughter of women spells trouble to those in power" (*Untamed* 21-22). However, women's humour is opposed to the creation and employment of any stereotype. For instance, the stereotype of the father-in-law does not exist in women's humour, in contrast to the stereotype of the mother-in-law, or a bachelor is not ridiculed as a spinster is parodied in men's humour. According to Gillooly, "feminine" humour can be distinguished from the other forms of traditional or "masculine" humour in different aspects of "production and consumption, in form, content, occasion, and psychological function" (*Smile* xx). For instance, in spite of conceiving humour as the disconnection between the norm and its violation, as the theories of *humour as incongruity* have argued, female humour reverses the standards by ridiculing the traditional patriarchal norms.

Based on Gillooly's study, another significant deviation of women's humour from the traditional, conventional, or masculine humour is that, by exercising various tactics and strategies in the text, feminine humour not only furtively attacks the dominating "ideological construction of 'woman,'" but also denounces "certain narrative and rhetorical tactics" such as used by the nineteenth-century writer Ribaldry (*Smile* 17). Furthermore, women do not employ satire in their writings: "Nor does satire – at least in concentrated form or in prodigious quantities – occur with any regularity" (*Smile* 18). The humour of *Vanity Fair* is an example of masculine humour which does not apply the "veiled tactics common to feminine humour to replicate." Masculine humour is, therefore, "too pronounced and transparent" compared to the covert tactics of feminine humour. Rather, feminine humour, works invisibly, to "unsay its sober expression, locally undermining the overt ideology of the text" (*Smile* 18). That is feminine humour does not express itself in a straightforward manner; instead, it topically subverts the open and visible notions of the text.

Similarly, Walker claims that unlike women's humour, which "is almost never purely comic or absurd" (*Very* xii), men's humour is carefree and playful. According to Walker, the melancholic mood and serious tone of women's humour can be regarded as the significant characteristics of their humorous expression since in referring to the infinite "absurdities that woman have been forced to endure in this culture, it carries with it not the light-hearted feeling that is the privilege of the powerful, but instead a subtext of anguish and frustration" (*Very* xii). Thus, the state of being carefree and playful is not consistent with women's humour wherein a troubled and melancholic ego exists underneath. The woman humour writer has her own way of healing for her troubled ego, or as Walker proposes, being "at odds with the publicly espoused values of the culture," the woman writer subverts the traditional and conventional grounds ridiculing the absurdities of "the politician, the pious, and the pompous." The woman humourist, then, "must break out of the passive, subordinate position mandated for them by centuries of patriarchal tradition and take on the power accruing to those who reveal the shams, hypocrisies, and incongruities of the dominant culture." A woman humourist's task, therefore, as Walker identifies, is an arduous one since it must face and overthrow the authority that keeps her unauthorised as well as "to risk alienating those upon whom women are dependent for economic survival" *(Very* 9). This is one of the reasons why women's humour has conventionally been subverted and ignored through the ages.

A major difference between masculine and feminine humour refers to the modifications feminine humour makes to the narrative conventions. While, as Gillooly points out, women's humour is subtle and "at least apparently unthreatening" (*Smile 118),* the narrative conventions of masculine humour are generally direct and threatening. One instance of such alterations is in decentring the marriage convention "as the authorizing textual principle." However, women's humour does not openly challenge the "authority of culturally dominant oedipal narrative" that mostly results in "the heroine's erotic and economic transformation from daughter to wife" (*Smile* 18). Thus, feminine humour does not make drastic changes to the narrative; instead, it undermines the authority of the dominant patriarchal ideology through gradual disruption of its power. For instance, Pym similarly undermines the mastering ideology by counteracting the power of marriage at the end of her novels. Her novels for the most part do not end in marriage and if, by chance they do, marriage is demonstrated as the reversal of the type of marriage depicted in the conventional comic novels. The marriage Pym presents is ineffective, and does not result in the coupling of the lovers.

Even though men and women reserve narrative motifs and themes for comic outcomes, feminine humourists, as Gillooly contends, employ "literary forms generally shunned by their fellows" (*Smile* 18). The reason for women writers' acting in this way might differ from writer to writer, but the most important cause is the limitation and restriction of their writings in terms of motifs and structure. Throughout history, women writers have been able to express their humour in a specific language and mode, different from men's. For instance, they picked out the genre of fairy tales and made radical changes to it. As Gillooly claims, "Fairy tales – which inform the content and closure of most narratives of the period – are openly exploited by writers like Gaskell, Bronte, and Austen for humorous purposes" (*Smile* 18). Much later, the form of the fairy tale is also used in the novels of Pym for the same humorous purpose.

Pym's novels reverse the narrative structure and the plot of the conventional fairy tale in all aspects. To make a relationship with Gillooly's statement, they typically revise the "family romance that pervades nineteenth-century British narrative." Pym's novels generally reverse the structure of the fairy tales in which, as Gillooly says, "paternal figures (fathers primarily) are customarily royal, powerful, and loving, stepmothers cruel and sometimes murderous" (*Smile* 19). Unlike fairy tales, Pym's novels are emptied of the royal, efficient, and powerful male figures and fathers. There barely exist any father-figures in her novels. If they do, they are all inefficient fathers and husbands. They are exceedingly common men without a single drop of royal blood. They are mostly clergymen or university professors who do not have the authority as the father-figure at home. They are mostly abandoned by their wives and their children and are left with nobody really to care for them. In contrast, the spinsters in Pym's novels are the ones with the authority. They are all efficient individuals, capable of not only solving their own problems, but also counteracting those of other characters. The world in which Pym's characters live is not even a nuclear family. Most men and women live lonely lives, without having any children. By drawing such a sketch and for comic reasons, Pym reverses the conventional structure of the nuclear family and family romance.

1.10 Women's Humour and Socio-Cultural Restraints

In women's use of language, the socio-cultural restraints are considered a more important obstacle than women's lack of a sense of humour or their intellectual inferiority, as has conventionally been claimed by the male humourists and theorists. Thus, the question of women's humour is not an issue isolated from social and cultural concerns; it is, in fact, "part of a complex web of cultural assumptions about women's intelligence, competence and "proper role"" (Walker, *Very* 98). According to Suzanne L. Bunkers, owing to their gender difference, women and men have a different sense of humour. She suggests that "any analysis of women's and men's uses of humour be informed by an understanding of power, past and present, in our culture, and by an awareness of the politics of power on interacting members in a power relationship" (169). Hence, men and women create different types of humour since their relation to power structures differs.

Gillooly also believes that the strategies and tactics that women use in creating their humour, in particular its "subversiveness, diffuseness, and self-deprecation," share much with the "humour of others who are similarly marginalized (and consequently gendered feminine)" in a society and a culture that is "dominated by white, heterosexual, able-bodied, Christian, middle-class masculinity" (*Smile* xxv). Likewise, by referring to the destructive effects of women's social control, Mahadev L. Apte asserts that such restraints "have a direct relationship to the free expression of the sense of humour." He also adds that women have rarely taken part in "both pre-industrial and industrial cultures, in such rituals as clowning and joking relationships" and this lack is due to "the social limitations on women's behaviour" (qtd. in Walker, *Very* 85). Likewise, Lakoff, who analyses the differences between the languages employed by men and women, considers "women's reluctance to be openly humorous" as "both source and evidence of discrimination." Moreover, she proposes that linguistic discrimination constrains women's use of language and this works in two ways: "in the way that they are taught to use language, and in the way general language use treats them" (qtd. in Walker, *Very* 86).

Further, according to Gillooly, feminine humour functions more with "tendentious jokes or other male-identified forms of humor (like irony)," as a "negotiatory mechanism" ceasing the "anxiety that arises in the conflict between aggressive urges and behavioral restraints." This conflict, for instance for many middle class women during the nineteenth century, focuses on the "desire for agency in a culture that insists upon female passivity." Therefore, feminine humour "mediates between the wish to avoid pain and the necessity of submitting to social codes," negotiating "between disagreeable feelings of subservience and the necessary recognition of female political inferiority." Consequently, "through a change in expression, such humor recasts the psychic impression of external reality – normally authoritative and determinant – as inconsequential and subordinate, thereby lessening its impact: the power of patriarchy is at least psychologically mitigated when it appears as the object of delicate ridicule" (*Smile* 24). Feminine humour, thus attempts to use the existing social conditions as a backdrop for its activities in order to adjust its discourse, which intends to make the social conditions more tolerable for women's survival, to the "circumstances at hand." Thus, without demanding any radical changes, it affords a flight from the existing weight of reality. In comparing it with satire, Gillooly describes the general orientation of feminine humour in the following words:

> Feminine humor – fostering harmony in the psychic economy while subtly disquieting the cultural one – represents the most efficient means of satisfying aggression without risking retaliation, affording a temporary escape from the burdens of reality (as opposed to their psychotic rejection) and just enough release of frustration and relaxation of conflict to make possible a more or less "healthy" adjustment to the peculiar constraints of nineteenth-century femininity. For in contrast to satire, the announced aim of which is to alter so-

cial conditions, feminine humor quietly enables the subject to survive the circumstances at hand. (*Smile* 24)

Humour for women writers, as argued by some theorists, has been the most natural way of expressing themselves in a patriarchal culture. In order to resist the culture in which she is born and later victimised, the woman writer employs the same device, language, of her oppressors in order to manifest her own marginality. In this case, Little suggests that "for several thousand years, any woman who became literate and who ventured to write learned to 'humor' the sentence which she borrowed from a culture and language very largely designed and dominated by her father, her husband, or her sons and brothers" (*Experimental* 19). Through humouring the sentence, Little signifies that women had to "get along" with language, "be nice to it, and give in to it enough so that she could make it give in to her at least some of the time. In doing this, women have also humoured the sentence in another way – they have carnivalized it" (*Experimental* 19). *Carnivalizing* the sentence helped women writers to make profit of the male-centred and male-created language and apply it according to their own need and use.

1.11 Ideology of Domesticity and Domestic Comedy

Right from the age of Industrialisation up to the present day, the ideology of domesticity has been a threat to women's free expression, and writing in a comic mode. Audrey Bilger asserts that the combination of woman writer and comedy in the 18th century was considered to be dangerous since it was a threat to the ideology of the domestic order: "Because the preference for sentimental comedy relied so heavily on images of domestic order and because domestic order required that women be subordinate to men, social fears of noncompliance and disruption made it difficult for a writer to be comic, critical, and female." To allay such fears, conduct literature and etiquette books of the time, according to Bilger, prescribed the "proper feminine behavior for middle class women largely in terms antithetical to the critical spirit of comedy" (21). The writers of such conduct books portrayed a diminished, false image of women, asking their readers to transform themselves into such an image. The literary theorist Mary Poovey calls such an image the "naturalization of the feminine ideal. They constructed an ideal of femininity and then redefined female nature in terms of that ideal" (qtd. in Bilger 21). This image was a complete contrast to the earlier image of the woman as being untamed and seductive. The new image was an image of a type, an obedient, a domestic, and tamed housewife, or, as Woolf puts it, an *Angel in the House*.

Such threats against and fears about women's creative writings continued until the twentieth century, especially in the aftermath of World War II, by the advent of domestic or housewife humour "in which the autobiographical persona of a harried housewife describes her frantic and often unsuccessful efforts to cope with life in the slow (family-and home-centered) lane" (Dresner 93). The socio-cultural conditions after World War II were in turmoil. As Orna Raz argues, "a new stress was posed on the nuclear family as a foundation of the new British welfare state" (99). Hence, women went back to their household dutifully and adopted the role of the housewife. Domestic comedy was partly the outcome of such a particular condition.

The primary purpose of the domestic humour, as Dresner argues, is that "by challenging the political, social, and economic systems that reinforced women's subjugation," it helped women "with a temporary tool for coping with those negative feelings about themselves and their lives" (95). Hence, domestic comedy changes into a means of escape for those women who had been "pressured, overtly or covertly, into acknowledging housewifery as their sole occupation and raison d'etre" (Dresner 93). Moreover, women, as being the essential agents of domestic life, were considered subordinate and thus unauthorised to act in a world abounding in male values; although, as Sochen suggests, they were the principal elements in "the domestic realm" (11). This realm was totally subservient to the public domain which devalued and dismissed women and their struggles. Thus, as Sochen argues, the writings of domestic humourists also have been deprecated because of their *insignificant* themes and subjects. For instance "humor associated with politics, business, and other male pursuits ranks higher in the hierarchy of humor than women's domestic humor," Sochen observes that male humourists such as "Twain, makes fun of politicians and

1 Characteristics of Women's Humour 51

current events" while "Whitcher jokes about gossipy women and the annoyances of homemaking" (11).

Likewise, Pym's humour deals with the domestic realm, with the *unpleasant tasks*, gossipy people, drawing room tea parties, and in particular with food and drinks. If there is a hint to a historical event or cultural change, it is stated in an indirect, and covert manner. The social turmoil after the World War II has also been mentioned subtly in the midst of some other main events. Indeed, in her novels Pym has combined the post-WWII horrors, losses, rationings, shell-shocks, and poverty in her typically humorous tone. Due to the particular socio-historical conditions of her time, Pym's humour strikingly deviates from the conventional, traditional humour.

The most significant factor that perplexes women's comic writings, as well as women's writings in general, is, according to Walker, the male belief in the false myths and stereotypes about women: "the cultural identification of womanhood with subordination rather than superiority, with passivity rather than prescience" (*Very* 28). Walker additionally suggests that possibly the most effectual way that women writers "have addressed male discourse is by revising the mythologies it has promulgated." These myths are the "myths and stories that have been used as paradigms for success, heroism, and male-female relationships." Moreover, such myths have been considered by women writers as "skeptical irony." For instance, the efficiency of the romantic love in fairy tales is "frequently deconstructed" (*Feminist* 50). Since the prevailing culture has commonly frustrated the woman writer's participation in its discourses, women have created a kind of literary work that has an inherent, ironic tone. Women have been consequently "mocking, appropriating, and revising the language and the stories of a culture" which have continuously been oppressing and degrading them (Walker, *Feminist* 50).

A crucial factor affecting women's humorous writing is, as Walker points out, "her very 'apartness' from the culture in which she lives" (*Feminist* 50). Women's oppression by the patriarchal culture banishes them from the dominant culture. Furthermore, Walker contends that from the beginning of the eighteenth century, which was the advent of domesticity as well, through the nineteenth-century "sewing society to the post-World

War II suburbs [...] women have in many ways inhabited a separate reality from that of men." The only reality of women's work, as Walker puts, has been "a largely domestic reality involving housework and children instead of business and politics" (*Feminist* 50). In Pym's novels, the ideology of domesticity of the 1950's is also aptly represented. According to Raz, "In the aftermath of the Second World War, a fresh emphasis was placed on the nuclear family as a foundation of the new British welfare state." And, by the end of the World War, "married women were encouraged to return home and assume the role of 'housewives.'" Raz, however, suggests that since most of Pym's heroines are single, "they are less affected by contemporary social changes brought about by the rise of the welfare state." Still, because they are living in the same society within the same dominant values and norms, "they are measured, judged and influenced by society's standards, and construct their identity according to the parameters of family situation, social class, and employment" (99). Thus, Pym's heroines, though single, are the victims of the society's false standards. Representing this situation in a humorous mode, Pym directs the attention of her readers towards the absurd and hypocritical nature of such standards.

1.12 Characteristics of Women's Humour

By emphasising the various functions of humour in women's social and mental lives and through reiterating the peculiar place of humour for women, Barreca argues that their laughter, being profoundly violating, is "confrontational and boundary breaking" (*Untamed* 12). In a parallel manner, Walker points out the similar function of comedy as a medium for representing the "shams, hypocrisies, and incongruities" (*Very* 9). Moreover, Barreca states that "anytime a woman breaks through a barrier set by society, she's making a feminist gesture of a sort, and every time a woman laughs, she's breaking through a barrier" (*They* 182). She stresses the widely held notion of the subversive nature of women's laughter by arguing that that "humor allows us [women writers] to gain perspective by ridiculing the implicit insanities of a patriarchal culture" (*Untamed* 12). Thus, being *transgressive, inherently subversive* and representing the *hypocrisies,* and *incongruities* of the dominating culture can be considered as some of the fundamental features of women's humour. By keeping an eye on the fact that Pym attempts to disrupt the well-established conventions related to the male and female roles distinctly observable in a patriarchal society, the significant features of women's humour are analysed in the selected novels in this study.

Through employing various strategies and techniques, women writers have not remained silent to the requirements of the patriarchy. Using proper language and diction, they have produced different forms in order to include their voice in the dominant discourse. In this regard Bilger states that "Although writing was itself a rebellious act – requiring that women reject the ideal of passive womanhood that has arisen during the eighteenth century – self-conscious, critical female writers could both seek shelter in and manipulate socially sanctioned domestic plots." Without appearing unfeminine, these women writers found out how to resist and control the improper by the use of various techniques and strategies in their writing. In other words, as Bilger says, "If the writing of critical comedy involved elements of aggression and overt self-assertion, careful women writers learned to disguise such unfeminine behavior with otherwise conventional characterizations and scenes" (25-26).

The aggressive and political nature of women's comedy is also given due consideration in this context. It is argued that the crucial factor in making women resort to writing in a comic mode has been their defiance of the oppressive patriarchal culture. Women's comic writings are produced as a strategy to guard themselves against the patriarchal ideology. Nonetheless, Gillooly contends that "to stress the defensive component of feminine humour is not, however, to argue that such humour is devoid of aggression." Moreover, according to Gillooly, women's aggression differs from the male aggression in the way that it is "more fully sublimated, or at least more thoroughly disguised, than the hostile impulse sparkling (for example) what Freud has termed "tendentious" humor" (*Smile* 23). Nevertheless, the aggression present in women's humour is the effect of the tension existing in the patriarchal system rather than the outcome of a moment of aggression on the woman writer's side. In this case, Barreca proposes that the motivation for women's comedy is aggression. It is the "aggression against culturally imposed restraints" ("Introduction" 6). The climax of women's comedy is not the annihilation of the patriarchal structure, revealed through daughterly marriages, and the renewal of the status quo through the progeny of the privileged, rather, it is "decentering, dislocating, and destabilising" authority. Thus, the delight of women's comedy comes from the destruction of the familiar, rather than the "perpetuation" of the familiar (Barecca, *Untamed* 30 and 19). Likewise, in her introduction to Gillooly's *Smile of Discontent: Humor, Gender, and Nineteenth-Century British Fiction* (1999), Catherine R. Stimpson asserts that "feminine humor" is a way of writing and speaking and a technique of resistance that is "discursive" (x).

The woman humourist, as having much in common with the feminine attitude in general, almost often upgrades the destiny of the helpless victims to the comic heroines in order to provide the required setting for her success against the current cultural obstacles. Barreca stresses the upgrading of the comic heroine to a "triumphant" heroine as "almost exclusively a product of the female writer" (*Untamed* 16). However, this kind of humour functions unlike the tendentious humour which arises from the aggression of the creator of humour towards the weak. As Gillooly proposes, the aim of "tendentious jokes is the release of aggression against the other" while "the aim of humor is the avoidance of pain and distress for the self" (*Smile* 24). Thus, the aim of tendentious jokes and humour differs with regard for whom the humour is intended; still, aggression, as the fundamental element of humour, underflows in the feminine humour. Or, as Gillooly argues, "Such avoidance of pain and distress, however purely defensive it may seem, has in feminine humor a combative component as well" (*Smile* 24). This aggression, nevertheless, is "aimed not at the Other but at the Law – the authority of the 'situation' – in relation to which one feels childlike and powerless." Feminine humour, rather than "providing momentary release from social inhibitions as tendentious jokes do," accordingly operates "as a sustained, if diffusive, undercover assault upon the authority of the social order itself." Thus, without seeking any superiority over the other, feminine humour "mocks the cultural construction of femininity in order to reduce its psychological power" (*Smile* 24). Similarly, the narrative voice in Pym's selected novels continuously undermines the socio-cultural abstraction of femininity by ridiculing the established rules and conventions.

Critics believe that the women writers' approach to the power structures and to the people related to authority is different from the male writer's approach to them. Bennett observes that while male writers might "attack the institutions of church and marriage," women writers "not only attack the institutions but also the male figures behind those institutions." These men however, according to Bennett,

> have traditionally dictated policy and behavior for women throughout the centuries, marking women as representatives of Eve, forever tempting men away from God with the apple of sex. In short, although men may view religion as absurd or meaningless, women may also see it as oppressive and destructive. (86)

Though Pym's novels usually deal with the institution of church, clergymen and parishes, however, she does not side with the influential and powerful oppressors. In the selected novels, clerics and the authority associated with the church are being ridiculed, and the relation between the common people and the clergy is usually counteracted. It is the clergymen who are in need of people's help, not the other way round as, according to Bennett, the combination of the "institution and man" is a good instance of the hegemony of the system which results in the figure of the "minister or preacher" that is a "common target of female satire." Thus, in Bennett's words, "by 'humanizing' preachers" women writers "decrease their authority and influence, thus, result in their appearing as absurd and comic" (86-87).

Whether women's humorous writing is political or not has long been a debatable issue. Barreca notes that that "much women's humor, while not explicitly political, nevertheless raises questions concerning the accepted wisdom of the system" (*Penguin* 1). Thus, although women's humour does not radically question or alter the existent ideological system, however, it certainly undermines and questions the existent order. Moreover, women's humour mostly questions the authority that suppresses and victimises them. In Barreca's words, "When it *is* explicitly political, women's humor often satirizes the social forces designed to keep women in "their place," a phrase that has become synonymous with keeping women quietly bound by cultural stereotypes (*Penguin* 1-2). Likewise, Pym's humour ridicules the authority that makes women obedient and subordinate. It does not subvert the existent order radically, nevertheless, it implicitly subverts the ideological authority that considers women as passive, subordinate, and dependent beings. Thus, being compatible with women's political purposes, women's humour is of a different type. Unlike masculine humour, women's humour "is not only about telling jokes; it is about telling stories, and about retelling stories that once might have been painful but can be redeemed through humor" (Barreca, *Penguin* 5). Thus, although women's humour does not have a political mission, it is at the same time a political tool.

Women writers generally employ two effective tools namely understatement and self-deprecation in order to make their writings more effective. The function of their humour, therefore, has some similarities with comedy. As Barreca understands, comedy often "turns directly against the self as the simplest target" (*Untamed* 30). In this case, Gillooly remarks that unlike the much aggressive "carnivalesque" which "overthrows convention and order" for a short period of time, "feminine humor is understated" (*Smile* x). That is, feminine humour does not seek for the temporary revolutionary changes that will cease their effects after a short while; however, it is rather, a type of humour which, according to Gillooly, "sews its stitches in nooks, crannies, and corners of a narrative," that is, indirect and subtle (*Smile* x). This type of comedy, according to Stimpson, controls and restrains "its aggressive impulses" in order to unarm "any counterattack" (x). Feminine humour mocks the absurdities, "the disproportions and incongruities within the (masculinized) norm" in a veiled and covert way (Stimpson x). However, as pointed out by Gillooly, this norm has always been the "traditional locus of cultural authority, which internalized carries the weight and force of law" (*Smile* xx). The subtle and indirect tactics that women apply in their writings might best be called "feminine" in being associated with traits, behaviours, perspectives, preoccupations, and dispositions that, with remarkable continuity and integrity, have been both historically and cross-culturally constructed, as appropriate to, or descriptive of, women. While the purposes of the different women writers are somewhat dissimilar in writing, nevertheless, Gillooly assumes that in every period and place, the strategies and "humorous tactics are strikingly similar." Gillooly further believes that the same tactics are largely "employed by other women in other periods and places" that are called "'feminine'" (*Smile* xix). Thus, this statement reminds us of Showalter's and other theorists' arguments about women's writings that are similar in all places and periods, and their discussion that women's writings, based on their specific conditions, are of the same nature.

1.13 Major Areas and Tactics of Female Humour

There has always been a controversy among the critics as how to distinguish feminine humour from masculine humour. In this case, Gillooly states that there are mainly two areas that humour "exhibits its femininity" which include "rhetoric and affect." Moreover, she proposes that while in some instances

> behaviors culturally attributed to British women of the middle-classes (such as self-denial and submission) become the objective of women writer's ridicule and mockery, however, in some other instances, the rhetoric is made up of these attributed behaviours giving a sort of humour that is gently delighting in shape, apparently "passive and modestly self-effacing. (*Smile* 15)

In order to subvert the force and authority of the "stereotypes," women writers reproduce feminine humour inclining to "hide behind" them. By highlighting them, she exposes them as "visible" and thus, ineffectual in face of cultural dominance (*Smile* 17).

Likewise, Pym's selected novels are full of the stereotypes that undermine the authority of the mastering culture. In order to undermine the foundation of authority, a good deal of tactics and strategies are used by women writers. As stated by Gillooly, "Feminine selflessness is (briefly) appropriated as a tactic of subversion" (*Smile* 17). Being selfless and offering services to the others are among the most crucial functions of women characters in Pym's novels. They usually attend to the others, mostly men.

Belinda in *STG*, for example, is a stereotypical sacrificial and selfless woman in Pym's fiction. Her main concern is to provide comfort and pleasure to the others while ignoring her own. Mildred, the heroine of *EW*, also cares about other people more than for her own self. Likewise, in *JP*, Jane as a clergyman's wife, cares for Prudence and other people more than for those of her own household. Similarly, the other female characters in the novel are seen attending to Fabian Driver, a handsome widower.

The topics and subjects of women's humour, as shown by Walker, have been chosen in accordance to the "experiences that must be survived – such as motherhood, waltzes with boors, and the double standard – it functions much as the humor of a racial or ethnic group does" (*Very* 36). Moreover, the woman writer considers her readers as being sufficiently familiar with the subjects, themes, and topics that she employs, presuming a

> shared discomfort or anger at the oppression they mutually endure." On the surface level, the text "appears to surrender to the status quo, carries within it the codes that members of the group recognize as part of their common heritage while superficially accepting the assessment of the dominant culture – e.g., women are frivolous, gossipy, inept – on a deeper level women's humor calls into question the values that have led to those assessments. (*Very* 36)

This is what exactly takes place in Pym's selected novels. On the surface, Pym's text seems to be in accordance with the values of the dominating culture – representing stereotypes such as gossipy spinsters, unloved, lonely women and inept housewives. On a deeper level, Pym's text questions the well-established prejudices and standards about women's behaviour. According to Little, the origin of this type of humorous writing goes back to the novels of Woolf and Muriel Spark. Any evaluation of the works of these writers, who in a way were marginal to the dominant culture, particularly during the period of "social change," demonstrates characteristics of reversal, as well as "mocked hierarchies, communal festivity, and redefinition of sex identity" in the texts of the writers "who perceive themselves as 'outsiders,' as persons assigned to the threshold of a world that is not theirs" (qtd. in Walker, *Very* 70). Thus, the humorous writing of such marginal writers does not affirm the existent values; rather, it resists and undermines them. Such a humorous writing, as Walker remarks, derides "the norm radically." Moreover, it "generates hints and symbols of new myths ... An essential purpose of humor is to call the norm into question. What Little suggests here is that the humor of those on the 'threshold' is apt to reveal a perception of incongruity that not only questions the rules of the culture, but also suggests a different order (*Very* 71). Therefore, unlike men's humour, women's humorous writing does not seek to ridicule the hypocrisies and absurdities of the dominant culture for the sake of humiliating and degrading an individual or a group, but to ridicule the ideological tradition and long-standing values and beliefs. Moreover, this sort of humour tends to be reformative. That is, it attempts to create and originate modern standards and reasonable belief systems.

The presented images of the submissive or incapable women in women's humour indicate the fact that rather than endorsing or even accepting the extremes of women's behaviour, the authors are rejecting the cultural forces that have created them. In Walker's words, such "negative satiric portraits" (*Very* 65) create a distance between the reader and the subject that it allows the reader to disclaim elements of similar behaviour in him/herself. However, the humourist's attitude toward these two different sets of images is not the same. The submissive women such as Belinda and Mildred are objects of pity as well as scorn. They have accepted the traditional notions of their subordinate role so completely that they negate any possibility of personal power or achievement. The author evinces some sympathy for the woman who is outstandingly capable or beautiful since her very accomplishments are a mirror that reflect the average woman's own shortcomings.

1.14 Self-Irony

Irony is a gender-based technique which is mainly utilised by male humourists. Although women writers seldom use this strategy, they usually make use of self-irony as a significant feature which exists in women's humour. Sparing feminine humour of "sentimentality and cynicism" in the late twentieth century, feminine humour, according to Gillooly, demonstrates "its postmodernity, in being heavily intermingled with self-irony – with the sense that its very identity lies in its ineffectualness." This type of irony, based on Gillooly's definition, does not depend on the "maternal consolation" (*Smile* 209). By getting through the humour, such irony does not affect the sympathetic bond between the narrator and the heroine. However, the lack of "maternal consolation," as Gillooly says, does not result in woman writers' "self-loathing" or "despair" since in spite of admitting the unapproachability of the mother touchingly, "feminine humor still offers comfort [...] in the process of trying" (*Smile* 209). The self-irony which can be traced in Pym's selected novels, originates from her particular condition and, as Walker suggests, does not affect the narrator-heroine bond.

1.15 Women Writers' Humour in the Nineteenth Century

In order to understand women's humour totally, one should trace its origins through women's literary tradition. Women writers dominated the nineteenth century literary scene in Britain. Gillooly traces a particular type of feminine humour in these writers' texts. She characterises feminine humour as being "affectively sympathetic (though often infused with a trace of bitter sarcasm), rhetorically self-effacing, and intellectually (if covertly) preoccupied with the injuries, inconveniences, and injustices of gender" (*Smile* 4)[13]. Thus, the nineteenth century woman had to deal with all the challenges related to marriage, family, gender, class, and age through employing various humorous methods and strategies that Gillooly labelled as "feminine humour." They, however, sought a way out in order to release themselves from such restrictions and limitations by the application of their

---

[13] According to Gillooly, feminine humour not only equipped nineteenth-century women writers with "a socially acceptable means of voicing their discontent," but also it "employed virtues and wiles traditionally gendered feminine with ironic aptness." Thus, humour both contributed to women's silent manifestation of their "legal 'selflessness,'" and had a powerful effect on the other prospects of nineteenth-century femininity. For instance, it persisted on "marriageability" as the essential factor of female value more sufferable for women. Added to the other criterions such as marriage, age was also "a gender marked value" that shaped a woman's "desirability at least as much as her beauty or wealth" (*Smile* 4, 10).

creative and artistic potential while using humour as a weapon to undermine the dominant patriarchal ideology.

Moreover, humorous writing, in Barreca's words, allows women to explore "their own powers; they are refusing to accept social and cultural boundaries that mark the need or desire for closure as a 'universal.' Comedy is dangerous. Humor is a weapon. Laughter is refusal and triumph" (*Untamed* 30). Likewise, "laughter," according to Cixous and Clément, "breaks up, breaks out, splashes over. ... It is the moment at which the woman crosses a dangerous line, the cultural demarcation beyond which she will find herself excluded" (33). According to Gillooly, the noticeable common characteristic of feminine humour that shows itself in the letters and essays of the nineteenth-century middle-class women writers is the "delight it concocts from the often deadening routines and duties of 'women's sphere'" (*Smile* 11). This assessment takes into consideration the specific socio-historical conditions of women writers along with their tendency to counteract the effects of self-deprecation. Thus, the 19th century women writers struggled to integrate the bitter realities of women's lives with the pleasantness of their humour, in order to make it more tolerable. Resounding the other theorists, Gagnier proposes that "however restricted they were in public, among themselves Victorian women used humour neither for disparagement nor temporary release, but rather as a prolonged anarchic assault upon the codes constricting them." In their own turn, these women broke "their own frames, codes, or sets of social premises" (929 and 930). Similarly, as we shall see in the ensuing chapters, Pym also employs humour "as a prolonged anarchic assault" to resist and subvert the conventions and codes that restrict women.

1.16 Humour as a Device of Sympathy

Sympathy is another important concept developed and elaborated by Gillooly, regarding women's humour. That women's humour is interwoven with sympathy towards the other, for the sake of making a community, is the major discussion in Gillooly's theory of women's humour. A critical reading of humour clearly distinguishes between feminine and masculine humour. The former tends largely towards sympathetic understanding of the other, as the "shared purpose," while the latter is concerned with the "aggressive humor of name calling." Moreover, the addressee of the humour in women's writing is not the "victim" humiliated in the masculine humour. Instead, s/he is treated with playful sympathy: "In feminine humor, the reference itself, founded in playful homage and sympathy of shared purpose, constitutes the joke rather than signalling an opportunity for the aggressive humor of name calling" (*Smile* 21). Pym's characters also experience situations in which the (implied) author or narrator addresses them with a pitiful playfulness. Pym makes a playful joke out of anything and anyone incongruous, not to ridicule, humiliate, or attack them, but primarily to create a community as well as to sympathise with them. Likewise, Walker and Dresner proposed that women's humour is normally "more gentle and genteel" than the traditional humour which is "more interested in ridicule than sympathy" (qtd. in *Smile* 22). This situation, as Gillooly contends, is due to "the cultural constrains imposed upon the rhetoric of women's humor" (*Smile* 22). Yet, such female rhetoric has also the "persona-protective effect" of disguising the hostility covert in the humour. Thus, female humour, as put by Walker and Dresner, decreases the dangers "involved in challenging the status quo" (qtd. in *Smile* 22).

The relation between the woman humourist and her addressee[14] goes far deeper than sympathy. While masculine humour creates a wide gap between the humourist and his victim through altering the addressee into a *victim*, and changing the humourist into a *victimiser*, feminine humour creates bonding. However, this bonding does not occur "between the humourist and the auditors but between humourist and victim, with the auditor participating vicariously in their relationship" (Gillooly, *Smile* 27). In addition, Gillooly states that such bonding in the nineteenth-century domestic fiction, however, "is performed by the narrator and heroine, who share an emphatic (as opposed to identificatory) closeness generally unmatched by the narrator/comic hero relationships found in Scott, Thackeray, or Dickens" (27). Thus, feminine humour is not only a humour to initiate laughter; it contributes to the relatedness of those involved in this humour. On the one hand, it relates the narrator with the addressee, and on the other, it

---

[14] Since the relation between the women humourist and her victim, unlike that of the male humourist, is one of friendship and sympathy, the term *addressee* instead of *victim* is used to refer to her.

bonds the reader with both the narrator and the addressee. Thus, the narration creates an intimate and friendly atmosphere in which the laughter is not to humiliate, ridicule or disempower. Rather, feminine humour is to create an intimate and friendly environment, as well as to manifest aggression and dissatisfaction at the existing order. As a result, Gillooly considers the psychological expression of feminine humour as "transitional, intersubjective, and relational"[15] (*Smile* 28). Thus, feminine humour is a way of women's defending themselves in the face of patriarchal system and rules to reunite with the lost mother[16]. Furthermore, in addition to forming a strong bond between the narrator and the heroine, feminine humour operates in other textual relationships. For instance, it connects "the narrator to witty characters" (*Smile* 30).

---

[15] In feminine humour, as Gillooly argues, the keen edges that distinguish and qualify masculine humor in such forms as "the oedipal joking relation," "the binarism of irony," and the "will to individuate into wit, comedy, satire ..." are all confused. The peculiar desire that is existent in feminine humour is "the longing for the infantile bond with the mother: the bond that, under the usually operative reality regime, has been displaced or 'lost.'" That is, the significant factor in determining feminine humor is its relatedness, its connection with the mother or the 'lost bond'. By working to recreate "the lost bond in the relation between narrator and heroine," feminine humour fights back the suffering, anguish and "disappointment of the original loss (of the preoedipal mother and of the child's early sense of omnipotence, which she represents)" as well as her "feelings of powerlessness, fear, anger, and guilt that generally accompany it." Dissimilar to the "hero (and Freud's typical son), whose lost union with the mother is largely compensated by his identification with the father as an active, desiring subject, the heroine [...] is fated figuratively and often literally to be simply a 'motherless' object of either male erotic desire or of female erotic neglect" (*Smile* 28).

[16] From one aspect, as Gillooly notes, "this longing for the lost mother constitutes the bedrock of nostalgia ... this congenial, if not innate, yearning to reunite with the lost mother, or at least to cling to her 'inner representation' (which is Winnicott's definition of nostalgia), expresses itself in feminine humor as an impulse to recreate the infantile conditions in which that "inner representation" had an unmistakable external potency." Instead of "characterizing the longing for an idealized father figure, that is, the nostalgia of feminine humor invokes a space of empathic identification in a time before the onset of the Law: 'a transient resurrection,' as Eliot describes it in *The Lifted Veil*, 'into a happier pre-existence.'" Therefore, the feminine humorist searches for shelter from "a magnified preoedipal mother-image" with which she is strong enough to refuse reality "by returning in fantasy to the mother-child dyad." This, however, is in contrast to Freud's beliefs on the authority "of the paternal superego" in the activities of humour (*Smile* 28, 37).

Likewise, as Walker understands, women's peculiar position in culture results in their purposeful use of humour in order to achieve certain ends. A prevalent subject considering women's humour is "how it feels to be a member of a subordinate group in a culture that prides itself on equality, what it is like to try to meet standards for behavior that are based on stereotypes rather than on human beings." Moreover, in Walker's words, "women have used humor to talk to each other about their common concerns" in order to work out a way to relate, to survive, and to resist (*Very* x). In contrast to men's humour, which is mostly a strategy for "self-presentation" and "a demonstration of cleverness," women's humour, according to Walker, is mainly "a means of communication" as well as "a sharing of experience" (*Very* xii). Thus, according to the theorists, creating sympathy and making a connection are the common features of women's humour that distinguishes it from the other forms of humour. Moreover, as Margaret Oliphant comments on Austen's humour, feminine humourists sympathise with those who suffer without pitying them:

> Giving them unconsciously a share in her own sense of the covert fun of a scene, and gentle disdain of the possibility that meanness and folly and stupidity could ever really wound any rational creature. The position of mind is essentially feminine ... feminine cynicism [...] It is something altogether different from the rude and brutal male quality that bears the same name. (Qtd. in Gillooly, *Smile* 37)

Thus, pitying the oppressed group, differs significantly from sympathising with them. In a sharp contrast to the masculine humour, which merely pities the oppressed group exhibiting its brilliance, feminine humour not only sympathises with the marginalised but also ridicules the follies and absurdities of the prevalent culture indirectly. Moreover, through pointing to the lack of women's comic tradition and the significance of women's stereotypes in comedies written by men, Andrew Stott states that "a woman's place in comedy has been defined by either her sexual identity or her availability for marriage. As a result, comedy engages in the repetition of negative stereotypes. Women are handed the role as the 'handmaid of laughter, not its creator'" (92). Thus, the stereotypes of women were the most significant source of humour for the male humourists, who employed them in various forms in their writings. However, according to Stott, only two types of women were kept traditionally as sacred by men: "the romantic partner or the mother could not be represented as either physical or humorous" while "the old or the unattractive" were the most important stereotypes (92).

1.17 Female Humour and Narrative Structure

Female humour and narrative structure are supposedly interconnected. The "relation between feminine humor and narrative structure," according to Gillooly, "differs from the norm" or the conventional humour (*Smile* 21). Likewise, gossip creates a "different narrative structuring" of the novel as the humour of the text operates through its gossip. As a type of unofficial way of conversation, gossip is "culturally identified as feminine. [… And] outside the boundaries of official discourse, gossip has constitutive power." That is, its "relational, intimate flow governs the narrative movement." In this manner, through creating an "unauthorized but nonetheless authoritative narrative community," gossip "challenges the traditional social order" (*Smile* 21). Likewise, as an *unauthorized* and *unofficial* discourse, gossip functions along with the subtle humour of the narrative, questioning the social and the conventional order. Moreover, it is embedded in the overall narrative structure through the dominant presence in the dialogues among and between the characters. In a similar manner, Pym's chosen narratives are filled with this kind of unauthorized discourse which may be regarded as the challenging force of the narrative to the conventional social order.

Moreover, considering the way feminine humour operates, Gillooly suggests that "syntactically, feminine humor occurs most often undercover: in self-effacing tropes and faint discursive patterns that work to conceal its existence" (*Smile* 22). Additionally, unlike masculine humour which is considered as the norm, feminine humour makes use of different "forms of representation" including "litotes, apophasis, and meiosis" that makes expression possible. Moreover, feminine humour apparently excludes tropes such as "hyperbole and metaphor" that are considered distinctly masculine.

It employs "italics and dashes over exclamation points to signal its presence," and applies "subjunctive constructions and periphrasis" in order to obstruct getting through it (*Smile* 22). Thus, the recognition of the subtle and covert structural strategies used by feminine humourists is a laborious task.

To conclude, the critical discussion on women's humour gains it legitimacy from the existence of a form of writing distinctly recognised as women's writing. The critics of women's humour, particularly Gillooly, argue that women's humour, in a similar manner to the historical underestimation of their affairs, has continuously been silenced, ignored and misread owing to the socio-cultural prejudices such as considering women's intellect as inferior, regarding them as mere Angels in the House, and their inferior economic, social and political position. Additionally, it has been argued that women's humour differs from male humour or deviates from the conventional or traditional humour. This study argues that women's humour attempts not only to unveil the absurdities and hypocrisies of the male society but also, by ridiculing the fundamental values, beliefs and stereotypes related to women, to resist and undermine the dominating patriarchal culture. Thus, women's humour, as critics argue, mainly revolts against the socio-cultural norms. That is to say, it does not attempt to alter the dominating political system; rather, through the implication of various methods, it subverts the foundation of the belief systems which have been functioning throughout the years in the collective consciousness of both men and women. Thus, they challenge the existent power structure by employing humour as a weapon for their survival within a cultural context that has a tendency to supress and undermine their intellectual abilities and capabilities as well as objectify their bodies.

1.18 Rhetoric of Humour in Pym's Novels

The skilful operation of women's humour in Pym's novels allows the author to undermine the current dominating socio-political system, as well as to challenge the long-held conceptions and stereotypes of women in a subtle and indirect manner. Through an artful use of humour, Pym creates heroines who are in sharp contrast to the longstanding values and conventions of the society. Thus, the present book is a study of Pym's rhetoric of humour by focusing on the principles of the kind of humour present in the central characters' speeches.

The central female characters' deriding views, in terms of the hypocrisies and absurdities inherent in the dominating culture, constitute the basic narrative element in Pym's fiction. This aspect generally contributes to the humorous nature of Pym's works. Thus, by applying feminine humour, these women cleverly deal with their difficulties and challenging conditions, as does their author. Moreover, the functioning of women's humour makes it possible for the creation of a sympathetic bond between the narrator and the heroine on the one hand, and between the narrator, the heroine and the reader on the other. Eventually, the problems and difficulties they encounter within a patriarchal society are altered into a sympathetic and light-hearted laughter at the end.

Critics of women's humour suggest that women's humour presents itself differently from the traditional, masculine humour in two ways, either through narrative and rhetorical strategies or through thematic tactics and subjects. The rhetorical and narrative techniques and strategies employed by women are capable of concealing the aggressive and hostile nature of traditional masculine humour. That is, by applying such narrative tactics, as well as by the employment of themes and subjects peculiar to women, women's humour diminishes the threats and dangers inherent in undermining the status quo (Gillooly, *Smile* 22). In subsequent chapters, the operation of women's humour in Pym's selected novels will be analysed structurally and thematically. By restricting itself to the three selected novels by Pym, the following chapters in particular explore Pym's application of narrative and rhetorical strategies such as the function of gossip, self-deprecation and understatement; the undermining process of the romantic love and happy ending by women humourists; double-voiced discourse in women's writers' texts; the sympathetic bond between the narrator, heroine and the reader; the thematic tactics and subjects, including images and stereotypes of women; the importance of domesticity and trivia; the *cult of domesticity*; humour as a means of women's power and control; and women's social critique.

2 *Some Tame Gazelle*: Construction of Women's Veiled Humour

> Belinda saw that it was no good trying to change the subject yet. He must be humoured out of it. (*STG* 38)

This chapter explores the function of women's humour in Pym's *STG* with reference to the discussed theories pertaining to women's humour as proposed particularly by Gillooly, as well as by the other critics such as Walker and Barreca. The chapter in general focuses on the rhetorical and thematic strategies exploring the ways in which they contribute to the construction of women's humour in *STG*. In the first part, the role of rhetorical strategies in the construction of women's humour is examined. In this case, the following issues are examined closely: the reversal of the romantic love plot through highlighting the discourse of trivia; the use of double-voiced discourse; the role of gossip in the construction of humorous narrative; the female characters' use of self-deprecating or understating language; and finally, the creation of a sympathetic bond between the narrator and the heroine on the one hand, and among the characters themselves on the other. In the second part, the chapter explores some motifs and themes that enhance the role of women's humour in *STG,* focusing particularly on the comic subversion of the images and stereotypes such as a spinster, a bachelor; the role of humour as a means of the narrator's power and control, and as a device for women's social critique through undermining the institution of the church and clergymen. The chapter highlights how, by employing some structural and thematic strategies, Pym in this novel builds up a distinct kind of women's humour that leads on to deconstruct the fundamentals of the existing dominant culture.

Pym's peculiar employment of humour, as Wyatt-Brown remarks, is to a large part due to her own life experiences. Since Pym judged her conduct by the traditional standards, she struggled hard "to hide all evidence of hurt and anger. Hence, her narratives reveal depression, not fury." Thus, an overwhelmed hostility in her novels is skilfully concealed behind her humour. According to Wyatt-Brown, Pym often expressed her emotions indirectly and "took pride in her self-control and paid the penalty of depression and low self-esteem" (3). Therefore, Pym's discourse of humour is distinguished from the conventional humour discourses in the way that, by applying both structural and thematic strategies, it subverts the discourse of patriarchy manifesting the particular viewpoint of women. Moreover, the consequence of Pym's subversive subtext, as Janice Rossen states, is sharply felt in association with her narrator's outward compliance to social expectations, coupled with their inward criticism. Simultaneously, these conflicts take place "in the realm of private thought, where the reader and narrator join the heroines in their isolation" (61). According to Wyatt-Brown, Pym's narrative strategy reveals that neither she nor her characters, in fact, face their situations directly, in case "they lose their sense of humor" (68). Rather, Pym employs a variety of tones, "from rueful self-effacement to occasional moments of sharp insight." Moreover, she produced narrative strategies that protect her characters from "uncomfortable self-scrutiny but allow for some expression of their true feelings" (Wyatt-Brown 68). This type of humour is mostly directed at the prevailing system which gives rise to the absurd, egoist and self-indulgent individuals rather than to the individuals themselves. Similarly, by directing humour at themselves, Pym's women characters undermine the various images of women as projected by the dominant culture and its false values.

2.1. Role of Rhetorical Strategies in the Construction of Women's Humour in *STG*

The rhetorical strategies employed by Pym in *STG* play a distinct role in the construction of humour through interweaving various narrative elements – such as the reversal of the romantic plot through domesticity, the employment of gossip, the use of double-voiced discourse, self-deprecating or understating language, and the creation of a sympathetic bond between the characters.

STG tells the life stories of people in a village, focusing on two sisters, Belinda and Harriet Bede. Belinda is represented as a modest and selfless sister who has been in love with the vicar, Archdeacon Henry Hoccleve, for thirty years while he is married to the unsympathetic Agatha. Belinda is a selfless helper in the parish and everyone expects her services and sacrifices. Her sister, Harriet, is presented as a selfish and well-dressed woman, obsessed with the young curates. She is forever occupied with strengthening her corsets, making fashionable dresses and serving young curates. Throughout the novel, she is busy serving and caring for Mr. Donne, the new curate in the village. She has a persistent admirer and suitor, Ricardo Bianco, who is shown being rejected by her continuously. Archdeacon Henry Hoccleve is a pompous, self-dramatising and pretentious person who does not do much, except reciting poems from the obscure English poets as well as pretending to be overworked and tired. During Agatha's holidays in Karlsbad, Belinda and Henry spend an evening together, in Agatha's absence. Henry reads poems aloud to Belinda, and then they converse. Dr. Parnell and his colleague, Mr. Mold, two librarians and old friends of Henry and Belinda, come to the village for a visit. Mr. Mold proposes marriage to Harriet and is refused. Another stranger, Bishop Grote also comes to the village, seeking a suitable wife. He chooses Belinda and proposes to her but she also rejects him. Both sisters prefer their comfortable spinsterhood lives to matrimony. Mr. Donne finally marries Agatha's niece, Olivia Berrige, and Harriet finds another young curate at their wedding. Belinda, however, continues her persistent love for Henry, without any change in her life and perspective.

2.1.1. Subversion of the Romantic Plot and the Discourse of Trivia

A significant structural element in shaping woman writers' humour, including Pym's humour, is believed to be the subversion of the conventional romantic love plot. Cooley stresses that although Pym employs romance, however, she subverts the romantic love plot in *STG* in which she, on the one hand, "celebrates" and on the other hand, "mocks romantic comedy." In other words, according to Cooley, Pym coincidentally "plays havoc with romantic convention as much as she exploits it" ("Barbara" 367). Barbara Brothers also points out Pym's romantic-minded characters and Pym's suppressing their romantic hopes and desires. Pym's heroines, as she argues, "nourish romantic aspirations but must learn to withstand emotional deprivation" (qtd. in Wyatt-Brown 6). Moreover, Brothers states that Pym's art is "subversive" in the sense that "her gentle ironies mock the romantic paradigm and her characters' acceptance of it." Brothers also maintains that since for Pym "romance in fiction and romance in real life are not the same," she refutes the thought that "women's images of themselves are formed by poets, novelists, popular culture, and magazines" (qtd. in Tsagaris 9). Similarly, Wyatt-Brown suggests that Pym was affected by previous writers among them "Austen and the Brontes," and thanks to her education, she "knew romances as well." However, her view of romance differs from the conventional views as "She borrows and rewrites the standard plots and characters of romance novels to create her own version of the heroine's quest for a meaningful life." Even according to Wyatt-Brown, Pym mostly subverts "the stock elements of romance" by employing various strategies (66).

It is argued that although in both male and female writers' narrative, certain themes and subjects are designed to achieve a comic effect, nonetheless, feminine humourists make use of the dominant strategies that are historically cast aside by others. The main reason for the woman writer's selection of particular topics and subjects refers to her limitations to some established motifs and structures. Nevertheless, women writers manage to convey their humour, by employing a different style and language. For instance, women writers chose the deep-rooted genus of fairy tale and altered it extensively. In this respect, Gillooly asserts that "Fairy tales – which inform the content and closure of most narratives of the period – are openly exploited by writers like Gaskell, Bronte, and Austen for humorous purposes" (*Smile* 18). Pym, in *STG* employs some elements of the fairy tale in order to undermine its comic effects. The conventions of the romantic love plot are subverted in the narrative that begins with an opportunity for a fairy tale romance; however, there is no considerable change in the fortunes of the characters at the end. Moreover, Pym constantly undermines the romantic conventions throughout the novel. Being educated in literature, she made use of the romance genre in order to undermine the existent tradition since, as Tsagaris puts it, "Like the romance writers, she is aware of literary history, as her allusions and quotes indicate. Unlike them, however, she uses her trivia to recreate the cozy but interesting world of her everyday heroines" (29).

The first paragraph of *STG* describes a scene in which the two sisters, Belinda and Harriet Bede, both unmarried, host a new curate at their house. The characters, the setting, and the action, entirely revert the conventions of the romantic love plot. The room is an ordinary drawing room in a village, and the hosts are two middle-aged women. Harriet has been obsessed with the young curates since her youth. However, she and the young Mr.

Donne, are not alone. Belinda, the elder sister is there too – not to admire the two, but to criticise them silently. Pym wrote about the common people, particularly marginal people. She "explored the lives of forgotten people in a most unusual fashion" (Wyatt-Brown 5). Unlike the traditional romantic plot, it is not the *man* who is peering at the lady and her clothes; it is the *woman* who is seen peering at the man's underwear, a piece of clothing supposed to be hidden. However, Belinda cannot help gazing at the curate's odd combinations and feel not embarrassed. Commenting on the anti-romantic plot of the first scene in *STG*, Cooley notes that "the ages and gender roles are scrambled. ... The woman is older and more judicious, the man young and somewhat dizzy." While Belinda "suffers from agonizing quixotic preoccupations with etiquette and propriety; the man is well pleased with himself and at ease. In Pym's world, the woman worries while the man talks on contentedly." Belinda is so preoccupied with the *rules of etiquette* that she always worries about the suitability of manners. As Cooley continues her discussion, "the rules of etiquette hem her in at every point; she can neither speak up about nor ignore the underwear" ("Barbara" 366). Therefore, the subversion of the traditional romance plot is threatened whenever Belinda notices an insignificant thing such as Mr. Donne's odd combination.

In *STG*, Pym reverses the conventional, gender-based roles. The central female character is much older than the man, and the trivial details, such as the combinations of the curate, are presented. In this way, Pym prevents the unfolding of the traditional romantic plot since, as Tsagaris (1998) puts it, "Pym takes the plot of the younger woman falling in love with a married, older man and subverts it through humor, and more important, through emphasizing the trivial and everyday" (10). In so doing, Pym disrupts the convention of an older man's courting a younger woman. Harriet, who in her mid-fifties, courts Mr. Donne, in his twenties. Furthermore, the man is not even aware of being courted by Harriet; instead, he behaves according to the social norms. According to Cooley, Pym deliberately creates unattractive but intelligent, middle-aged spinsters in order to undermine the conventional image of the heroine as represented in the romantic love plots. Moreover, these women, as Cooley points out, are not beloveds, rather they are the *lovers*: "Spinsters for her far from beautiful spinster-observers, Pym lowers the level of physical attractiveness required for literary heroines and raises the level of mental acuity. Her spinster heroines tend to be the only characters who are clear-headed and generous-minded." In contrast, the beloveds are men. They are, as Cooley states, "muddled by self-absorption and vanity. Thus Pym alters the "rules' of romantic comedy by having plain heroines and handsome but vain and foolish heroes; a dowdy woman and a silly man replace the beautiful couples of romantic comedy" ("Barbara" 9). As Gillooly states, *STG* subverts the narrative structure and the plot of the conventional fairy tale reversing the "family romance that pervades nineteenth-century British narrative." Moreover, according to Gillooly, *STG* also reverses the structure of the fairy tales in which "paternal figures (fathers primarily) are customarily royal, powerful, and loving, stepmothers cruel and sometimes murderous" (*Smile* 19).

Unlike the usual fairy-tale plots, Pym's *STG* is devoid of any strong and effective male figures. Married men are generally inefficient and weak. In the novel, Henry Hoccleve, though having the position of the Archdeacon, is ineffective as a man and a husband. His not being a father in his fifties, indicates his impotence. He does almost no work in the vicarage and the church. However, he pretends to be very busy with the affairs of the parish and church. The entire burden falls on his wife, Agatha, the curate and the parishioners. Similarly, the unmarried men are shown as being extremely vain and egoist. In contrast, the spinsters in *STG* possess authority. All of them are efficient individuals who, apart from being able to solve their own problems, are also capable of handling another's troubles. Henry himself admits to their role and contribution in the parish affairs. There is, however, hardly any household in the village which can be considered as an instance of a happy nuclear family. Unlike the big households of the romance narratives, in *STG* two unmarried women are shown living together, the two Bede sisters live together, also Edith lives with Connie. While Ricardo Bianco, Mr. Mold, Dr. Parnel, and Lady Clara all live alone. The only married couple, Agatha's and Henry's nuclear family, is also incomplete since they do not have any children. Accordingly, by breaking down its conventions and rules, Pym reverses the conventional structure of the nuclear family and family romance.

Being an attractive woman and the younger sister, Harriet has the advantage of having many suitors. She rejects her persistent suitor, the Italian Ricardo Bianco, although he has the characteristics of the persistent and romantic lover. Harriet's other suitor, Mr. Mold, in contrast, is not the romantic lover of the romantic plot. Pym undermines the concepts of the *lover* and *suitor* by portraying the humorous character of Mr. Mold, as Harriet's suitor. The scene where Mr. Mold is shown proposing marriage to Harriet, cannot be considered as romantic since both are in their fifties, and are not in love with each other. The proposal scene takes place in the morning because Mr. Mold must go back to his job in another city. He is unsure about proposing to Harriet and has decided to change the subject, in case Harriet does not turn out to be beautiful. However, we are told that "She was even more handsome in daylight than she had been in the evening, he decided, which was indeed very surprising. He had almost expected to be disappointed at their second meeting and had planned an alternate course of action should this happen" (*STG* 134). Harriet's beauty, nevertheless, is not natural. She is not the young and beautiful virgin of the romantic plots. Her main occupation at home is the strengthening of her corsets with elastic threads to hide her plumping figure. In order to hide the trace of the passing years, she usually puts on heavy makeup, as she does on the day of Mr. Mold's proposal: "her face rather heavily powdered and her hair neatly arranged" (*STG* 134). When Mr. Mold decides that Harriet is pretty enough to propose, he has difficulty in proposing to her. Although he is in his fifties, however, it is his first proposal. Moreover, he does not quite know what to say. In contrast to the chaste lovers and suitors of the romantic plots, he has had relationships with various women who were unsuitable for marriage: "His intrigues had been mostly with the kind of women who would hardly make suitable wives for the deputy Librarian of one of England's greatest libraries; nor had they ever been considered as such" (*STG* 135). Unlike the hero of the romantic plots, Mr. Mold is unable to propose, although Harriet is experienced enough to recognize that he needs help: "She determined to put him at his ease, so she said in a light joking way, 'Now, I do hope you haven't come to say goodbye. It will be very naughty of you to run off and leave us so soon.' She found this way of talking very good with curates and it certainly seemed to make Mr. Mold less shy" (*STG* 135). However, before Mr. Mold could propose, Harriet is certain of his proposal. Since she is used to Ricardo Bianco's unceasing marriage proposals, this proposal does not surprise her. For she has been expecting it.

However, even before Mr. Mold could propose, Harriet thinks about her own response. Unlike the young, inexperienced girls in the romantic plots, she does not accept him without further thinking: "She began to see that there were many reasons why she should refuse his offer when it came. To begin with she had known him for such a short time; indeed, this morning was only their third meeting" (*STG* 135-136). Moreover, Harriet is not the kind of sentimental heroine of the romantic plots for whom love is considered to be everything. She judges rationally and does not believe in love at first sight: "Harriet was not the kind of person to believe with Marlowe that *Where both deliberate, the love is slight / Whoever loved, that loved not at first sight?* Obviously that was quite ridiculous. How could one possibly know all the things that had to be known about a person at first sight?" (*STG* 136; emphasis original). Unlike the romantic heroine who marries for love's sake, Harriet analyses Mr. Mold's economic position, social status and his house: "Belinda had said, she believed Mr. Mold had a very nice house, but then poor Belinda was so vague, and for all that the house might be semi-detached and not at all in an advantageous position," Finally, she concludes that her spinsterhood life is, in many respects, preferable to a married one: "who would change a comfortable life of spinsterhood in a country parish, which always had its pale curate to be cherished, for the unknown trials of matrimony?" (*STG* 136) Thus, after having explored all the details, she decides to reject him; however, she is cautious to do it without offending him: "If Mr. Mold were very much in love with her it might be unkind to hurt his feelings – Harriet did not stop to consider how many times she must have hurt the feelings of her faithful admirer, Count Bianco" (*STG* 136). Unlike the eloquent lover of the love plots, Mr. Mold is unable to express himself and propose. He does not directly go to the main point declaring his love, rather he states: "'You know, I feel that you and I have so much in common ...'" (*STG* 137). When she thinks about their shared interests, she discovers that Mr Mold does not share her interest in the curates which makes her more firm in refusing him: "the suspicion that Mr. Mold was the kind of person who was not entirely at his ease with the clergy" (*STG* 136). His declaration of love comes at the end of Mr Mold's talk, and it seems that he is rather reluctant to express it mainly because, compared to love, any other factor, such as his economic situation and his house, is more important to him: "'What I mean to say is, that I think we should be very happy if we married. My house is large and comfortable and my financial position is sound ... and,' he added, rather as an afterthought, 'I loved you the moment I saw you'" (*STG* 136). Even in his uncertain expression of love, he is not honest and Harriet is not impressed: "she was disappointed" (*STG* 137). In comparing him with Ricardo, she finds him inadequate as a lover:

> Proposals from Ricardo several times a year had accustomed her to passionate pleadings, interspersed with fine phrases from the greater Italian poets. Besides, Ricardo never proposed sitting down. Always standing or even kneeling, indeed, his courtly manners had often caused Harriet some amusement. Compared with Ricardo, Mr Mold sounded so prosaic and casual. He didn't sound as if he really cared at all. She glanced at him hastily; little beads of sweat were glistening on his forehead and his face was crimson. Harriet could not help remembering that Ricardo always looked pale. (*STG* 137-38)

Moreover, Mr. Mold's heart does not break at Harriet's refusal as he thinks that he had proposed to her only because he pitied her. However, he is offended that his proposal is rejected: "he was now annoyed rather than hurt at her refusal, and did not consider that she had sufficiently realized the compliment he had paid her in asking her to be his wife" (*STG* 138). Nonetheless, not being disappointed, Mr. Mold goes to have a drink after being refused, feeling that he is free again:

> Perhaps after all the Librarian was right when he said that marriage was a tiresome business and that he and Mold were lucky not to have been caught. He looked at his watch. There

would be plenty of time for a chat with the landlord of the Crownwheel and Pinion before lunch. Marriage might put a stop to all that kind of thing. (*STG* 139)

Later on, when he sits in the train to go back home, he feels happy that he "had a lucky escape. And indeed, he reflected, *Love is only one of many passions and it has no great influence on the sum of life*, as the Librarian was so fond of quoting" (*STG* 144; emphasis original). Harriet's preference to remain single contributes to Pym's reversal of the romantic plot. Neither the proposal scene nor Harriet's response is compatible with the conventions of the romantic plot. Thus, Pym's *STG* has no happy ending with the marriage of the hero and heroine.

In the same manner, Bishop Grote's marriage proposal to Belinda undermines the conventional styles of courtship and marriage proposal. Belinda's appearance is not suitable for such an important event. She is making supper and is *floury all over*. Since their helper is not at home, she opens the door but is embarrassed and uncomfortable about her appearance. She does not look like the elegant heroine of the romantic love plots, but a dull, and old spinster. The bishop does not propose to Belinda because of his love, rather it is totally for profit-seeking reasons. He thinks about his loneliness in old age. Belinda is merely one among so many efficient, qualified women in the village, who can be considered as his wife. He initiates his proposal by telling Belinda: "'Miss Bede, I am sure you must have realized – have noticed, that is – my preference for you above all the other ladies of the village'" (*STG* 222). In response, without really meaning it, Belinda humbly tells him that she is not different from the others. However, Bishop Grote takes her understatement literally, charging her for not being pretty: "Ah, well, one hardly looks for beauty at our time of life,' he said, with a return of some of his usual complacency. 'She is not fair to outward view ... how does Wordsworth put it?'" (*STG* 223) Belinda is surprised by the bishop's tactlessness and straightforward manner: "Not even a middle-aged spinster likes to be told in so many words that she is not fair to outward view. Besides, she felt that the Bishop had taken an unfair advantage of her, calling on Emily's afternoon off, when she had had no opportunity to tidy herself." Bishop Grote takes Belinda for granted and believes that he does her a great favour by asking her to be his wife; he even humiliates her by saying, "'Perhaps you are not accustomed to receiving such offers?' he went on. 'Or perhaps it is some time since you last had one? After all, this is a quiet country village; it is unlikely that you would meet many strangers.'" When he wants to propose, he directly tells her that he wants her to marry him, not asking her in the form of a question, but in the shape of an order: "'I am asking you to marry me'" (*STG* 223). When Belinda rejects him, he misreads her reluctance as considering herself not an appropriate wife for a Bishop:

> My dear, you are equal to being the wife of a bishop,' he said kindly, making a movement towards her. 'You need have no fears on that account. When I was a younger man I held views about the celibacy of the clergy, young curates often do, you know,' he smiled indulgently, 'it is a kind of protection, if you see what I mean. But a man does need a helpmeet, you remember in Paradise Lost. (*STG* 224)

As suggested, Bishop implies that his decision to marry is not because of love, since he successfully escaped marriage in his youth, but it is mainly because of his fear of being lonely and he is in need of a helpmate to do odd jobs for him in his old age. Ironically, Belinda remembers Dr. Parnell's thoughts on men's marriage that resembles the Bishop's. However, she believes that she is not to be his wife: "A man needs a woman to help him into his grave, thought Belinda, remembering a remark Dr. Parnell had made. Well, there would be plenty who would be willing to do that." Belinda is surprised at the Bishop's self-indulgence and is taken aback by his suggestion of Milton who is known for his misogynistic views: "Belinda interrupted him with a startled exclamation. 'Paradise Lost!' she echoed in horror. 'Milton ...'" (*STG* 224). However, Belinda is incapable of imagining a marriage without love. When she tells Bishop that she cannot marry him as she does not love him, she learns that he does not consider love as a significant factor in marriage: "'But you respect and like me,' said the Bishop, as if that went without saying. 'We need not speak of love – one would hardly expect that now'" (*STG* 224). He regards love as something unreal, inaccessible and imaginative and considers himself certainly a likeable and respectable person. Moreover, in his mind, he turns Belinda into a *tragic figure* who still mourns for her dead beloved. While leaving, he is not disappointed, and asks Belinda to forget everything that happened: "'Do not give it another thought, Miss Bede,' he said briskly" (*STG* 225). Later on, Belinda hears of his proposal to Connie, and her acceptance. Pym's undermining of the romantic love plot and ending is portrayed here since neither of them is young, or in love. The woman is not beautiful, as the man points out to her. The man is quite ugly, but he is not aware of it and maintains a great self-esteem. He thinks that he is doing a favour to Belinda. His proposal is not due to love, he is searching for a wife to serve him in his old age, and when Belinda rejects him, he runs to another candidate.

The unromantic notions about marriage are replete in *STG*. Mr. Mold is the one who believes in marriage for marriage's sake, not marriage for love's sake. Dr. Parnell's thoughts about marriage are utterly unromantic and rational. His profit-seeking mind argues that "'Of course, I never advise anyone to enter into that state without long and careful thought'" (*STG* 145). According to Dr. Parnell, money and common interests must be considered in a marriage, rather than love. He criticises Harriet for rejecting Mr Mold: "there would be plenty of money, so that if there had been love, which Dr. Parnell rather doubted, it would have been less likely to fly out of the window, as he had been told it did when poverty came in at the door" (*STG* 145). When Harriet mentions that there is no common interest between them except "'a love of good food'" which she regards as insignificant, Dr. Parnell replies that liking the same food "'for dinner is one of the deepest and most lasting things you could possibly have in common with anyone,' argued Dr. Parnell. 'After all, the emotions of the heart are very transitory, or so I believe; I should think it makes one much happier to be well-fed than well-loved'" (*STG* 145). Dr. Parnell's profit-seeking and materialistic notions about the benefits of marriage are in complete opposition to the love-seeking ideology of the romantic love plots. Even the relationship between Agatha and Henry is absolutely unromantic and practical as it is restricted to daily rituals. There is no sign of romance and intimacy between them, and there are some hints in the novel that Henry would prefer Belinda as his wife, while Agatha would prefer Bishop Grote as her husband. Henry kisses Agatha out of habit. He expects her to take care of him and his clothes. When Agatha is on a holiday and Belinda asks Henry whether there is any news from Agatha, he takes out Agatha's letter from his pocket and gives it to Belinda. She thinks that Henry should not have given Agatha's private letter to her: "Belinda took the letter rather gingerly, thinking it odd that he should hand it to her so willingly." However, after reading it, she finds out that there is no sign of romance in it: "she saw that the letter contained nothing private. It seemed to be a long list of things he must not forget to do. It was admirably practical, but unromantic." Despite that, Belinda, in her internal monologue, thinks that Agatha is doing the right thing since "after so many years of being married to a charming but difficult man like the Archdeacon, perhaps it was rather too much to expect that Agatha should dwell on the desolation of life without him" (*STG* 147). The love letter from Agatha turns out to be a very practical one, contrary to the expectations of Belinda and the readers too.

Pym presented the persistent undermining of the romantic love plot and reversal of all romantic notions about marriage in *STG*. The scene in which Harriet and Bishop Grote see each other after thirty years can be considered as the most significant scene that undermines the conventional romantic plot. Harriet has prepared herself for the reunion after many years, and Belinda, Edith and Connie are looking forward to it. Connie, in particular, has a romantic tendency: "'I do wish I knew what they were saying,' said Connie, though of course it's the most unpardonable curiosity. Meetings like this ought to be really *sacred*." Connie, like Belinda, is a character who is preoccupied with romance and has many false notions about love and the reunion of lovers. However, when the critical moment comes, and the two see each other, Harriet bends "graciously and extended her hand as if to take his, but received instead the box of lantern slides" (*STG* 175). Bishop Grote does not even remember Harriet while she hoped to affect him with her intentionally arranged appearance. All the three expectant women are disappointed. The romantic minded Connie comes down to earth when Edith says: "'He's obviously saying something about the slides,' ... 'Connie is much too romantic. I suppose she thinks he ought to be quoting poetry'" (*STG* 176). The unromantic ending to an expected romance has taken place and everybody is surprised and disappointed to find their hopes for a happy reunion of lovers shattered.

Pym also hits hard at the long-held images and stereotypes of women in *STG*. She does so through using various strategies. One of them is the women shown proposing to men. Agatha implies that she had proposed to Henry thirty years ago, and now her niece Olivia proposes to Mr. Donne. Unlike in romantic plots, here it is the woman who proposes to the man. While talking to Belinda, Agatha believes that many women propose: "'I've often wondered if it was done very much. I suppose it must be done a good deal more than one realizes'" (*STG* 216). The conventional role of the man, as being the main role player in the play of courtship, is reversed since the woman takes over his role, leaving him powerless and ineffectual. Thus, Agatha's statement undermines the patriarchal tradition in which marriage takes place after a man proposes to the woman. Moreover, the practical- minded Agatha takes this matter as a common practice: "'it is not at all unusual. Men are understandably shy about offering what seems to them very little and when a woman realizes this she is perfectly justified in helping him on a bit, as it were'" (*STG* 216). Although women proposing to men is not a new practice; however, it is not generally talked about much within the society. Conventional Belinda has never heard of such a thing and is surprised and comforted to find out that Henry has not proposed to her:

> At this moment an idea came into Belinda's head. At first it seemed fantastic, then quite likely, and finally almost a certainty. Agatha had proposed to Henry. Why had this never occurred to her before? And now that it had, what was the use of it? Belinda could not answer this, but she knew that she could put it away in her mind and take it out again when she was feeling in need of comfort. (*STG* 216)

Belinda's romantic notions about love and marriage prevent her from thinking practically. She cannot imagine that she could ever propose to a man. Since she is still bound by the restrictions imposed upon women by the patriarchal order, she is even unable of thinking about such a thing: "'I don't think I should ever feel certain enough to take on that responsibility myself. I know men have to take it'" (*STG* 216). In contrast to Belinda, Harriet is rational and practical. When she hears about Mr Donne's engagement, she does not make a scene or get depressed, instead "her attitude was rather one of indignation and pity for Mr Donne." And unlike Belinda, who has not heard of women's proposals to men, she replies: "'I expect she proposed to him.'" However, Belinda cannot think of it without the fear of being refused: "'It wouldn't have occurred to me, I'm afraid. And think how dreadful it would be to be refused'" (*STG* 217).

Harriet is aware of Belinda's romantic point of view regarding people and things and tries to help her to look beyond her romantic perspective. While Harriet wants to sell Belinda's old and shapeless clothes to a wardrobe woman, Belinda tries to prevent the woman since she loves her old dresses; Harriet is however unaware of it: "'It's no use being sentimental about things,' said Harriet. 'You shouldn't keep a clutter of clothes you never wear just because you once liked them.'" Harriet is aware of Belinda's obsession with love of the past and old things although they are now useless. Belinda nevertheless hopes to get rid of the old things in her mind: "Belinda made no comment on this, for she was thinking that Harriet's words might be applied to more serious things than clothes. If only one could clear out one's mind and heart as ruthlessly as one did one's wardrobe" (*STG* 220). Henry too, time and again undermines Belinda's romance, by involving her in his domestic and trivial problems. Belinda's excitement in seeing him at the garden party is reversed due to Henry creating a scene about his grey suit. He does not care for her sentiments and undermines them by domestic trivia. For instance, at the garden party he is seen continually complaining to Belinda about Agatha lacking a wife's skills in preserving his suit.

Thus, while marriage is the most prominent factor in the romance genre, it is questioned in *STG*. As Wyatt-Brown states: "Her best novels challenge comedy's complacent endorsement of the importance of marriage" (5). Moreover, according to Benet, *STG* "develops finally as an unmarriage plot: Belinda and Harriet Bede, the recipients of the two proposals, are not the ageing stars of the weddings. When each sister confirms spinsterhood as her happiest choice, the novel suggests that while love is essential to the emotionally fulfilled life, marriage is not. The author, then, turns the staples of the romantic novel upside down" (16). As stated before, the ending of the novel, in contrast to the endings in romantic plots, does not end in marriage or any kind of fundamental change in the states of the characters. In this way, as Cooley suggests, Pym "alters what is generally considered the most essential characteristic of romantic comedy – the happy ending. Her novels do *not* end in the usual shower of wedding rings." Cooley moreover asserts that although "Some characters do marry at the end in some of her novels," however, the hero and the heroine remain unmarried: "If the heroine has a marriage possibility that may develop beyond the end of the novel, both the heroine and the reader know that the union will be at best a very modest blessing" (*Comic* 9). Belinda is quite happy to have passed all the dangers that might have changed their lives: "For now everything would be as it had been before those two disturbing characters Mr. Mold and Bishop Grote appeared in the village" (*STG* 250). For Harriet and herself, she imagines a future, not different from the past:

> In the future Belinda would continue to find such consolation as she needed in our greater English poets, when she was not gardening or making vests for the poor in Pimlico. Harriet would accept the attentions of Count Bianco and listen patiently and kindly to his regular proposals of marriage. (*STG* 250)

Indeed, Belinda does not even dare to imagine a different future for herself and her sister: "Belinda did not go any further than this in her plans for the future: she could only be grateful that their lives were to be so little changed" (*STG* 250-51). Likewise, Benet believes that "The sisters' relationship, as Pym presents it, is a satisfactory alternative to the male-female relationship conventionally accepted as being primary. Unquestionably, Belinda and Harriet are happier with each other than they would be with the bishop and Mr. Mold" (27). In like manner, Tsagaris undermines the reversal of the romantic ending in Pym's fictional world: "'happy ending' so crucial to romance is subverted because it does not necessarily involve marriage to the hero or 'prince.'" Despite that, Tsagaris argues that although the ending in *STG* is not a happy ending in the common use of the term, however, it is "happy because the sisters refuse their suitors. For them, the desire to remain in the home they have built together is stronger than the social pressure to find husbands" (34). Following that, according to Tsagaris, it is a *happy ending* for the Bede sisters to stay together in their own house after having rejected their suitors.

As will be pointed out in the discussion on double discourse in *STG*, Belinda's internal thoughts alter the happy ending of the traditional love plot and marriage. Unlike the conventional love plots, maintenance of the single state, as Wyatt-Brown underlines, seems to be Pym's preference: "the author asserts that the spinster's life has many advantages over the matron's. The action of the novel, as Long observed, is a 'parody of romance.' Pym makes fun of all marriages, both those that have endured and those that are solemnized at the end" (67). Pym's spinsters remain unmarried, since they believe that their single status is of greater benefit to them. In this case, Tsagaris hints at a research article, "Cumbered with much Serving," carried out by Robert J. Graham in which he explores the significance of home for unmarried women, arguing that "to single women, home represents control over their environment. Moreover, Graham argues that ritualized housework provides affirmation of unmarried women's single householder status and a 'substitute for social exchange and intimacy.'" Thus one could regard "the sisters' decision as 'overt love displacement,' where feelings of love are linked to home and garden" (Tsagaris 34). Belinda and Harriet are happy and satisfied with doing their ritual housework and garden work. Although "the Misses Bede had a maid they were both quite domesticated and helped her in various small ways, clearing away the breakfast things, dusting their own bedrooms and doing a little cooking when they felt like it" (*STG* 19). Both Belinda and Harriet have certain duties at house and both take pleasure in shopping. Belinda regards gardening as a safe outlet for her anxieties and when she wants to escape from her romantic imaginings about Henry, she does some work in the garden. Therefore, the main strategy employed by Pym to undermine romance is the trivia and domesticity. The romance of Mr. Donne and Harriet is reversed in the very first paragraph due to the former's odd combination of clothes. The romance of the scene in which Bishop Grote proposes, is reversed by Belinda's dishevelled and unkempt appearance since she was making ravioli in the kitchen. The romance of Mr. Mold's marriage proposal to Harriet, is also reversed by her refusing him for the very reason of her obsession with the curates. Additionally, the romance of Bishop Grote and Harriet is undermined by a little lantern box that Bishop Grote gives Harriet, instead of taking her hand. Accordingly, as Cooley suggests, Pym modifies "the beat dictated by literary convention." Her strategy of arousing the conventional rules goes as far as reminding the readers of the romance plots, of "beautiful heroine, admirable hero, happy ending – and then reverses it." Cooley asserts that "Part of this bending of the rules is undertaken, no doubt, for the pure comic delight of turning rules upside down" (*Comic* 10). However, overturning the rules is intentional. Pym deliberately breaks down the rules of the patriarchal romantic novels by avoiding climaxes, undermining romance through domestic trivia, and eliminating the happy ending of marriage, in order to ridicule all the serious conventions of the love plots that have symbolised the patriarchal values. She demonstrates that the hero and the heroine of the romantic plot do not inhabit the real world. Pym, moreover, subverts the romantic plot through the discourse of the trivial.

Pym employs the discourse of trivia in *STG,* not only for the subversion of romance, but for creating significance out of the trivial and unimportant matters. Throughout history, women have generally been kept away from the issues conventionally considered as important such as politics, sports, and economics. They have remained isolated from the power structures, and have dealt with issues regarded as insignificant, such as domestic matters: children, gossip, parties, and cooking. However, Pym indicates that trivial issues are not actually insignificant; rather, they are intentionally made insignificant by the patriarchal culture's values and criteria. Nonetheless, by stressing the significance of the domestic trivia in the lives of her female characters, Pym, as Tsagaris points out, "highlights that their lives and affairs are also of profound significance" (29). Judy Little demonstrates how Pym, by positioning "the discourse of the trivial" with "the ordinary and the everyday" (*Experimental* 76), creates a significant discourse out of the insignificant one. Moreover, Woolf argues that since women's humour originates from "women's distinct experiences" (Little,

Comedy ix), men's and women's "values," thus, are to some extent different. The problem arises when the prevailing values becomes men's values. Woolf also maintains that "the values of women differ very often from the values which have been made by the other sex" (*Room* 76). Therefore, placing the values of men higher than those of the women, according to Woolf, has resulted in a double standard:

> Speaking crudely, football and sport are 'important'; the worship of fashion, the buying of clothes 'trivial'. And these values are inevitably transferred from life to fiction. This is an important book, the critic assumes, because it deals with war. This is an insignificant book because it deals with the feelings of women in a drawing room. A scene in a battlefield is more important than a scene in a shop - everywhere and much more subtly the difference of value persists. (*Room* 76-77)

Domesticity and trivia constitute a major part of *STG*. Pym highlights the descriptions of the tea parties, foods, clothing, cooking, sewing, knitting, washing, cleaning and the other trivia, making them the dominant motifs in her work. Nevertheless, she does not consider trivia as mere trivia; rather, she gives significance to the insignificant and trivial. She ridicules the characters who degrade trivia and domesticity. One such character is Henry who, in his visit to the Bedes' house, surprises the sisters – he finds Harriet busy with strengthening her corsets with elastic thread and Belinda cleaning the tea table. He does not apologise for interrupting them; rather, he says that "'I am glad to find you both engaged in the trivial round, the common task'" (*STG* 74). His tone is not a complimentary tone, but a deprecatory one, mocking the Bede sisters' preoccupation with domestic tasks.

Another such example is Mr. Donne, who believes that domestic tasks and trivial issues are specific to the less-gifted people, such as women. The gifted people like himself ought to give their time to the more important issues such as reading, religion, and sports. When Belinda self-deprecatingly says that her work is considered as insignificant, he takes it seriously and remarks humiliatingly: "We cannot all have the same gifts" (*STG* 68). Additionally, when Mr. Mold comes to Bede's house to propose marriage to Harriet; while waiting for Harriet, he spends his time reading the magazine *Stitchcraft*. Harriet mocks him reading "'a frivolous feminine paper'" (*STG* 134). However, she does not laugh at him because he is reading a woman's magazine; rather, she indirectly mocks and subverts the underlying tradition of considering domesticity as insignificant. She undermines the patriarchal culture's criteria concerning the value of women's issues as unimportant and those of men as important: "'I suppose you would be much too important to have anything to do with them now'" (*STG* 134). The trivial discourse of the narrative thus acts as a threat to the dominant male discourse by highlighting the insignificant and the trivial.

Belinda's preoccupation with the domestic chores is the most significant instance of Pym's highlighting of the trivia: "The new curate seemed quite a nice young man, but what a pity it was that his combinations showed, tucked carelessly into his socks, ... but Belinda rather doubted whether he thought at all, if one were to judge by the quality of his first sermon" (*STG* 7). Belinda cannot take her eyes off Mr. Donne's combinations. His underwear initiates a stream of thought in her mind. It gradually moves from the thought of his underwear to the issue of the low quality of the sermons he gives. Thus domestic trivia often ends in a more significant matter. According to Deborah Donato, the first paragraph touches this point. Donato argues that "what Pym lightly shadows in the progress of Belinda's thoughts is a mind that is expanding to something more and something larger through the provocation of something small" (25). Mr. Donne's disorganised appearance, as Donato continues her argument, is a manifestation of his disorganised thoughts:

> This movement from the smaller to the larger remains within the modest, essentially insignificant context of the curate's negligible untidiness. But the note that carries through all of Pym's work is, however sparely, sounded here – that the trivial in life, and in literature, is more than merely trivial. (25)

Henry is sketched as a character who publicly humiliates women and believes that their proper role is to be men's helpmates. When Agatha says that she is fond of scholarly work and has done academic research in the past, he tries to suppress her telling that: "'After all, academic research is not everything'" (*STG* 68). He goes on to quote lines from George Herbert's poem, stressing the value of trivial housework, implying that it is better for women to busy themselves with housework rather than academic research, even though they might be bright. Nevertheless, it is ironical that Olivia changes into a helpmate for Mr. Donne. As soon as Belinda sees her and hears her talk, she decides that she is superior to Mr. Donne, though a few years his senior: "It was obvious that she would take care of him, not letting him cast a clout too soon. She would probably help with his sermons too, and embellish them with quotations rarer than her husband, with his Third Class in Theology, could be expected to know. A helpmeet indeed" (*STG* 235). Since she is an academic, she will help Mr. Donne write more learned sermons, as she also affirms: "'I daresay I shall find myself encouraging Edgar to write more literary sermons'" (*STG* 236). She will be comfortably suited to the role as a clergyman's wife, caring for his affairs and writing his sermons. However, this is ironically in opposition to what Mr. Donne believed about men and women's jobs.

Household tasks have always been considered as inferior and unimportant in comparison to the other jobs. However, Pym demonstrates that the *domestic trivia* is as important as, and even more difficult than, the other jobs. Belinda and Harriet, though having a home maid, still help with the house work. One day, having been extremely tired after working on a paste in the kitchen for some time, when Belinda finds out that it needs twenty more minutes to be done, she ironically remembers Keble's lines in praise of housework:

> The trivial round, the common task – did it furnish quite all we needed to ask? Had Keble really understood? Sometimes one almost doubted it. Belinda imagined him writing the lines in a Gothic study, panelled in pitch-pine and well dusted that morning by an efficient servant. Not at all the same

thing as standing at the sink with aching back and hands plunged into the washing-up water. (*STG* 227)

Thus, Belinda questions the poet in writing about the matters of which he has no experience. The discourse of domesticity and trivia is considered to be inferior to that of poetry. While the poet pretends to be aware of the domestic chores when he praises them, Belinda ridicules him in writing about matters he has no experience. She ridicules Keble's opinion about the housework as being simple and easy. However, by subverting the role of the poet However, Belinda also undermines the patriarchal beliefs and presuppositions about domesticity and housework.

2.1.2 Belinda's Double Text Discourse

"Double-voiced discourse" or "double-text," according to Showalter, is a prominent factor distinguishing women's writing from that of men. Women have a specific purpose in employing double-voiced discourse in their writings. This discourse, as Showalter notes, includes "the inscriptions of both the dominant male culture and the oppressed, muted female one. Nevertheless, the two discourses are not segregated; instead they are interwoven and simultaneous" (*Literature* 34). In the same manner and in order to undermine the dominating patriarchal order, Pym extensively makes use of double-text speech in *STG*. As pointed out by Showalter, the dialogues of Belinda and Harriet, and their inner thoughts include many examples of such double-texts:

> Women's fiction can be read as a double-voiced discourse, containing a 'dominant' and a 'muted' story [. ...] I have described it elsewhere as an object/field problem in which we must keep two alternative oscillating texts simultaneously in view: 'In the purest feminist literary criticism we are ... presented with a radical alteration of our vision, a demand that we see meaning in what has previously been empty space. The orthodox plot recedes, and another plot, hitherto submerged in the anonymity of the background, stands out in bold relief like a thumbprint. (*Literature* 34)

Although at the surface level it is the "orthodox" discourse that controls the narration, however, at the undercurrent level a resistant or an already oppressed, but disrupting, discourse lies at the centre of the textual orientation. This disruption is achieved mainly by the function of humour in the selected narratives in which the humorous voice operates chiefly as a strategy to *resist* and *survive* within the general culture.

Pym's double-voiced usage is compatible with her humorous discourse. Despite the fact that Belinda recognises the truth in people and in things, she usually does not speak-up because of her fear of losing suitability and politeness. She seems to be a subservient character, obedient to the laws of the dominant culture. Pym, nevertheless, gives her a chance to express herself through the tactic of inner speech which is closely related to feminist humour. According to Walker, Humour, in order to be considered as feminist, takes two shapes. The most usual form of feminist humour "makes use of a double text to pose a subtle challenge to the stereotype or the circumstance that the writer appears superficially merely to describe" (*Very* 13).

The two central characters, Belinda and Harriet, in *STG* are middle-aged spinsters, living in a quiet village. They are not rebellious or modern figures. Instead, as Wyatt-Brown states, "Pym wrote about women who are too polite for open rebellion" (68). Pym's women characters employ a subversive strategy to help them express their thoughts in a sub-text. According to Bowman, when Pym's sense of outrage at women's victimisation got the better of her, she "constructed an alternate system of linguistic codes" (qtd. in Wyatt-Brown 68). Her characters moreover make wry asides expressing their dissatisfaction. Wyatt-Brown further proposes that Pym's only release was to "create a subversive subtext, one which reflects the way women have traditionally talked about men behind their backs." Following that, she suggests that some of her "excellent" heroines like Belinda Bede and Mildred Lathbury "exact a delicate revenge upon the pompous or unreliable men in their lives by means of their interior monologues" (Wyatt-Brown 3).

Pym's style of writing in a double-discourse has made her text to signify more than what is apparent at the surface level. Besides paying attention to the narrator's critical comments, the reader of Pym's narrative should take into account the deeper textual meaning which is usually subversive and undermining, That is so because, as Doan (1991) argues, "Pym understands that without a newly conceived narrative structure, the process of self-definition stands in danger of achieving only minor revisions," Thus, Pym's strategy, as highlighted by Doan, is to create a new type of narrative which includes two levels: the surface level and the deeper one:

> Since fundamental change must occur at the level of narrative structure, Pym adopts a way of writing that allows for the insertion of critical commentaries into the text so that, in effect, two voices articulating different positions resonate from a unitary text. The development of this strategy aligns Pym with a tradition of women writers who, as Sandra Gilbert and Susan Gubar explain, 'managed the difficult task of achieving true female literary authority by simultaneously conforming to and subverting patriarchal literary standards'. Like Austen's and Bronte's fiction, Pym's narrative works on two levels, where the surface meaning disguises the "deeper, less accessible (and less socially acceptable)" meaning. ("Pym's" 149)

Belinda's dialogues in the novel can be considered as a fine example of double-voiced discourse since her inner thoughts differ largely with her deeds and her words or her behaviour. There is a subversive subtext at the deeper level that opposes the seemingly obedient Belinda's words and conduct. Although Belinda loves Henry and defends him in front of the others, however, she often makes witty asides that undermine Henry's sense of dignity in his presence. In this way, as Doan states, most of her inner speeches mix a "dutiful and subversive voice" (qtd. in Wyatt-Brown 45). Pym employs the double-voiced discourse in varied situations. Belinda, being a spinster in her mid-fifties, is aware of her unmarried status, gender, economic and social position and tries to adapt her conduct and language to the criteria of the patriarchal order. She is aware of the fact that a middle-class, middle-aged spinster cannot expect much from her society and pretends to be the obedient gentlewoman. However, she expresses the signs of disobedience in her inner thoughts. By undermining the language of the dominating patriarchal culture, she subverts the rules and values associated with it.

Belinda is critical of both Harriet and Mr. Donne on the day of the curate's first visit to their house. Although she sympathises with Harriet, however, she is amazed at her obsession with the young curates. True that she does not criticise her sister and does not express her views regarding her behaviour; in her inner speeches, nevertheless, she cannot keep up with this odd situation although she is used to her sister's habit of flirting with the young curates:

> The evening promised to be just like so many other evenings when other curates had come to supper. There was something almost frightening and at the same time comforting about the sameness of it all. It was odd that Harriet should always have been so fond of curates. They were so immature and always made the same kind of conversation. (*STG* 16)

Harriet never learns of Belinda's opinion about her relation with the young curates since the latter behaves extremely politely towards the curates and never criticises them in her presence. However, she always criticises them in her inner thoughts. The first sentence of the narrative begins with Belinda's inner speech regarding the appearance of the new curate. She criticises his inconsiderateness in the manner of his clothes although, she tactfully avoids speaking up: "The new curate seemed quite a nice man, but what a pity it was that his combinations showed, tucked into his socks, when he sat down. Belinda had noticed it when they had met him for the first time at the vicarage last week and had felt quite embarrassed" (*STG* 7). She is neither capable of hiding her disapproval nor of mentioning it to Mr. Donne. Thus, through Belinda's inner thoughts, the narrative demonstrates her disapproval of the established conventions.

When Agatha goes on a holiday, Belinda suddenly feels happy and to a great extent "relieved" (*STG* 72). Her sudden feeling of happiness, she reasons to herself, is that she is happy for Agatha's sake since the waters in

Karlsbad will do well to relieve Agatha's rheumatism. However, as it is expressed in her inner speech, the real source of her happiness derives from the fact that she and Henry will be able to spend some time together without Agatha's presence. However, she continually negates this thought reminding herself of the fact that she loves Agatha, and wishes well for her and Henry:

> Of course she was glad that Agatha was to have a well-deserved holiday and the waters would undoubtedly help her rheumatism, so there was room for gladness, but she ought not to have to tell herself this after the first thought that came into her mind had been how nice it would be to be able to ask Henry in to tea or supper without having to ask Agatha as well. (*STG* 72)

Through such a double-voiced narration, as Doan states:

> On the surface, the reader is presented with a narrative voice fully compliant with normal social expectations – a voice politely civil even when answering an impudent, audacious query. Yet underneath this veneer of mild-mannered conformity, another voice speaks to challenge, even to ridicule, a social order that calls for the repression of unkind retorts. ("Text" 63-64)

Belinda's real thoughts are thus artfully concealed behind the text. The narrator shows the difference between how she appears publically and how she violates the social laws privately. Feminine humour, in this case, lies mostly in the subtext of the narrative.

Another instance of Belinda's employment of double text refers to the time when she runs into Henry one day, and he invites her to the vicarage in order to have a cup of tea. She outwardly rejects his invitation although she covertly desires to go with him. Her excuse in refusing his invitation is: "Harriet will be expecting me." However, the main reason for refusing him is the fear of being the subject of gossip, though she is aware that the invitation was "the kind of spontaneous invitation that comes perhaps only once in a lifetime" (*STG* 86). In this way and behind such false excuses, she hides her real intention for the refusal. The reader is aware that her main fear is being left alone with Henry. She fears that the past emotions and memories might reach an uncontrollable level. Later, when Belinda tells Harriet about Henry's asking her for tea, Harriet is surprised that she did not go: "'I can't believe you didn't want to.'" However, Belinda's reply does not satisfy her: "'No, it wasn't exactly that,' said Belinda slowly. 'I didn't really mind one way or the other,' she lied, 'but I knew you would be expecting me back and I thought you might wonder where I was.'" As suggested, her words do not reveal her actual thoughts since she tries to hide her real intentions:

> And then Florrie and the cook might have thought it funny if I went there the minute Agatha was out of the house. You know how servants gossip, especially in a small place like this. I don't want to be silly in any way, of course there would have been nothing in it, but I decided it would be better if I didn't go.' (*STG* 88)

Nonetheless, there is no end to what she can imagine. She does not limit herself to what has happened. In her imagination, she regrets for a short time about not going and imagines what they would have talked about if she had gone. However, she reveals her main intention through her inner speech:

> Of course there was a certain pleasure in not doing something; it was impossible that one's high expectations should be disappointed by the reality. To Belinda's imaginative but contented mind this seemed a happy state, with no emptiness or bitterness about it. She was fortunate in needing very little to make her happy. (*STG* 89)

Thus, her main intention in declining Henry's invitation is that while, on the one hand, she prefers to love at a distance, on the other, she fears to face her romantic feelings and emotions. Since she feels that many people would not understand her wish to be satisfied with too little, she does not dare to voice her thoughts.

Belinda's willingness to sacrifice herself and help the others paves the way for other people to take her for granted and in many ways even to misuse her. The most abusive person is Henry. At the time of Agatha's return, Henry asks Belinda to go with him to the station since she is the most convenient person. Although Belinda does not like the idea, she accepts Henry's suggestion with an ironic thought: "On this day she was classed with Agatha's nearest and dearest in a way which seemed to her rather ironical. Who but a man could be so lacking in finer feelings as to think of such a thing? She wondered. But of course she said she would go" (*STG* 160). After Agatha's arrival, when they are having tea in the vicarage, Belinda's sense of self-sacrifice and good-will again overtakes her at the time Henry informs her about the fact that he is too overloaded to take the responsibility of distributing collection boxes. As he expects, Belinda takes on the burden and volunteers to do the job: "Belinda could only wonder how he was to be made to realize this, but, loyal as ever, she agreed that the Archdeacon was much too busy and, much to her own surprise and dismay, heard herself offering to take on the organization and distribution of the boxes." Both Bishop Grote and Henry praise Belinda for taking the responsibility. When Bishop Grote mistakes her for another woman who had done "splendid work for the Guild of St. Agnes" (*STG* 167), Henry replies: "'Oh, Belinda is a very excellent person altogether,' ... 'I don't know what we should do without her.'" Belinda, however, is not content with their compliments on her way back home, she "reflected a little bitterly on these words" (*STG* 168). The reason being she feels that she is respected and loved not because of herself, but because of what she has done, and will do in the parish. She is loved because of her willingness to take on the other's responsibilities. However, she never dares to speak up her thoughts. It is through the narration of her inner speech that her private thoughts become known to the reader.

No matter how deeply Belinda loves Henry, she is critical of him since she is aware of all his defects and shortcomings. However, because of her love for him, she mostly does not speak up against him. On one occasion, she hides her criticism of Henry when she reads Agatha's letter finding out that there is no sign of romance in it: "she saw that the letter contained nothing private. It seemed to be a long list of things he must not forget to do. It was admirably practical, but unromantic." However, Belinda, in her inner thought, finds Agatha absolutely right in being so practical about Henry since he is not an easy person to handle: "after so many years of being married to a charming, but difficult man like the Archdeacon, perhaps it was rather too much to expect that Agatha should dwell on the desolation of life without him" (*STG* 147). She remains silent, not expressing any opinion about Henry. By taking into account such characteristic, Doan states that the double-voiced discourse has got a prominent function in Pym's characters:

> Pym rescues the spinster from a debilitating sense of guilt and facilitates a psychological release by overriding the voice of the dominant social order to insert a more subversive voice into the text. When personal desire collides with duty, the dual voiced narrative mediates between the two through the juxtaposition of inner thoughts with conversations and actions. ("Pym's" 149).

Although Belinda is aware of the extent of Henry's self-indulgence and pretentions, she does not let their mutual friend, Dr. Parnell, think of him as a lazy, self-important person and defends him loyally. However, her inner thoughts are functioning differently. When Henry protests that he is too overloaded and tired, she confirms him by telling Dr. Parnell: "'You don't realize how hard Henry works. I mean,' she added obscurely, 'there are things to do in a country parish that people don't know about unless they live in one. Your work in the Library has its fixed hours, but a clergyman is at everybody's beck and call'" (*STG* 98-99). Both Henry and Belinda are aware that she is being dishonest; however, Belinda defends Henry in this particular situation. She explains in detail, the imaginary tiresome tasks that Henry must perform. But later, she "reflected sadly, people would never dare to trouble the Archdeacon with their worries; they would go hurrying along Jubilee Terrace to Mr. Donne" (*STG* 99). Belinda's ability to say something and think otherwise is her unique characteristic in dealing with people and different situations. Her intention in talking or performing a task is mainly to please others, but there is an underlying disobedience in all her thoughts and deeds. Some days later, when Henry preaches his famous sermon, Belinda is thinking about its aftermath, trying to find a way in order to criticise him politely although Henry does not approve of being criticised. She also thinks about how she can defend Henry in case of any criticism. She reflects that "He might welcome intelligent criticism, she thought, knowing perfectly well that he would not" (*STG* 112). When Henry's sermon gets unusually long, she becomes frustrated since their lunch and also the other people's Sunday lunch, is on the verge of burning and yet, Henry does not care. She wonders whether Henry does not even think of his own burning lunch. At home, the Bede sisters become aware of the truth of the matter. Henry was not in a hurry since they were going to have duck for dinner and Belinda "said thoughtfully, as she watched her sister carve the over-cooked beef, 'duck needs to be very well done, doesn't it? It can't really be cooked too much'" (*STG* 113). Although not stated directly in the text, the implication is that Henry's egoistic self-indulgence does not let him care for the others since his own food needs a longer time to cook. His unkind and unsympathetic behaviour towards other people originates from his self-centredness. Whatever he does, or says, is not for the sake of the people but primarily for his pretention. He believes that the village people are "so sunk in lethargy that they do not know their own wickedness" (*STG* 98). This is an ironic remark since he excludes himself in his criticism. Ironically, he himself is the one who is ultimately ignorant of his defects and wickedness. Belinda's awareness of this is shown in her inner thoughts. By addressing them directly, Henry insults and abuses the congregation throughout his sermon deliberately. Belinda reflects that "Of course dear Henry had not really meant to insult them. He had obviously been carried away by the fine poetry, and naturally he must have meant to include himself among those he condemned" (*STG* 112). Being doubtful of Belinda's remark, the reader finds her comment is ironical. Pym's style of double-text functions in a way that, on the one hand, through the narration of the character's words and actions, and, on the other hand, by expressing Belinda's covert and indirect remarks and thoughts, the narrator helps the reader realise the truth of the matter and know the undeclared intentions behind the words and actions.

Belinda's employment of the double-voiced discourse is also obvious in her letter to Agatha. She censors her real intentions, thoughts and feelings writing down what she thinks would be appropriate. Her purpose is to make Agatha happy. For example, she gives compliments to Agatha's flowers and garden saying: "I have noticed your pink chrysanthemums showing buds, which is very early for them, isn't it?" She writes that they were all "impressed" by Henry's Judgment Day sermon while the reader already knows that many were afraid and bored with it. She, moreover, tries not to appear intimate and interested. When she writes that "You will be glad to hear that he is looking well and has a good appetite" (*STG* 139), she rewrites this sentence many times carefully since she thinks that it would be "perhaps a little presumptuous? Ought an archdeacon to be looking well and eating with a good appetite when his wife was away? And ought Belinda to write as if she knew about his appetite?" (*STG* 140) Thus, she decides to add "'as far as I know'" to the sentence in order to neutralise its implication. Even when she writes her thoughts about Mr. Mold and the type of person she thinks he is, later on she feels that she had been unfair towards him and blames herself for regarding him as such: "Here Belinda laid down her pen again. Was she being quite fair to Mr. Mold? She had allowed herself to get so carried away by her own feelings about him that she had rather forgotten she was writing to Agatha, in whom she did not normally confide." Therefore, she completes her paragraph by adding: "'Still, I daresay he is a very nice man,' she went on, 'when one really knows him'" (*STG* 140). While the letter gives too little information about Belinda's thoughts, the narration gives a full account of her inner thoughts before, while and after writing the letter. In this way, the reader is able to trace the truth about what Belinda meant to write and what she actually wrote.

Harriet's discourse also contains instances of double text discourse. When she hears the rumour of Mr. Donne getting engaged, she gets angry; however, after knowing that the news has been a rumour, she alters the usual order of the supper and serves sherry to her guests out of happiness. She, nonetheless, is tactful enough to hide the reason of her hospitality although the narration makes it clear that her sudden hospitality arises from her happiness. When she suddenly decides to serve sherry, she excuses her behaviour by telling that: "'After all, we might have been going to drink to Mr. Donne's engagement'" (*STG* 92). Her words do not betray her thoughts and she is in control of her words and behaviour so that she would not appear odd.

2.1.3 Function of Gossip in the Construction of Humorous Narrative

Gossip functions as the connecting bond and the shaping power in *STG*'s narration. Pym shapes her narrative through her peculiar employment of gossip. She does not consider gossip as an insignificant trivial, but a considerable and guiding force in the formation of narrative. Pym foregrounds the function of gossip in the fictional society represented in *STG* according to which she creates the plot of her narrative too. The topics women writers wrote about have been considered as unimportant for many years and gossip has always been among them. When women wrote about gossip, they were, according to Barreca, accused of being "the unimportant discuss the unofficial" (*Untamed* 20). However, Pym disrupts the distinction between the important and unimportant by making the latter the shaping force of her narrative.

Female humour and narrative structure are supposedly interwoven. The "relation between feminine humor and narrative structure," according to Gillooly, "differs from the norm" or the conventional humour (*Smile* 21). Similarly, gossip creates a "different narrative structuring" of the novel as the humour of the text operates through its gossip. As a type of unofficial discourse, gossip is "culturally identified as feminine. ... [And] outside the boundaries of official discourse, gossip has constitutive power." That is, its "relational, intimate flow governs the narrative movement." Thus, gossip questions the traditional patriarchal order through creating an "unauthorized but nonetheless authoritative narrative community" (Gillooly, *Smile* 21). Likewise, gossip, being an "unauthorized discourse" as well as an unofficial one, functions along with the subtle humour of the narrative, challenging the social and the conventional order. Gossip is also woven into the overall narrative structure through its dominant presence in the dialogues among and between the characters. *STG* is filled with the *unauthor-*

ized discourse that can be taken as the challenging force of narrative to the patriarchal social order. Gossip is represented as an empowering female device in *STG*. Little argues that the discourse of trivial and gossip is "solidifying, communal link for women." According to Little, every matter relating to life can be a subject of gossip:

> the language about home life, meals and gardens (one's own or the neighbor's seen through a window) in Pym's fiction often draws people together, as Patricia Spacks claims for gossip. Domestic trivia, then, constructs a communal subjectivity, a self that finds its identity in shared everyday activities or observations. (*Experimental* 88)

All the new and important matters of the village are spread through gossip. Gossip is the most significant way of acquiring news and information about the others. Following that and being constructive, it is a way of making connection and creating intimacy, not enmity. Harriet's preoccupation with the young curates has been the topic of gossip for many years. However, seeing them as being harmless, she does not care about it. She lets people talk about her as they wish: "her frequent excursions to the curates' lodgings had often given rise to talk, for people did like a bit of gossip, especially about a respectable spinster and church worker like Miss Harriet Bede" (*STG* 1). When Harriet sets out to Mr. Donne's lodgings one day, she can sense that the people behind the curtains are following her and gossiping about her:

> Every window had its lace curtains and she imagined that she detected stealthy movements behind them as she walked along to the house where the curate lodged. Well, let them watch her and gossip about it too if they liked, she thought stoutly, it would do some of them good to realize that charity began at home. (*STG* 55)

Unlike Belinda, who fears people's gossip, Harriet undermines it by ridiculing the very act of gossiping and ironically wishing them to learn how to help the needy. She reverses the effects of the gossip through ignoring it as well as by the strong belief that she does not do anything wrong. In contrast, Belinda worries that she might become the unfortunate subject of gossip. When she sits down at a table for two at the garden party in order to have tea with Henry, she fears that she may be the subject of the gossip: "what would people think to see her having tea with the Archdeacon while his wife was still working tirelessly at the garden-produce stall? It was a pity really to worry about what people thought" (*STG* 37).

Moreover, Gossip is so prevalent in the community of *STG* that people are no longer ashamed of gossiping. When Agatha is setting out for a holiday, we are told that Belinda and Harriet "watched her departure out of Belinda's bedroom window" for the sole reason that "from here there was an excellent view of the vicarage drive and gate." Thus, gossiping and following someone is a usual practice in the fictional community, although Belinda excuses herself by showing "the duster in her hand" (*STG* 70). Accordingly, Pym subverts the effects of gossiping by demonstrating that gossip is not considered as a threat but it can be regarded as a source of excitement and hope:

> To watch anyone coming or going in the village was a real delight to them, so that they had looked forward to this morning with an almost childish excitement. And yet it was understandable, for there were so many interesting things about a departure, if one could watch it without any feeling of sorrow or regret. What would Agatha wear? Would she have a great deal of luggage or just a suitcase and a hat-box? Would the Archdeacon go with her to the station in the taxi, or would he be too busy to spare the time? If he did not go to the station would he kiss Agatha goodbye before she got into the taxi, or would he already have done that in the house? (*STG* 71)

As it is suggested in the part, being interested in other people's affairs is not considered as intrusion; however, Pym reverses the threatening tone of the gossip into some kind of homely remedy for the characters, since their gossip would not do any harm to anybody. Belinda's and Harriet's gossip begins immediately after they find out that the Palmer's car had arrived to pick up Agatha. Harriet disapproves of this saying that "the Archdeacon was too mean to order Haines" (*STG* 71). Belinda, nevertheless, defends Henry. They carefully observe Agatha's departure and comment on the event elaborately. Having been aware of their curiosity, Belinda immediately turns away and continues her cleaning, while Harriet is taking great joy in watching Agatha and commenting. Belinda is certain that "nothing would move Harriet from the window," she also knows that "others in the village were doing exactly the same thing" (*STG* 72). In this way, gossiping is considered to be so essential for the villagers that they hardly lose any opportunity to gossip or keep track of the others. Gossiping is also a necessary way of socialisation for the characters in the novel since through it the characters get to know each other's thoughts and emotions. The news about each other does not come through television, wireless, the newspaper, or the internet, but from the people's talk about each other and in this way the villagers learn about one another's happiness and misery.

2.1.4 Understatement and Self-Deprecation

Pym uses the strategy of understatement in order to produce a significant effect. Through it, the women characters are represented as struggling hard to resist and survive the suppressions of the patriarchal order. By employing self-deprecation, women characters, on the one hand, highlight the subservient position of women in the society. On the other hand, by the use of self-irony as well as through detaching from self-importance, they look at themselves critically through taking the perspective of the patriarchal order and looking at themselves as objects. By doing so, they hope to prevent further oppression and suppression by the patriarchal culture. Related to this, Gillooly, stresses the covert and self-effacing nature of female humour maintaining that "syntactically, feminine humor occurs most often undercover: in self-effacing tropes and faint discursive patterns that work to conceal its existence" (*Smile* 22). Considering form, feminine humour makes use of different "forms of representation" including "litotes, apophasis, and meiosis" that makes expression possible. Moreover, feminine humour mostly do not use tropes such as "hyperbole and metaphor" considered as masculine tropes. It employs "italics and dashes over exclamation points to signal its presence" (Gillooly, *Smile* 22).

Additionally, understatement is considered as an efficient method that women writers employ in order to make their writings effective. Based on Barreca's, definition of comedy it often "turns directly against the self as the simplest target" (*Untamed* 30). Walker also suggests that female humour is more self-deprecatory and more disguised than feminist humour. Ackley's proposal is also in line with the women writer's self-deprecatory methods. She argues that Pym's handling of misfortunate and pitiful conditions are "gentle, subtle and understated, seldom acrylic" (20).

Belinda's use of self-deprecation as a strategy noticeably contributes to her determined resistance or survival in the patriarchal society, and the subversion of its presupposed values and beliefs. Through Belinda's understatement, Pym shows the destructive effects of patriarchal culture on women, particularly, on unmarried women. Belinda's self-deprecatory remarks in fact, function as a weapon to resist the devastating effects of the patriarchal culture. Her inner speeches are the most prominent instances of understatement and self-effacement. Additionally, her habit of accepting the blames of the others can be considered as her self-effacing strategy. When she is accused or attacked verbally, she takes the blame without even trying to defend herself. Her acceptance of all the responsibilities implies that she is already weak and defenceless and has given in. Moreover, Belinda's strategy does not reduce or humiliate her. On the contrary, it gives her the strength to face difficult people and conditions. When Henry praises her as being a tolerant listener to his nonsensical talk, the narrator shows how Belinda herself, in her thoughts, agrees with Henry. She considers herself as an exceptional person "somehow exalted above the groups of bust women, who had been arranging pyramids of apples, filling bran-tubs and decorating stalls with coloured paper. Once, she knows, she *had* been different, and perhaps after all the years had left her with a little of that difference" (emphasis original, *Pym, STG* 29). The narrator, therefore, represents her as truly believing that she is *different* since she has always acted as a silent listener to Henry's pretentious and pompous words. Her satisfaction with the little and ordinary issues does not depict her weakness; instead, it suggests her strength in being content with very little. In her heart, she is loyal to Henry, as his praises still make Belinda fairly satisfied even after thirty years. Further, Belinda's self-effacing nature makes her feel ashamed for other people's actions. When Edith asks Henry about the arrangement of the cloakrooms, Belinda "turned away in embarrassment" (*STG* 29). Unlike her, Henry and Edith are not embarrassed and Henry even "appeared to be enjoying the conversation and entered to the discussion with great courtesy" (*STG* 29).

Rules of etiquette force Belinda into distancing herself from the matters dealing with bodily functions. Moreover, she is equally embarrassed at Harriet's flirtations with the young curates in public. In vain, she always tries to control and suppress Harriet. At one point when she witnesses Harriet's flirtatious chat with Mr. Donne, she decides that "it would be as well if they went home to luncheon" (*STG* 31). On the day of their party, Belinda takes the blame for not entertaining the guests and offering sherry: "I feel that I have been lacking in manners for not offering it sooner,' said Belinda quite sincerely, thus taking upon herself the blame for all the little frictions of the evening. But it was so obvious that women should take the blame; it was both the better and the easier part" (*STG* 119). By expressing Belinda's loyalty to the rules of etiquette, the narrative voice ridicules her efforts to control and reform others' conducts and words, as dictated by the patriarchal voice. Moreover, the narrator violates and subverts the moralising tone of the narration by presenting the absurdity of such etiquettes and conducts. For instance, when Miss Prior states that Agatha's "clothes are from the *best* houses" (*STG* 48), Belinda is shocked thinking that: "It isn't right, thought Belinda indignantly, for a clergyman's wife to get her clothes from the best houses. She ought to be a comfortable, shabby sort of person, in an old tweed coat and skirt or a sagging stockinette jumper suit. Her hats should be shapeless and of no particular style and colour. Like my old gardening hat" (*STG* 49). Her strict codes for certain conducts are mocked and undermined by the narrative voice. Moreover, Belinda thinks that certain things are unsuitable for her, while the same things are suitable for others. For instance, at the lecture day, when Edith offers her cigarettes, she does not smoke since she believes that "it would be unbecoming for her to smoke, though it seemed right that Edith should do so. Anything that she did seemed to be in character" (*STG* 176). The narrator undermines the patriarchal order by ridiculing Belinda behaving as the obedient follower of the conduct rules of the patriarchal order. Another source of Belinda's self-deprecatory manner is her discontentment with her clothes and general appearance. It is ironic that although she does not like simple clothes, she usually wears shapeless ones suitable for spinsters. The narrative voice ridicules her by stating: "Her appearance tonight in a homespun skirt with white blouse and Albanian embroidered waistcoat made Belinda feel dowdy and insignificant, one of the many thousand respectable middle-aged spinsters, the backbones or busybodies of countless parishes throughout the country" (*STG* 176). The sense of her humbleness affects her relations with other people and results in her understatement: "She glanced down at her own – long, English gentlewoman's feet she always thought them" (*STG* 32). She considers herself as a middle-aged unattractive spinster. At the garden party, she wears low-heeled: "at our age, surely all that was necessary was to dress suitably and if possible in good taste, without really thinking of fashion" (*STG* 32). However, she cannot prevent Harriet from wearing her high-heeled shoes and fashionable dresses. In her shaping of an image of herself as a spinster, the narrative voice undermines the images and stereotypes of the spinster created by the dominant culture through ridiculing Belinda's obsession with suitability and the rules of etiquette. In contrast to her, Harriet does not limit herself with the restricting stereotypes and rules. Belinda's understatement related to the stereotype of spinster is not restricted to herself alone. In her view, all unmarried women are, in some way, incomplete. Nonetheless, she does not have the same opinion about Agatha and the other married women in the village. She is always tolerant to Agatha's sarcastic remarks and humiliating behaviour. Nonetheless, she underestimates the unmarried Edith to the extent that she cannot imagine her being once loved: "it seemed odd to think that anyone could have loved Edith, who seemed a person to inspire fear and respect rather than any tender emotion" (*STG* 33). Belinda thus represents the views of the patriarchal society about the spinster, although the voice of the narration mocks her discourse.

Belinda's tendency towards self-deprecation, further manifests itself when Henry indicates the importance of housework for women, by quoting lines of Herbert. Belinda is visibly affected, since according to her the housework she does cannot be considered as a useful job. She does not really "sweep rooms, Emily does that. The things I do seem rather useless, but I suppose it could be applied to any action of everyday life, really (*STG* 68). Belinda's self-deprecation results in Mr. Donne's humiliating her: "'Oh, certainly, Miss Bede,' said Mr. Donne, with curately heartiness. 'We cannot all have the same gifts,'" which Belinda interprets as Mr. Donne's "insufferably patronizing air" (*STG* 68). Mr. Donne implies that men's intellect is superior to that of women. However, ironically, Belinda is superior to him in character and intellect; even the collection of the books in his lodgingç as noted earlier by Harriet, is not "a particularly original selection." Moreover, as he himself once remarked, he was not much of a reader since he spent his time outdoors: "'I don't work very much in the evenings, except when I'm preparing a sermon. The Boys' Club and the Scouts take up most of my time" (*STG* 56). Even the qualities of his sermons are lower than those of Henry's, as all the parishioners are aware. The unintelligent curate, nevertheless, ridicules the highly-educated and intelligent Belinda and other women. Considering women's intellect as inferior to that of men is a long-held presupposition of the patriarchal order, which is being undermined by the humour of the narrative voice in *STG*.

The issue of women's self-deprecation and understatement also manifests itself in Pym's presentation of men and women's food. In *STG*, the best foods and drinks are cooked and offered to men while the less nutritious foods of inferior quality are offered to women. According to Tsagaris, food plays various roles in Pym's novels. She restates Penelope Lively's view that food "has a rich, subtle language of its own" (49) in Pym's novels. For instance, Harriet is forever shown providing the young curates with the best of foods and fruits since she believes that they are not well-fed. Foods provided to women are very simple and ordinary. For instance, when Connie and Edith come to Bede's house, the Bede sisters ask them to stay for supper; however, they do not put much effort in cooking special food. Belinda "wondered whether they ought perhaps to open a tin of tongue and get Emily to make a potato salad. Or would a macaroni cheese be better? With some bottled fruit and coffee to follow that should really be enough" (*STG* 89). This was going to be the four women's supper if Mr. Donne had not arrived to the Bedes' house. Being certain that Mr. Donne would stay for supper, Harriet changes the order of the supper and makes the servant cook special foods. When Belinda enters the dining-room, she instantly realises that Harriet made the servant cook the meat she had bought for the next day's luncheon. Still, Edith ironically thinks that, "They would all benefit from Mr. Donne's presence, she knew, and noted with sardonic approval that there was a large bowl of fruit salad on the table and a jug of cream as well as a choice of cold meats" (*STG* 92). Harriet's hospitality toward Mr. Donne is not limited to food alone, she even serves sherry because she is happy that Mr. Donne is not going to be engaged. Therefore, parties for both sexes contain rich and exotic foods and drinks. People in *STG* consider men's need for food more than for the women, thinking that men need more and better food than women. Such an instance can be observed on the day when both Miss Prior and Mr. Donne are coming to the Bedes' house, Mr. Donne for lunch and Miss Prior for dinner. After a long discussion over who ought to have the duck, Mr. Donne is chosen as the right candidate since Harriet finds it unacceptable to have him eat cauliflower cheese. Following that, Miss Prior's inferior position and her gender both make her eligible for the cauliflower cheese. Although Belinda insists on giving the meat to Miss Prior since she is too sensitive, Harriet however says: "Miss Prior will just have to put up with cauliflower cheese,' said Harriet firmly. 'If you expect Mr. Donne to, why shouldn't she?'" (*STG* 46) Harriet is so obsessed with Mr. Donne's food that she continuously thinks about how to make it more delicious: "Harriet's thoughts were already with Mr. Donne and the duck they were to have that evening. Could they perhaps have something original served with it, like the orange salad they had had at Count Bianco's? One wanted to give people really interesting food" (*STG* 52). However, Harriet in her plans excludes women. She also does not care much about her other women friend's food when they come to her house, considering them as inferior to the curates. In another instance, when Belinda informs her of the low quality of the meals at the vicarage, she does not care about the people living in the vicarage. She only thinks about Mr. Donne: "'Well, it's a good thing Mr. Donne doesn't have to live there'" (*STG* 53).

Harriet manifests the values and beliefs of the patriarchal culture about the different needs of men and women. Men's food, similar to men's jobs and values, has been considered more important than those of women. By mocking gender discrimination, the narrative voice undermines this situations. When Belinda becomes aware of the caterpillar in Miss Prior's cauliflower cheese, she is greatly embarrassed. Nonetheless, Cooley asserts that "since this is an amiable and laughing comedy, all ends happily" (*Comic* 60). Belinda makes an excuse and, as usual, she takes on the responsibility. Pym's humour makes the scene end in friendship and sympathy. Miss prior talks about the matters that cheer up Belinda, re-establishing their friendship and intimacy. They sympathise with each other while they discuss the short-comings of Agatha Hoccleve who is considered as a common enemy. The main source of their sympathy comes from the fact that Agatha too, like Harriet, deprecates Miss Prior since she is beneath her in social status. Although she is a bishop's daughter, Agatha is said to keep a mean house. When Miss Prior goes to the vicarage, Agatha gives her only "a dried-up scrap of cheese" and sometimes no sweet (*STG* 48). Miss Prior is aware that Agatha gives her scraps because she considers her beneath her social class so that food becomes "a social marker" (Tsagaris 37) which distinguishes people based on their class and gender. Belinda and Miss Prior undermine the tendency of the patriarchal culture to discriminate people according to their gender and social class. They do so through humour directed at Agatha's inadequacy to provide good meals, besides her lack of hospitality.

Belinda's manifestation of her self-deprecation takes place in another scene, in a wool shop. She sees wool with suitable colour for clergy: "here was an admirable clerical grey. Such nice soft wool too." She wonders whether she would "ever dare to knit a pullover for the Archdeacon?" Then, she thinks about the way of presenting it to him so that it might not raise doubts: "It would have to be done surreptitiously and before Agatha came back. She might send it anonymously, or give it to him casually, as if it had been left over from the Christmas charity parcel. Surely that would be quite seemly, unless of course it might appear rather ill-mannered?" (*STG* 82) Her sense of self-deprecation and fear of Agatha, make her change her mind in a way that she decides to knit something for herself rather than for Henry: "After all, she might make a jumper for herself, now that she came to think of it she was certain that she would, either that or something else equally safe and dull." However, the main reason for her mental change is her lack of self-confidence to knit for Henry whatever she wishes. She is concerned with the thought that she is unable to face the consequences of knitting a pullover for Henry: "When we grow older we lack the fine courage of youth, and even an ordinary task like making a pullover for somebody we love or used to love seems too dangerous to be undertaken." She is concerned that "Agatha might get to hear of it; that was something else to be considered. Her long, thin fingers might pick at it critically and detect a mistake in the ribbing at the Vee neck; there was often some difficulty there. Agatha was not much of a knitter herself, but she would have an unfailing eye for Belinda's little mistakes." Belinda's self-deprecation thus results in her inability to even imagine the possible consequences of knitting for Henry: "the pullover might be too small, or the neck opening too tight, so that he wouldn't be able to get his head through it. Belinda went hot and cold, imagining her humiliation. ... Obviously the enterprise was too fraught with dangers to be attempted and Belinda determined to think no more about it" (*STG* 83). She decides that it is better not to act. By her self-effacing manner and non-action, she prevents the blows that might come towards her. Thus, she protects herself by self-deprecation. However, Belinda makes indirect sacrifices for Henry. The narrative voice ridicules her when she feels sorry that she could not attend Henry's evening sermon due to the preparation for the party. She comforts herself by reflecting on the situation: "looking after his material welfare was just as important as her own spiritual welfare, if such it could be called, and that she was making the sacrifice in a good cause" (*STG* 114).

Another source of Belinda's self-effacing manner is her fear of Harriet's marriage, which she thinks will add to her own isolation. Having already lost Henry, she is haunted by the threatening dream of being left alone and having to find a companion for herself:

> All, all are gone, the old familiar faces ... Dear Nicholas was back in the Library, John Akenside was in heaven, while his earthly remains rested in an English cemetery in the Balkans, and if Harriet married Theodore Mbawawa, even she would be gone ... Who was there apart from the forbidden Archdea-

2 Some Tame Gazelle: Construction of Women's Veiled Humour 111

> con? One's women friends, of course, people like Edith Liversidge and Connie Aspinall, but they were a cold comfort. Belinda grew even more melancholy, and then she remembered Count Bianco. There was always Ricardo. Perhaps they could read Dante together and find some consolation in the great Italian poet. (*STG* 160)

As suggested, without altering the plot of the story, the narrator represents the reverse process of Belinda's imaginations about being abandoned. Moreover, Belinda is concerned about her being left alone in her old age, ill and incapacitated, when Bishop Grote comes to visit them: "Harriet was going to marry the Bishop and Belinda would be left in her old age to die a lonely death, or with nobody but a paid companion to cheer her last hours. Surely that was enough? She had been trying to prepare herself for the worst and did not wish to be unsettled" (*STG* 191-92). By employing the strategy of self-deprecation, Belinda resists the ills that may happen beforehand. When Harriet decides to sell their old clothes to the wardrobe woman, Belinda is happy that she does not have to talk to her about the price since she is too embarrassed to offer high prices: "'What a good thing you are seeing her,' ... 'I'm afraid I never have the courage to ask a big price but just agree to what she offers'" (*STG* 220). All in all, Belinda employs the strategy of understatement, not to humiliate or efface herself, but primarily as a useful weapon to resist against the abuses and misdeeds directed at her by the dominating patriarchal culture.

2.1.5 Sympathetic Bond between Narrator and Heroine and among Characters

The sympathetic bond functions significantly between the narrator and the female characters as well as among the female characters themselves in Pym's *STG*. The narrator apparently makes a sympathetic bond with the main female character, Belinda. For although the narrator ridicules her, it does not result in her humiliation. Moreover, instead of creating stereotypes, the narrator, as Ackley remarks, presents Belinda through both "humour and irony" (28). The narrator sympathetically takes side with the victimised women in the oppressing patriarchal culture. This humour is aimed at the prevailing authoritarian system within the fictional society, rather than at any character. Through relating it to the heroine, the narrator depicts her innocence and helplessness. Thus, the woman writer's, or Pym's, relation to the heroine is not authoritative and mastering; on the contrary, it is protectively sympathetic, mainly because of the homogeneous socio-cultural experiences women (writers) universally face within the social context.

The relation between the woman humourist and her woman characters even goes beyond sympathy since a sympathetic bonding usually takes place in the feminine humour. This humour, according to Gillooly, occurs "between humourist and victim, with the auditor participating vicariously in their relationship" (*Smile* 30). Thus, feminine humour represents the inter-relatedness of all those involved in this humour. On the one hand, it relates the narrator with the heroine through the former's representation of the inconsistency between the latter's inner thoughts, perceptions, actions and her behaviour. And, on the other hand, it bonds the reader with both the narrator and the heroine since through following both diverging and sometimes converging moments of their discourses, s/he is able to get connected to different levels of textual meaning. Moreover, feminine humour creates a sympathetic bond among the female characters, too. For example, the narration represents an intimate and friendly atmosphere in which the laughter is not to humiliate, ridicule or disempower. Rather, feminine humour is to create an intimate and a friendly environment as well as to express their dissatisfaction with the existing order. In addition to forming a strong bond between the narrator and the heroine, feminine humour operates in other textual relationships too. For instance, according to Gillooly, it connects "the narrator to witty characters" (*Smile* 30). In contrast to men's humour, which is mostly a strategy for "self-presentation" and "a demonstration of cleverness," women's humour, as Walker says, is mainly "a means of communication" as well as "a sharing of experience" (*Very* xii).

Thus, in the opinion of theorists, creating sympathy and making connections are the two common features of women's humour. As mentioned earlier, the functioning of women's humour makes it possible for the creation of a sympathetic bond between the narrator and the heroine on the one hand, and among the characters, on the other. Finally, the female characters' problems and difficulties in the patriarchal society change into sympathetic and light-hearted laughter at the end. Gillooly, moreover suggests, that women's humour essentially creates a "narrator-heroine bond," and provides a sense of pathos "if no longer reassurance and comfort, to the discontented heroine" (*Smile* 207). The narrator's relation with Belinda is neither authoritarian nor suppressing. Although the narrator, through employing various strategies, ridicules and laughs at her internalisation of the patriarchal beliefs and presuppositions as well as their manifestation in her words and deeds. The narrator, however, does not humiliate or victimise Belinda. Rather, by the application of sympathetic humour, the narrator, on the one hand, manifests all the ills, absurdities, and deficiencies of the patriarchal culture and, on the other hand, creates a sympathetic bond with Belinda. At the same time, the narrator ridicules her internalisation of the values and beliefs of the system and undermines the patriarchal order.

The sympathetic bond between the female characters is traceable in Belinda's and Harriet's relationship. Although their personalities differ sharply, they understand, protect, and support each other in many ways. One prominent instance of this sympathetic bond can be observed when Belinda returns from Henry's house. Harriet immediately recognises her feelings and helps her to express herself although Belinda is reluctant and embarrassed: "'there's really nothing to tell. Henry read aloud to me and then we talked a bit and then he persuaded me to stay to supper, which I did. But I don't know whether I ought to have done that,' she added rather unhappily'" (*STG* 153). Sympathetically, Harriet makes an Ovaltine for Belinda in order to ease her: "'Now wouldn't you like a nice cup of Ovaltine?' she said, fussing round Belinda like a motherly hen ... Harriet had already gone into the kitchen and soon returned with the Ovaltine and a selection of biscuits and cakes. 'Now,' she said, as if speaking to an invalid, 'drink it up while it's hot and don't try to talk till you've finished. There'll be plenty of time for you to tell me all about it'" (*STG* 154-55). In order to persuade the reluctant Belinda into talking about her feelings, Harriet "chose a chocolate biscuit" (*STG* 155). However, although it might be difficult, Harriet tries her best to make Belinda express her feelings: "Then he's been telling you that he's very fond of you, and hinting that he wishes he'd married you instead of Agatha,' went on Harriet, gallantly persevering" (*STG* 155). Belinda, however, gradually decides to confide in Harriet. Her main purpose is to make Belinda happy and to "make something interesting out of Belinda's evening at the vicarage" is mainly because of the sympathetic bond with her sister and also because she understands Belinda's persisting love for Henry. Harriet, therefore, does her job cleverly and humorously to persuade Belinda to speak up. She soothes Belinda by assuring her that their love is mutual and Henry prefers Belinda to Agatha. Harriet's statement might not be true and Henry might not have loved and preferred Belinda, but by doing so, she creates a sympathetic connection with her sister. Moreover, Harriet cares and sympathises with Belinda. For example, when she is unwell, Harriet provides her with everything she needs. She brings her books and food to her bed and gives everybody lengthy accounts of Belinda's illness.

Similarly, Belinda is supportive and protective of Harriet and does not like any kind of gossip spread about her. On the day Bishop Grote gives his lecture about the tribal costumes in Africa, Belinda is careful not to allow any rumour to spread about Harriet. When Edith asks her questions about Harriet and Bishop Grote's familiarity, she replies in a low voice, since she did not want Miss Beard and Miss Smiley, who were sitting in front of them with a group of fellow teachers, to hear all their conversation: "Things half heard were apt to be wickedly exaggerated and Miss Beard, in spite of being an excellent Sunday school teacher, was very much inclined to gossip" (*STG* 175). Even when Harriet is not near, Belinda keeps a sympathetic connection with her sister, and does not let anything go against her. When Belinda thinks about Harriet's prospective marriage with Bishop Grote, she gets distressed and in her thoughts compares Mr. Mold with Bishop Grote, regretting that Harriet has not married Mr. Mold since he seems to be superior to the Bishop: "almost wishing that Harriet were even now Mrs. Nathaniel Mold. Then at least there could be no danger of having the Bishop of Mbawawa for a brother-in-law" (*STG* 170). On another occasion, when Belinda finds that Bishop Grote does not even recognise Harriet after so many years, she feels a deep contempt for him and in her inner thought, in contrast to her usual manner of covert and embarrassed discourse, accuses him of being uncaring and impolite:

> Harriet's position on the table made it necessary for the Bishop to gaze up at her. She bent graciously and extended her hand as if to take his, but received instead the box of lantern slides. Belinda was indignant. How rude and casual of him! she thought. How like a bishop! ... Theodore Grote was cold, a cold fish as she remembered their dear mother calling him. Legless, unloving, infamously chaste, she thought detachedly, remembering Ricardo's goldfish, and was then ashamed of herself for thinking of it. There could be no excuse, for Leigh Hunt was not even one of our greater poets. Still, there was something fishlike about Bishop Grote. Fish and sheep. Was that possible? (*STG* 175)

Bishop Grote's lack of respect and interest in Harriet makes Belinda angry. Acting against the true nature of her character, Belinda searches among animal names to call him by. Moreover, her sympathetic bond with Harriet makes her care even for Harriet's reactions in a specific situation. When Bishop Grote imitates the African songs: "Belinda glanced at Harriet to see how she was reacting. As far as it was possible to see, she was displaying remarkable self-control, for she was very prone to giggle, and appeared to be gazing at the Bishop with rapt attention" (*STG* 179). The sympathetic bond between Harriet and Belinda is strong enough to make Belinda forget her love or prejudice about Henry as well as side with Harriet the moment Ricardo tells her about Henry's rumour concerning Harriet. Henry told Ricardo that Harriet is going to marry Bishop: "The wicked liar, thought Belinda angrily. An archdeacon making mischief and spreading false rumours, that was what it amounted to" (*STG* 212). At Mr. Donne's wedding, when she sees Harriet "approaching with the new curate" (*STG* 251), she welcomes them, and the last scene of the novel ends with a depiction of the sympathetic bond between Belinda and Harriet. When Belinda sees that Harriet has forgotten Mr. Donne and found a new curate, she helps Harriet to invite him to their house for dinner: "Belinda smiled. 'Of course, dear.' Asking the new curate to supper seemed a particularly happy thought" (*STG* 251).

Belinda also sympathises with Connie, while watching Harriet and Bishop Grote's reunion. Connie talks of romantic ideas about the reunion of the beloved and the lover. While Harriet extends her hand to reach that of the bishop's, Connie's imagination takes her to the stories about the beloved's soft hands, when Edith suddenly blurts out her unkind and unsympathetic opinion: "Edith looked down complacently at her own fingers, gnarled and stained. 'Not in the country,' she said, 'though Connie's always fussing about hers, rubbing them with lotion and all that sort of nonsense. I always tell her that nobody's likely to want to hold her hand now, so why bother.'" Belinda thinks that Edith's response is "rather unkind and sympathizes with Connie. It wasn't exactly that one hoped to have one's hand held ..." (*STG* 176). However, Belinda ultimately understands why Connie wishes to appear beautiful – creating a sympathetic bond with her. At the end of the lecture, when she sees that Connie likes to go to the vicarage, she persuades Edith to let Connie go and have fun instead of going home. Again, at Edith's house, she sympathises with Connie and creates a connection with her when she sees Edith's disordered and disorganised home: "everything was so primitive and comfortless that Belinda felt really sympathetic towards poor Connie" (*STG* 183). Connie is a lonely, poor and unprovided woman. Although Edith provides for her as a far relation, however, she also suppresses her because of her lower social and economic position. Belinda's sympathising with her is due to her oppressed and subservient position.

In the middle of their party, Belinda is seen suddenly making a sympathetic bond with Agatha, when she senses that nobody has noticed Mr. Mold's abusing joke towards her. At one moment she forgets her sense of understatement, embarrassment, and self-sacrifice when she, upon awaking, finds out that nobody really cares for her as she is surrounded by all self-important people with their ridiculous obsessions: "she thought doubtfully, the Library, great though it was, did not always attract to it cultured and intellectual persons. Nicholas himself, obsessed with central heating and conveniences, was perhaps not the best influence for a weak character like Mr. Mold." At that moment, she wishes to be in

2 Some Tame Gazelle: Construction of Women's Veiled Humour

> Karlsbad with dear Agatha, helping her to get cured of her rheumatism. She imagined herself in the pump-room, if there was one, drinking unpleasant but salutary waters, and making conversation with elderly people. Perhaps taking a gentle walk in the cool of the evening with an old clergyman or a retired general ... (*STG* 123)

Her sudden wish to be with Agatha, far from the circle of serious and pretentious men, is mainly due to her sympathy with Agatha. She sympathises with Agatha at the moment since she understands the burden Agatha is bearing while living with Henry, and being surrounded by pretentious, self-indulgent men. Thus, Pym makes use of the sympathetic bond among the characters and between the narrator and the heroine as a humorous strategy, in order to produce an intimate and sympathetic atmosphere. Such a narrative technique enables her to protect the interests of the heroine and the other female characters, and simultaneously to undermine the presuppositions and beliefs of the patriarchal system.

2.2. Function of Themes and Motifs in the Construction of Humorous Plot

2.2.1 Subversion of Female Stereotypes

The narrative voice in *STG* questions the long-held beliefs and presuppositions about the images and stereotypes of men and women mostly through the practice of humour. Pym occupies a prominent position among such writers. By skilfully employing the already existing stereotypical images, she attempts to change their implications. Images and stereotypes of women have existed in literature. They have mostly been created by the conduct literature and etiquette books which are believed to prescribe "proper feminine behavior for middle class" (Bilger 21). These books sketched diminished and false images of women, persuading the female readers to transform themselves into such images. The literary theorist, Mary Poovey calls such an image the "naturalization of the feminine ideal since they constructed an ideal of femininity and then redefined female nature in terms of that ideal" (qtd. in Bilger 21). The new image of woman was the image of an obedient, domesticated housewife. It was a stereotype, or as Woolf puts it, an *Angel in the House*. The image of the angel in the house and other such images in literature, implied obedient and subservient women. Woolf mentions some of the socio-historical implications of the concept (Parsons 85). Woolf tries to describe such a fictional woman as following:

> She was intensely sympathetic. She was immensely charming. She was utterly unselfish. She excelled in the difficult arts of family life. She sacrificed herself daily. If there was chicken, she took the leg; if there was a draught she sat in it – in short she was so constituted that she never had a mind or a wish of her own, but preferred to sympathize always with the minds and wishes of others. Above all – I need not say it – she was pure. Her purity was supposed to be her chief beauty – her blushes, her great grace. (2012)

Woolf maintains that women strengthened the ideal of womanhood by internalising it through the years. Moreover, the patriarchal order has created hypocritical, indolent and pretentious males mainly through giving them powerful and influential positions. Considering them as stereotypes, Pym exhibits their peculiar manners and behaviour in different situations, as also their relations with spinsters, in order to ridicule their sense of self-importance, indolence and lack of self-irony. In this way, the narrative voice in *STG* subverts the image of the powerful and influential men, as well as the system that creates them.

The narrative voice in Pym's *STG* presents women as domestic angels. At the same time, it primarily undermines such conventions. Belinda Bede is the untiring, self-effacing, and self-sacrificing woman whose good deeds go ahead of her. Everyone is aware of her tendency to serve, and thus takes her services and sacrifices for granted. Still, Belinda's inner thoughts, in opposition to her deeds, undermine the ideals of womanhood. Although she appears to be an obedient and submissive woman, nonetheless, the narrative voice mocks such values and conventions by subverting Belinda's severe disciplines and strict etiquettes. In fact, since conduct books hold little meaning in the fictional society, nobody acts according to them. Her insistence on right conduct and behaviour seems extremely absurd and ridiculous. The narration, however, mocks her at such occasions. Belinda is so obsessed with the image of the respectable spinster that she does not protest even when she disagrees with something, instead she bears its unsatisfactory consequences. At Edith's house, while Edith is cooking food, Belinda sees "a grey wedge of ash drop into the beans," When Edith asks her whether she cares, Belinda unwillingly replies that she does not mind: "remembering Miss Prior and the caterpillar. Perhaps there was something after all in being a gentlewoman" (*STG* 184). Her concern for the etiquettes and suitability prevents her from giving her true opinion on any matter.

The conventional stereotype of the spinster is loaded with some negative connotations. Nevertheless, Pym's spinsters are considered as most joyful, and humorous characters who are not humiliated through humour. Pym does not create stereotypes out of her spinster characters, rather she creates individuals similar to the stereotypical spinsters. She selects spinsters as her main characters in order to manifest their marginal role in the society and, through employing humour, she challenges the society's presuppositions concerning them. Having an unidentified role in the society, the unmarried woman turns hardships into humour, since she is capable of creating satisfaction "despite unrequited love, solitude, and tedious work" (Cooley, *Comic* 4). The stereotype of the spinster carries with it the socio-cultural burdens which are evident in Pym's novels too. Doan, proposes that Pym, through the application of the tactic of the "dual-voiced narrative," voices two opposing viewpoints towards the spinster: "the voice of the patriarchy and the voice challenging that authority." According to Doan, Pym presents spinsterhood as the embodiment or synthesis of all the better things life has to offer. Spinsterhood, then, is an alternative life-style which offers women an active role in society allowing them the opportunity to examine others critically ("Pym's" 152).

As stated in the theoretical chapter, women's literature, according to Walker, "has described myriad aspects of women's lives, employing familiar stereotypes about women for the purpose of mocking those stereotypes and showing their absurdity and even their danger" (*Very* 10). Pym employs these stereotypes in her *STG* in order to display the absurd and subordinating view of the patriarchal culture in relation to these stereotypes.

Similarly, Pym's *STG* is filled with spinsters and unloved women. She depicts these stereotypes not primarily to exhibit their ineffectiveness, but to display the shortcomings of the male-centred culture in dealing with them. Walker, also observes that: "What female humorists have done with these stereotypes, however, is to subvert them" (*Very* 11). Pym likewise resists and challenges the dominant order by ridiculing the standards that the prevailing culture defines for women. Women's humour, in addition to questioning the standards prescribed for women, attacks the institutions and individuals associated with the power structure too. Women's humour questions the authority that suppresses and victimises them or, as Barreca points out, "When it *is* explicitly political, women's humor often satirizes the social forces designed to keep women in "their place," a phrase that has become synonymous with keeping women quietly bound by cultural stereotypes (*Penguin* 1-2).

Henry can be considered as representing the patriarchal order since his deeds and beliefs regarding women, conform to the social values and conventions of this culture. Despite benefiting from women's services and sacrifices, Henry ridicules them. When Belinda and Henry are having tea at the garden party, Belinda tells him that it's time for her to go and take Agatha's place at the stall in order to have tea. Henry accuses both Agatha and Belinda of being pretentiously austere: "'It will please her not to have any,' said the Archdeacon. 'I wonder that you have had any. I thought women enjoyed missing their meals and making martyrs of themselves'" (*STG* 39). He emphasises on the image of the self-denying women. Nonetheless, Belinda and Agatha imply that they do not comply with his mental image. Both women are keen on their food and clothing. They never miss a meal. As Miss Prior suggests, the Bede "always have such nice meals" (*STG* 52). In fact, contrary to Henry's presupposition, Agatha responds that she "'shall really be glad of a cup of tea'" (*STG* 40). Thus, in opposition to Henry's beliefs, neither Belinda nor Agatha take pride in remaining hungry and thirsty, nor do they pretend to be selfless and self-sacrificing as they take great joy in eating, drinking and other everyday pleasures.

Women's internalisation of the images ascribed to them is another significant issue that Pym ridicules in *STG*. For instance, when Edith, Connie, Belinda, and Harriet gather to have a gossip about whether Mr. Donne's engagement to Olivia Berridge is true, they all agree that she cannot be a suitable wife for Mr. Donne since doing scholarly job "doesn't seem a very good training for a wife.'" Olivia, Agatha's niece, is an intelligent and hard-working woman doing an academic research on *The Owl and the Nightingale*. Belinda at this point remembers "Agatha and her inability to darn" (*STG* 90). Olivia cannot be regarded as an efficient wife since she is not good at knitting: "Well, I hope she knows how to graft a toe by now,' said Harriet bluntly" (*STG* 203). When Agatha in defiance of her niece says that "'her work on *The Owl and the Nightingale* has really been a most substantial contribution to Middle English studies,'" Harriet reminds her that her ability to knit a sock is more important: "'all the same, it is important to know how to graft a toe,' persisted Harriet" (*STG* 204). Pym, therefore, ridicules women's internalising womanly ideal by narrating women's gossip about Olivia's inefficiency as being a clergyman's wife. Henry, too, does not think of her as a *girl* since she has passed her thirtieth year: "'I should hardly call her a girl,' said the Archdeacon spitefully. 'But I suppose women like to think of themselves as girls long after they are thirty'" (*STG* 203-04). Preference of the younger women in patriarchal society is for their desirability in marriage. Older women are not regarded as desirable for the purpose of marriage. Age is considered as a significant factor in determining women's destiny in matters such as these. No matter how talented Olivia is, she must be efficient enough in the art of housekeeping.

Women's selflessness and their self-sacrifice originate from the ideology of the ideal woman. Pym undermines this image by ridiculing such traits in women like Belinda. Women have always been regarded as "helpmate, sex object, and domestic servant" (Walker, *Very* 98) rather than individuals capable of acting by and for themselves. The prevalence of images concerned with depicting the submissive or incapable women in women's humour, suggests that the authors, rather than sanctioning or even accepting these extremes of women's behaviour, are rejecting the cultural forces that have created such stereotypes through the years. Such negative satiric portraits create a distance between the reader and the subject allowing her/him to disclaim elements of similar behaviour. However, the humourist's attitude toward any one on the two different sets of images is not the same

(Walker, *Very* 65-66). Nevertheless, Belinda's role is not that of the submissive woman who can be the object of pity. She has not completely accepted the traditional notion of her subordinate role in a way that to negate any possibility of personal power or achievement. The humour originates from the paradox between Belinda's words and her inner thoughts. Despite Henry's humiliation of the spinsters, he still expects their unending services. Although he says that his rival, father Newman's church, solely consists of "doting spinsters," nonetheless, he needs and expects these spinsters' voluntary help and contributions. Belinda retorts to his mocking remark: "'You need not make fun of doting spinsters,' said Belinda, ... after all, it isn't always our fault ..." (*STG* 27). However, Henry goes on with his self-dramatization, and pretending to be the helpless victim in the hands of some oppressive spinsters, while the truth is totally the other way around: "'Women like to have something to dote on,' he said mildly enough, 'I have noticed that. And we in the Church are usually the victims'" (*STG* 28). The mocking tone of the narration stresses Henry's pretention and self-dramatization in order to attract attention to his helplessness.

Everybody expects Belinda's services and help and, being a spinster, she is doubly oppressed. As Doan observes, the spinster who is sensitive to attending "this voice of duty, rarely eludes acting responsibly because all actions are measured against an invisible public standard," Thus, to ignore carelessly and egoistically "the properties of the social order is to risk personal guilt" ("Pym's" 149-150). Not caring much about her own clothes, Belinda acts as Harriet's dress-maker. Putting a lot of effort to make Harriet's crepe de Chine dress before the garden party, she "ran around her with her mouth full of pins" while Harriet "was having one of her tirades against the Archdeacon" (*STG* 20). Harriet always takes Belinda's sacrifices for granted and believes that she does not need much. At the beginning of the novel, Harriet asks Belinda to answer the door since she is too busy combing her hair. Belinda too is getting ready, but she does not care and she goes to answer the door feeling that she is not ready. Harriet, moreover, borrows Belinda's clothes and even asks her to mend or knit her clothes. Although Belinda is displeased at Harriet's high expectations, nonetheless, her protest is not loud, but silent and covert: "She hoped that Harriet had not also borrowed her black velvet bridge coat, as she wanted it herself on these late September evenings" (*STG* 9). Belinda also selflessly serves Henry and the other men. Ackley argues that "both married and unmarried women alike can be irritatingly preoccupied with deferring to men, serving them, and inflating their already healthy egos" (34). However, unmarried women can be better servers due to their unrelated status.

Henry also takes for granted Belinda's services, expecting from her even more. When Belinda asks Mr. Donne what Henry says about her, he replies: "'He – er – said you did a lot of good work in the parish.'" However, Belinda does not like to feel like a servant, attending to people's needs: "Belinda could not help feeling disappointed. It made her sound almost disappointed. It made her sound almost unpleasant" (*STG* 10). When in their house, Belinda darns Henry's sock, he unashamedly expects more: "'My dear Belinda, you have done it quite exquisitely,' said the Archdeacon. 'I must take care to be passing your house every time I have a hole in my sock'" (*STG* 78). However, Belinda is obsessed with pleasing the others, and satisfying their needs and desires. She, at times, acts ridiculously. At the party, she does her best to please Henry and Dr. Parnell. She "brought out a photograph of Nicholas Parnell in his academic robes and put it on the mantelpiece; she also displayed on a small table a little pamphlet he had written about central heating in libraries" (*STG* 116). She is acting in this way since she is aware of Dr. Parnell's obsession with the conveniences in the library. Although she knows that men's preoccupation with their trivial affairs is ridiculous, however, she takes them seriously in order to please them. Woolf states that: "Women have served all these centuries as looking-glasses possessing the magic and delicious power of reflecting the figure of man at twice its natural size" (*Room* 35). The patriarchal values and standards have given men an image of self-importance in society. Henry, Dr. Parnell, and Mr. Mold are examples of such types – serious and self-important men who take themselves and their work much too seriously. Woolf asserts that patriarchal culture has taught women to regard men greater and more important than they really are. This situation, according to Woolf,

> serves to explain in part the necessity that women so often are to men. And it serves to explain how restless they are

under her criticism; ... For if she begins to tell the truth, the figure in the looking-glass shrinks; his fitness for life is diminished. How is he to go on giving judgement, civilizing natives, making laws, writing books, dressing up and speechifying at banquets, unless he can see himself at breakfast and at dinner at least twice the size he really is? ... The looking-glass vision is of supreme importance because it charges the vitality; it stimulates the nervous system. Take it away and man may die ... They start the day confident, braced, believing themselves desired at Miss Smith's tea party; they say to themselves as they go into the room, I am the superior of half the people here, and it is thus that they speak with that self-confidence, that self-assurance, which have had such profound consequences in public life and lead to such curious notes in the margin of the private mind. (*Room* 36-37)

Women's internalisation of the patriarchal ideology has also taught them not to regard themselves equal to men. Belinda and Harriet do not care about Edith and Connie in their party. They are invited only to prevent further gossip by the village people. They do not even have a particular place at the supper table: "Belinda had taken care to arrange the table so that Harriet should sit between Ricardo and Mr. Mold, when she might see how superior dear Ricardo was. Belinda herself sat by the Archdeacon and Dr. Parnell, while Miss Liversidge and Miss Aspinall were fitted in where there happened to be spaces" (*STG* 120). Underestimating themselves, Belinda and Harriet overestimate men. However, women are not to blame for humiliating other women since it is the ideology of patriarchy that has trained women, as well as men, not to care about women and their needs. Even a person as caring as Belinda does not care about the two women-guests at the party. She and Harriet attempt to satisfy men's needs, providing them with the best food and drinks. The next morning Belinda feels exhausted since "The effort of trying to talk to so many people last night and keep them at peace with each other had quite exhausted her. But there was some satisfaction mixed with her tiredness, for she felt it had been quite a successful party" (*STG* 128). Her anxiety to please men continues even after the party and she wonders whether the guests are satisfied or not. Pym ridicules Belinda's tendency to please people (especially men) by doing the foolish things she does, only to please them. She becomes an unappreciated male server, which is what the patriarchal system expects. Nevertheless, the tone of the narration and her inner thoughts undermine her actions. The narrative voice also mocks the serving female when Belinda goes to a wool shop. Seeing that Belinda is looking at the clerical grey wool, the seller encourages her to buy it by telling her: "'This is a lovely clerical grey,' said Miss Jenner, as if sensing her thoughts. 'I've sold quite a lot of this to various ladies round here – especially in Father Plowman's parish" (*STG* 82). She implies that women in the parish buy the wool only for the sake of knitting for the clergymen. According to Dr. Parnell, the most significant reason for men to marry after a certain age is their need to be served and cared for by a woman. However, he believes that young and middle-aged men should not marry since marriage restricts their freedom. Nevertheless, marriage benefits men in the old age since they need a woman to take care of them. According to Doan, the narrative voice mocks Dr. Parnell by undermining his high self-esteem and misogynistic beliefs: "an interrogatory tone works far more effectively than a stronger, more censorious comment to suggest the dubious nature of Parnell's own self-esteem. Pym uses both understatement and humour to belittle her bachelor" ("Text" 65).

Henry also expects Agatha's ongoing services. He is extremely angry when Agatha "had been grossly neglectful" (*STG* 24) to let the moths get into his grey suit and cries out to Agatha so that everyone could hear him, although Agatha herself ignores him. Henry is so preoccupied with his desires and needs that even when he imagines Belinda as being his wife, he does not dream of his romance with her, rather he only thinks that of what she can do for him, the things Agatha fails to do. He is so much obsessed with his affairs that a few hours later, in the garden party, he still discusses his ruined suit and suddenly tells Belinda: "I don't think you'd have done that" (*STG* 37). Although Agatha humiliates and ridicules Belinda, still she takes advantage of her when she needs her. For example, when Belinda visits Agatha, Agatha tells her worries about the tasks that will remain undone in the church and the parish during her holiday. She expects Belinda to take on the responsibility. Although Belinda is disinclined to do so, nonetheless, she cannot refuse her and says: "I'm sure I should be very willing to do what I could,' she said doubtfully" (*STG* 64).

Harriet also tries to please men, particularly young curates, by serving them. Belinda, herself a serving woman, cannot understand Harriet's obsession with the young curates: "It was odd that Harriet should always have been so fond of curates. They were so immature and always made the same kind of conversation" (*STG* 17). Harriet does all she can for their well-being and comfort. She invites them to dinner and takes foods, clothing, and fresh fruits to their lodgings. In the first scene, she even regards Agatha as her rival in serving and hosting curates. When Mr. Donne tells her that Agatha promised him some apples, she "looked rather annoyed. 'Their apples haven't done at all well this year,' she said, 'and I always think those red ones are rather tasteless. You must take some of our Cox's Oranges with you when you go'" (*STG* 13). Harriet is so devoted to the curates that she also expects Belinda to attend them. Harriet scolds Belinda for not being hospitable to Mr. Donne: "You are hopelessly inattentive. When Mr. Donne was here the other night you never passed him anything. If it hadn't been for me he would have starved.'" Although Belinda acts as if she is sorry for being inconsiderate and tells: "'I must try not to be so absent-minded,'" however, she mockingly thinks about "How many curates would starve and die were it not for the Harriets of this world" (*STG* 80). By ridiculing Harriet's obsession of serving curates, Belinda undermines the patriarchal value of serving the clergymen. Nevertheless, although she detests serving the curates, she feels obliged to play the role of the sympathising, kind-hearted Christian. Women function as men's servants wholeheartedly. Harriet is usually seen "carrying a large basket" (*STG* 54) to the curates' lodgings. She provides the curates with the food and fruits they themselves see nothing of: "Besides a cake and some apple jelly, she was taking some very special late plums which she had been guarding jealously for the last few weeks" (*STG* 54). However, like many other curates before him, Harriet loses Mr. Donne too. Not feeling disappointed, she expects another curate, and gets ready to pamper him. As she hears that the new curate is recovering from an illness, she makes special preparations: "'Oh, Belinda, he will need such special care!' Later that evening she could be seen studying a book of Invalid Cookery, and was quite annoyed when Belinda pointed out that he would probably be eating with a normal appetite by the time he came to them" (*STG* 241). Harriet's obsession with the curates and their well-being is, on the one hand, triggered by her unfulfilled desires and, on the other hand, it is the outcome of the presuppositions imposed by the patriarchal system about serving the clergymen and the church. The narrative voice mocks Harriet's preoccupation with the curates and all the foolish things she does for their sake. The curates whom Harriet serves selflessly are not impoverished and ill-fed as she, on entering Mr. Donne's sitting room, observes: "This was quite a nice room, not as meanly furnished as Harriet could have wished, though Belinda was relieved that they did not have to provide the curate with furniture as well as food" (*STG* 56). Women in *STG* are shown obsessed with the long-held belief that men cannot do without them – cannot keep houses, cook food, and do the other chores – and women must take care of men. When Harriet enters Mr. Donne's living room, she is surprised at seeing the comfortable and cosy atmosphere of the living room.

2.2.2 Subversion of Male Images

Pym employs stereotypical male characters in *STG* in order to demonstrate their absurd and hypocritical behaviour. However, her aim in representing such characters is not merely to ridicule their peculiarities; rather she portrays the reasons for such behaviour and the culture which creates such characters. Men in *STG* are generally indolent and unresponsive. They expect everything to be done by women. They tend to self-dramatise. Archdeacon Henry Hoccleve is one such instance. Long argues that "Hoccleve is not merely self-centered but also self-dramatising" (33). Hoccleve pretends to be overloaded, however, he finds it is "very difficult to get up in the mornings, and of course one knew that he always made his curates do the early services which was really rather slack, because it wasn't as if he were very old or weak in health" (*STG* 3). Male indolence and self-dramatization also manifests itself in Henry's words when Belinda gives him a list to choose the children who should recite poems, to which he "smiled with an affection of weariness and then sighed. 'Ah, yes. There is so much to be done before this afternoon. I haven't been able to sleep for thinking about it. Nobody can possibly imagine how much I have to do'" (*STG* 26). Everybody in the village is aware that he always wakes up very late and does not do any worthwhile job in the parish or the church. Nevertheless, his mind is so obsessed with reading poetry aloud that he forgets everything and everybody around him while reciting poetry. Once, he recites a horrid and depressive poem in his sermon merely for the sake of pretention. The poem, as Harriet remembers later, was "all about worms, and such stilted language," The congregation was so affected that a woman "walked out in the middle" (*STG* 20). When Belinda asks him to choose the list of children, instead, he begins to recite Milton to her, while a lot remains to be done in the garden before the garden party: "his first words were already out of his mouth when Belinda interrupted him, and directed his attention to the matter in hand" (*STG* 26). Usually he does not care about the situation, or the addressee, and selfishly pretends to be knowledgeable by reciting poems to the audience who are not the least interested. His indolence and pretention can also be traced to the time his friend, Dr. Parnell, pays him a visit. When Belinda and Dr. Parnell reach the vicarage, they see that he is sitting indolently on the bench under a tree. Henry pretends to be reflecting on the sermon he is going to give on Sunday:

> the Archdeacon was sitting in his favourite seat under the yew trees. She felt a faint irritation to see him sitting there in the middle of the morning when so many people, women mostly, were going about their household duties and shopping. She supposed that men would be working too, but somehow their work seemed less important and exhausting. (*STG* 96)

However, Henry is cautious to pretend that he is too busy and that his life differs much from that of normal people who have time to take a walk: "When the Archdeacon saw them he smiled benevolently, but at the same time condescendingly. It was as if he were letting them see how fortunate they were to be able to stroll in the village on a fine October morning, while he was condemned to sit among the tombs thinking out his sermon" (*STG* 96). Later on, when Belinda invites them for supper on Sunday, Henry, although wanting to accept, pretends to be too busy and tired to go to such parties: "'Sunday is always a heavy day for me,' said the Archdeacon 'and this Sunday will be particularly so. I intend to preach myself both morning and evening," Further, he makes a shocking comment that reveals his sense of self-importance: "These people are so sunk in lethargy that they do not know their own wickedness'" (*STG* 98). When the day of the party arrives, Henry self-dramatises the time he enters the Bedes' home: "The Archdeacon advanced towards an armchair by the fire and sank down into it rather dramatically, as if exhausted" (*STG* 116). Another instance of Henry's pretention is the time he includes an unsuitable poem in children's poetry citation so that he might be able to "explain to an audience not really interested in such linguistic niceties, the history of the rare word dingle. How it is first known in the twelfth or thirteenth century in a work called Sawles Warde; then it is revived by the Elizabethans, who gave it to Milton – you remember it in Comus, of course..." (*STG* 42). Thus, by employing various methods, he makes a pretence of his knowledge about literature to the uninterested audience. One evening in the vicarage, when Agatha regrets that she cannot do scholarly work since she does not have enough time, Henry disagrees with her and pretends to have taken all the burdens of the church and parish, and in this way plays the role of an overloaded clergyman: "'Well, my dear, there is no reason why you shouldn't get down to something like that yourself,' said the Archdeacon. 'I am sure you have more time to spare than I have'" (*STG* 67-68). Nevertheless, the truth of the matter is that Agatha, the curate and the parishioners, are in charge of the church affairs and Henry does almost nothing other than reciting poems and pretending to be thinking. Therefore, Pym ridicules the peculiar traits and characteristics of the indolent and pretentious clergymen, by revealing their true intentions, under their outward actions and words.

Henry's self-dramatization and indolence are manifested excessively after Agatha's departure for a holiday, when he immediately comes to the Bede's house, where his pretention as a kind-hearted and self-sacrificing husband, shocks and annoys both Belinda and Harriet. However, they do not mention it. Henry behaves as if he was the one who took Agatha to the train station, while they saw from their window, that it was Mr. Donne who took her to the station. Henry behaves as if he is extremely tired:

"'Such a business getting her to the station, I really feel quite exhausted. These departures are always more tiring for those who are left behind.'" When Belinda offers him a cup of tea, he says that he had already had his tea at the vicarage: "Well, that is kind of you, but I had some refreshment at the vicarage,' said the Archdeacon. 'I really felt justified in having something'" to which Belinda "nodded sympathetically" being aware of Henry's dishonesty (*STG* 75). The voice of the narration, combines with Belinda and Harriet's voices, and affirms Henry's hypocrisy and dishonesty. The narrator, accordingly, does not let Henry deceive Belinda and Harriet by his untruthfulness. Along with them, the reader too, aware of Henry's dishonesty and pretentions, laughs mockingly at him. Henry's untruthfulness and hypocritical intentions are also narrated at the garden party. Though Henry detests annual garden parties, he feels that he "had to put in an appearance to fawn on the more distinguished visitors. There was always a possibility that Lady Clara Boulding might decide to come to his church" (*STG* 26). His hypocrisy, craftiness, and dishonesty in wanting to meet the influential and rich people in control of power demonstrate his ambition for power and position. Though he humiliates and ridicules his parishioners and detests those beneath him, however, he is weak and obedient when facing persons of influence and power. Henry is also too lazy to write his own sermons. When Harriet criticises Archdeacon's sermons as "horrible and intolerable," though Belinda defends him, the narrator engages the reader in Belinda's inner speech since she knows the truth of the matter: "Of course the real truth of the matter was that poor Henry was too lazy to write sermons of his own and somehow one didn't think of him as being clever in a theological kind of way" (*STG* 21). However indolent, unintelligent, and inefficient Henry might be, being the religious and moral leader of his community, he is considered as the most significant person for the community. Still, the irony lies in the fact that he cannot be considered as a moral or religious person. All his works are being done by the others and his sermons and talks contain traces of his literary pretention.

Mr. Donne also expects Bede sisters to serve and make sacrifices for him from the time of his first visit. For instance, on hearing Belinda saying that she loves September, since she loves sitting by the fire and knitting, he answers: "Ah, knitting,' he smiled, and Belinda could see him glancing round the room as if he already expected to see the beginnings of a pullover for himself" (*STG* 3). Belinda's mocking tone and comments make Mr. Donne's words and behaviour appear as being extremely ridiculous and egoistic. When he is reminded of the garden party at the vicarage, Mr. Donne dramatises and pities himself, though he has no responsibility at the garden party: "The curate sighed with an affection of weariness. 'shall be almost glad when it is over,' he said. 'These functions are always very tiring for us'" (*STG* 18). The narration makes it clear that talks and manners of the clergymen are mere self-dramatizations, implying that the whole burden of such gatherings lies solely on women.

Dr. Parnell, an old friend of Belinda and Henry, visits the village during Agatha's absence. However, like every other male character in this novel, he also has his strange habits and pretentions. The main source of his pretention is the library he works in, and the conveniences recently made in the library, such as central heating and cloakrooms. He takes pride in having provided such facilities in their library, and talks about it no matter where he is. In a café, where he and Belinda go out to have coffee, he describes the conveniences of the library with great enthusiasm, to almost a relative stranger: "'Of course we have central heating there now,' said Dr. Parnell. 'There have been great improvements in the last ten years or so. We also have a Ladies' Cloakroom in the main building now,' he added, his voice rising to a clear, ringing tone. 'That is a very great convenience'" (*STG* 94). Dr. Parnell is so greatly obsessed with the idea of the conveniences in the library that he repeats the entire conversation to Henry. He is thankful to Belinda since she had introduced him "to a charming lady who showed great reverence when the Library was mentioned. It is really rather gratifying. I should be delighted to show her round,' he added. 'She would find every convenience" (*STG* 97). He is not content with merely talking about present conveniences in the library; he also talks about the extra conveniences that will be added to the library: "The next thing will be to have some kind of a restaurant where readers can take luncheon or tea together. Do you know,' – he tapped his walking stick on the ground – 'I have had to have notices printed requesting readers not to eat in the Library? One would hardly have thought it possible" (*STG* 97). The narration ridicules Dr. Parnell's obsession with the affairs of the library, his lack of self-irony, and taking his job too seriously, so that he cannot recognise how comic his preoccupation with the affairs of the library is. Doan argues that "Pym creates an unsympathetic portrayal by appropriating spinsterish qualities and embedding them into the character of the bachelor. Parnell's pettiness ... reflects stereotypically spinster-like attitudes toward life" ("Text" 66).

Male pretention is also evident in Bede's party when male guests are shown fussing over trivial issues and turning every insignificant thing into a controversial matter. This makes the women rather uncomfortable. Belinda reflects that

> Perhaps it was a mistake to have any kind of serious conversation when eating, or even anywhere at all in mixed company. Men took themselves so seriously and seemed to insist on arguing even the most trivial points. So, at the risk of seeming frivolous, she turned the conversation to something lighter. (*STG* 122)

Nonetheless, Belinda is aware that her struggle to lighten up the atmosphere has been in vain as men have again taken her humorous story, which she had mentioned in order to change the heavy atmosphere seriously. Soon there is an argument among men about the trivial matter that Belinda proposed for a change: "Belinda felt rather flustered at the interest which everyone was taking in her silly little story" (*STG* 122). The narration ridicules men's rivalry and pretention towards each other and their struggle to show themselves more knowledgeable and wise than the others. However, Pym depicts this habit as mere pretentions and self-indulgences since the arguments and discussions among men are not for the sake of coming to a conclusion, solving a problem, or exchanging knowledge or experience, rather, they are primarily for mere pretention. Belinda's narration ridicules men's sense of self-importance and lack of self-irony and humour. By taking everything seriously, men cannot view themselves and things from a distance and are unable to perceive their flaws and deficiencies. Unlike women, they do not have any sense of humour.

Pym portrays the bachelors' characteristic traits as the extreme opposite of those of her spinsters. While the spinster is self-effacing, self-sacrificing, sympathetic, and humorous, the bachelor is self-confident, self-indulgent, insensitive, and lacking in self-irony and humour. Bachelors who are refused by Belinda and Harriet become extremely annoyed because of their feeling of self-importance and their lack of self-irony. In this case, Doan states that

> Pym implies that from the bachelor's point of view, to be refused in marriage is the ultimate insult. Since bachelors feel somehow privileged in their single states, when they elect to marry, they believe that a woman should feel honored. Everything, especially a marriage proposal, is confidently expected to go their way." However, when things do not go as they wish, they get frustrated and as Doan suggests, "The irony again is that since the bachelor is so self-absorbed, he fails to understand that being married to him might not in fact, be so appealing. ("Text" 73-74)

The male and female characters represented in Pym's *STG*, do not conform to the stereotypes and images of women and men, created in the conduct literature based on the patriarchal culture. The narrative voice ridicules the image of the ideal woman as well as the stereotypes of the spinster and the bachelor. Pym's spinsters are not the dull, conventional ideal women, but strong, caring and humorous characters in sharp contrast to the images of women created in the already existing literature. Although they are shown as conforming to the conventions of the patriarchal order at the surface level, however, on a deeper level, they undermine its fundamental presuppositions, injustices, and prejudices through applying humour in their discourse. The narrative voice also threatens the image of the strong, active, and responsible male characters. Married men and bachelors in *STG* are generally indolent, passive, and self-important individuals who lack enthusiasm in their lives because of their lack of self-irony. The narrative voice reverses the image of the strong and honest male characters by portraying their absurdities, hypocrisies, and pretentions in a humorous manner. Additionally, the narration questions the very foundation of the patriarchal culture that is responsible for creating such individuals.

2.3 Women's Humour as Social Critique: Undermining the Institution of Church and Clergymen

Being a church-going Anglican, Pym was closely familiar with the Church of England and the characteristics of the Anglican clergymen. As Long states, she exploits both "the figure of spinster and the Church of England as the material of her satire" (15). Not being an exception, the represented community in *STG* consists of the pretentious, inefficient, and lazy churchmen, as well as efficient, and intelligent parishioners. Among these parishioners, Belinda, a spinster and a devoted church worker, subtly ridicules the authority and power associated with the church and clergymen. In this way, she undermines the authority and the power they represent by pointing out their absurdities and hypocrisies.

Throughout history, women have intentionally been kept away from the power structures. The institution of church is one of them. Therefore, women's relation to the power structures have always been different. Similarly, the women writers' approach to the power structures and the people associated with authority is different from the male approach. Bennett argues that women, in addition to questioning "the institutions of church and marriage," also challenge "the male figures behind those institutions" since they, being the agents of the authority, have

> traditionally dictated policy and behavior for women throughout the centuries, marking women as representatives of Eve, forever tempting men away from God with the apple of sex. In short, although men may view religion as absurd or meaningless, women may also see it as oppressive and destructive. (86)

In the same manner, although Pym's novels commonly deal with the institution of church, clergymen, and parishes, nevertheless, she does not regard them as infallible and perfect. In *STG,* clergymen and the authority associated with the church are being ridiculed and the relation between the common people and the clergy is continually counteracted. As Bennett asserts, "minister or preacher," being a combination of "institution and man" has always been the target of women's humour and women writers, "by 'humanizing' preachers," diminish their authority and power (86-87).

The institution of church is the representative of the authoritative or patriarchal order. Women's relation to the church has been paradoxical throughout history. While they do not have the right to preach or gain the status equal to men in the church, they can still be nuns or voluntary church workers. However, the burden of the church affairs has always been on women. Pym mocks this tradition in *STG,* undermining the convention by creating clergymen, commonly weak, lazy, and egoistical, as opposed to the energetic, intelligent, and efficient spinsters. Belinda and Harriet are among such spinsters. When Belinda sees the ongoing quarrel between the priests, she wishes that she were a priest, to take charge of the church herself. However, she knows well that a woman cannot enter the pulpit: "thought Belinda, almost wishing that she were Deaconess Bede and could enter the pulpit herself to celebrate Holy Communion – it was of course the *early* services which had been cancelled" (*STG* 7).

Clergymen have ordinarily been considered as being satisfied with very little, in terms of luxury and material goods. Nonetheless, the clergymen in the novel prefer good food and luxury. When Belinda thinks of the curate, we are told that

> the Reverend Edgar Donne was surely a simple young man and would not expect much. Naturally one did not think of the clergy as expecting anything in the way of material luxuries ... Belinda paused, for she was remembering the vicar, Archdeacon Hoccleve, and how one couldn't really say that about him. (*STG* 2)

Later, when Harriet visits Mr. Donne's lodging with the same idea of a clergymen's limited needs, she finds out that she has been mistaken, since Mr. Donne's house turns out to be a very comfortable, beautiful house.

Henry is the main target of Pym's criticism since he is a character who tries to progress through making himself closer to the institution of the church to gain personal power as well as the favours of influential people. For example, his intention in participating in the garden party is to persuade Lady Clara in order to give some money to the church. He is "wondering whether Lady Clara would give some definite contribution to the church-roof fund as well as buying things at the stalls" (*STG* 33). Even Belinda knows that when Henry is not around, he must be "probably attending on some more distinguished visitors" (*STG* 36). However, Belinda at times attacks Henry's ego and his sense of self-importance, either by her words or in her inner speech. In these rare moments, she mocks the institution of church and also the clergymen, undermining the power attributed to them. At the garden party when she notices Henry fussing over his ruined suit, she attacks him from the aspect of Christian principles: "'We are supposed not to take heed of what we shall wear'" (*STG* 38). However, Henry finds an appropriate answer for such a slight criticism: "I am sure that you would have seen that it was put away with moth balls" which reveal his unceasing expectations. It is ironical that Archdeacon Henry, a sworn Christian, is the one who does not act according to Christian teachings, and Belinda undermines his status by reminding him the Christian principles. Henry's egoism, however, does not prevent him from desiring a better serving woman than Agatha, and believes that if Belinda had been his wife, she would not let moths eat into his suits. Henry, on another occasion, ridicules the Christian doctrines. For example, when Belinda suggests him to go on a holiday, with "a mocking tone" he responds: "'One cannot leave the flock without a shepherd'" (*STG* 39).

Additionally, the church in *STG* does not play the conventional role and the prominent function it had before. It is a fast decaying, forgotten old place where people gather not for the sake of praying, but mainly for gossiping, pretention, and making some money. It seems that people do not attend church because they believe in the Christian doctrines anymore; instead, they come to church out of their long-established communal habit. When Henry preaches his famous sermon about the Judgment Day, although the congregation is Christian, still they all get anxious and afraid when they are reminded of the "Day of Wrath" as they "reminded themselves that of course such a thing couldn't really happen." Their reactions to the sermon demonstrate that they just attend church and do religious worship habitually, and do not believe in their religion's principles. Ironically, they believe in scientific facts:

> Why, scientists told us that it would take millions of years for the sun to move sufficiently far away from the earth for life to become extinct. At least it was perhaps not exactly that, but something very like it. They knew enough to realize that the Archdeacon was being ridiculous and that the Judgment Day could not possibly be tomorrow. When the first uncomfortable shock had passed they were able to laugh at themselves. How could they have been so silly as to be alarmed! (*STG* 109)

As suggested, through the employment of humour, Pym challenges the institution of church and clergymen by ridiculing their influence and power as well as revealing the fact that it is the church and the clergymen who are in need of people, not the other way around. The church's burden is on the people's shoulders, while the clergymen do almost nothing other than preaching terrifying sermons to the discontent and unbelieving congregation. Spinsters, who have been commonly ignored and deprecated, play a major role in the church and the parish affairs. Moreover, as represented in their thoughts and actions, they are also able to trace the ills and absurdities carefully.

As shown in the on-going discussion, the structural and thematic strategies contribute to the construction of women's humour in *STG*. Rhetorical strategies include the reversal of the romantic love plot and the employment of the domesticity, double-text discourse, gossip, self-deprecation and sympathetic bonds. Pym turns every romantic incident into its opposite by making use of various strategies – including pairing unlikely couples such as old women and young men; omitting the happy ending of marriage; subverting the normal ritual of courtship; the reversal of the gender roles; and the employment of the domestic trivia in the romantic moments. Moreover, Pym's discourse of trivia, in addition to subverting romance, creates significant out of the insignificant and ordinary. By making the women's so-called unimportant matters and subjects as significant, Pym's humour undermines the patriarchal culture's long-held values and criteria. Similarly, her use of the double-voiced discourse" or double-text, including both the discourse of the dominant patriarchal culture and the oppressed muted women's culture, is a strategy to survive in, or resist the dominating system. Belinda's employment of double-text is in harmony with her self-deprecating, covert language, as her inner speech reveals her real thoughts. Through undermining the prevailing patriarchal culture, these inner speeches are in opposition to those uttered in public.

Further, gossip plays a major role in the shaping of the narrative in *EW*. Functioning alongside the humour of the narration, gossip has a shaping power in creating bonds in the represented fictional society in *STG*. Gossip functions as the main source of acquiring news and information and plays the role of today's media, newspaper and the internet, undermining the patriarchal system. Understatement and self-deprecation is a strategy through which women characters in *STG* effectively resist the oppressions of the patriarchal society and thus survive in that culture. By employing self-irony and self-deprecation, Belinda does not humiliate herself, rather she strengthens herself by preventing further oppressions attacking her from the male-centred culture and its values. By regarding herself critically and understating herself Belinda does not let the dominating culture's blows harm her. She also undermines the patriarchal culture's values and beliefs by presenting their absurdities.

A sympathetic bond exists between the female characters and narrator, as also among the female characters themselves. The female humour in the narration creates a sympathetic relationship between herself and Belinda by mildly criticising her for obeying the laws of the patriarchal society. Moreover, the female characters also sympathise and make a sympathetic bond with each other. Belinda and Harriet particularly make such a bond and support and protect each other, wherever they might be. Through such a bond, the narrator protects the female character in the face of patriarchal oppression. Additionally, it undermines the authority of the patriarchal order. The factors related to themes and motifs also affect women's humour in *STG* – subversion of images and stereotypes of women, as well as the subversion of images of male characters; criticising the public culture by women's humour; and undermining the institution of church and clergymen. Pym subverts the images and stereotypes of male and female characters by ridiculing the long-held beliefs and presuppositions of the male-centred society. Belinda's internalising of the images of the *angel in the house* and the *ideal of womanhood*, as well as, the male self-importance and self-dramatization are equally ridiculed. Moreover, Pym highlights the paradoxical relationship between women and the religious institutions through presenting Belinda's delicate undermining of the power of the authoritarian institutions, represented mainly by the church and its people or clergymen.

3 *Excellent Women*: Humour of Mildred Regarded as an Excellent Woman

> 'On the threshold of sixty,' mused Dr Parnell. 'That's a good age for a man to marry. He needs a woman to help him into his grave.' (*STG* 148)

This chapter explores the humour of central character Mildred's being presented as an excellent woman in *EW*. The chapter primarily examines the rhetorical as well as thematic strategies that help create women's humour in *EW*. By highlighting Mildred's understatement and self-deprecation, this chapter firstly explores the role(s) of rhetorical strategies in the construction of women's humour in *EW*. Secondly, the chapter examines women's humour in the novel by exploring Mildred's double voiced discourse. Finally, the roles of thematic and rhetorical strategies are explored by emphasising the subversion of the images and stereotypes of both female, such as spinsters, and male characters, such as the Byronic hero. The chapter concludes that through the application of women's humour, Pym in *EW* achieves the disruption of the established and dominating patriarchal culture.

In *EW*, Pym creates the stereotypical concept of excellent woman by presenting the central character Mildred Lathbury, as an excellent woman. However, as Ackley observes, "Pym's excellent women are not the totally selfless, charitably-spirited people the world would see them as" (9). Pym portrays the discontented and unrelated Mildred as the stereotype of a woman whom everybody turns to in time of trouble and need, confides in, and approaches for help in difficult situations. Mildred is thoroughly dissatisfied with her situation although she does whatever she is able to do for her friends and neighbours. Her sense of guilt in delaying or refusing somebody's request for help demonstrates her internalisation of the stereotype of an excellent woman.

Regarding women as helpmates of men has been a long-held belief and practice. In this case, Ackley argues that:

> The opinion that men's needs are superior to or more pressing than the needs of women is reiterated with the same sort of bemusement throughout the novels. Countless women

perform domestic tasks and menial clerical labor for men. We see this attitude expressed in Mildred's falling under Rocky's spell and then acting as drudge for him and Julian, not to mention Everard, in *Excellent Women*. (46)

Nevertheless, although Mildred plays the role of the serving spinster in front of the others, she is fully aware of her ironic situation and during her every comment or in her inner thoughts, she is able to humorously ridicule and subvert the long-held beliefs and values concerning the image of a spinster. As Cotsell states, Pym's "chief quality is a dry wit, of which she herself is often the subject ... the irony extends to other, for Mildred is an observant person ... but the chief satisfaction is in self-recognition" (50). Cotsell also argues that Mildred's "determined self-knowledge that is also a repression leaves one open to subsequent humiliating self-knowledge and to the easy condensation and pity of others" (51).

3.1 Rhetorical Strategies in the Construction of Women's Humour

Rhetorical and structural strategies are extremely effective tools in the construction of women's humour in *EW*. Through them, Mildred's understatement and self-deprecation are embedded into the general structure of the narrative plot. But, before their examination, an overview of the synopsis of the novel will be helpful. *EW* recounts the story of Mildred Lathbury who considers herself on the verge of becoming a spinster in her early thirties. She is the daughter of a country vicar. Following the death of her parents, she resides all by herself in an unfashionable part of London in the post-world war II era. She lives on a small inherited salary and undertakes a voluntary job for the impoverished gentlepeople. She spends most of her time with the church and in local parish affairs. Her life undergoes a great change when new neighbours move into the flat situated beneath her living quarters. Helena is a serious anthropologist and her husband Rocky has served as a Flag Lieutenant to an Admiral in Italy during the war. His responsibility has involved entertaining the Wren officers. Mildred takes a fancy towards him and plays the role of a serving spinster and makes an approach when Helena leaves Rocky to be with Everard Bone, her fellow anthropologist whom she is in love with. Everard rejects Helena because of his principles and requests Mildred to inform Helena that she should leave him alone because he does not love her. However, his interest in Mildred grows because of the various jobs she can undertake on his behalf. Mildred also serves and saves Julian Malory, their vicar and her sister Winifred from the questionable widow, Allegra Grey, who plans on marrying Julian and turn abandon Winifred. Mildred hosts Winifred and is able to console the heartbroken Julian after Allegra leaves him after she had done the same to Rocky. Rocky leaves for his country house asking Mildred to send his furniture. Finally, due to Mildred's attempts, Rocky and Helena are able to unite and vacate the flat. Following their departure, two spinsters replace them. Everard invites Mildred to dinner in his house, suggesting she undertakes a worthy job – indexing and proofreading his manuscripts. However, Mildred misunderstands this suggestion as a proposal for marriage.

3.1.1 Understatement and Self-Deprecation

Mildred's strategy of understatement during the course of her discourse produces a significant effect. Her self-understatement does not result in the humiliation of the spinster; instead, it strengthens the resistance against the oppressions of the dominating patriarchal society. On the one hand, Mildred refuses to comply with the laws of the patriarchal society by means of self-deprecation and, on the other hand, she covertly revolts against the existent injustices of the dominating culture. While thinking about her house, she remembers the condition of her flat from time to time. Self-deprecatingly, she thinks that she is not worthy of having a bathroom for herself: "There were offices on the ground floor and above them the two flats, not properly self-contained and without every convenience. 'I have to share a bathroom,' I had so often murmured, almost with shame, as if I personally had been found unworthy of a bathroom all my own" (*EW* 6). Here, Mildred's implied underestimation goes beyond self-humiliation representing her defiance in the face of a discriminating society as she reacts to Helena when the latter states that she and her husband do not "'like the idea of sharing a bathroom.'" In a self-deprecating manner, Mildred again responds by stating, "'I am always *very* quick in the mornings and on Sundays I usually get up early to go to church'" (*EW* 7). Mildred's intentional underestimation demonstrates that she ought not to be considered as a threat to Helena and Rocky. Thus, she defends and strengthens herself through her self-deprecating actions. However, Long asserts that Mildred's underestimation is primarily due to her sexual suppression:

> her sense of guilt appears in the opening when she explains that she has to share a bathroom with the people in the flat below. Her embarrassment amounting to shame over the shared toilet implies sexual repression, since the sharing of toilet connotes physical-sexual contact, from which she shrinks. (47)

Moreover, Mildred's habit of self-underestimation extends to other people that are similar to herself. For example, when she and her friend, Mrs Bonner, come across Everard Bone in the church, Mildred automatically thinks that he is completely different from the other church goers because of his different complexion and outfit: "we certainly seemed harmless enough, elderly and middle aged people with one or two mild-looking younger men and women. Indeed, Everard Bone had been the only person one would have looked at twice" (*EW* 51). Mildred's self-deprecating perception of herself and of fellow church goers points towards their shared lower status and also to their unnoticeable situation. However, through such emphasising, she highlights the conditions in which these people live by offering them the status they previously lacked since she is able to bring to attention the socio-culturally insignificant groups. Later, when Mildred informs Rocky and Helena about seeing Everard in the church, Helena self-understatingly responds when inquired whether she spoke with him and Mildred: "'Oh, no, I don't think he saw me, or if he did he didn't recognize me. People don't, you know. I suppose there's nothing outstanding about me'" (*EW* 55). By highlighting her insignificance and through self-criticism, Mildred makes an entrance into the group of unnoticed people in the church and prevents Rocky and Helena's further criticism of her while being an unrelated spinster. Mildred's self-deprecation is demonstrated when, after a difficult day, she has to wash her clothes. She is fully aware that her clothes appear to be nothing more than a pile of unfashionable old items: "Then I went back to my flat and collected a great deal of washing to do. It was depressing the way the same old things turned up every week. Just a kind of underclothes a person like me might wear, I thought dejectedly, so there is no need to describe them" (*EW* 85). By criticising her unfashionable and old clothes without describing them, Mildred is able to neutralise the reader's possible humiliation regarding her outfits. This also indicates the possibility of a sympathetic bond between her situation and the reader's reactions.

Anthropology is another subject about which Mildred is not well informed. For her, this results in embarrassment and humiliation when she is among her anthropologist friends. After Everard and Helena present a shared seminar at the Learned Society, Mildred feels that she ought to leave earlier because she is unable to make conversation with Everard about the event:

> Everard Bone had broken away from a group of Americans and was standing by my side. I was grateful to him for rescuing me though I could think of no conversation beyond a polite murmur and was quite sure that he was one thing to get back to discussing his paper with people who were able to. 'I think I must be going home now,' I said. 'Thank you very much for asking me.' (*EW* 93)

Mildred wishes to escape from the group of anthropologists because she thinks that her conversation would not be appropriate. By doing so, she does in fact prevent her humiliation among the scholars. When Everard pays attention to her, she misunderstands his actions because of her extreme self-deprecation. As Cooley suggests: "Mildred's misreading of Everard is of a piece with her general underestimation of the impact she has on others. As the novel progresses, we see more and more incidents in which Mildred tries to ignore the fact that she has attracted interest and affection" (*Comic* 88). Not only is she embarrassed among scholars, but she usually prevents herself from holding any conversation about matters she is unaware of.

Similarly, Mildred deprecates herself among women who are younger and prettier than herself. When she sees Helena for the first time, she compares her complexion and outfit with hers and feels ashamed for appearing dowdy: "She was fair-haired and pretty, gaily dressed in corduroy trousers and a bright jersy, while I, mousy and rather plain anyway, drew attention to those qualities with my shapeless overall and old fawn skirt" (*EW* 7). Mildred's strategy involves placing stress on her unattractive complexion and outfit as well as describing herself with adjectives such as plain and mousy. With this, she is able to control other characters', as well as the reader's, perceptions on her own appearance. By using self-deprecation, she is able to turn the irony toward herself and prevent further humiliation. Later, she compares herself with Allegra Grey, another attractive woman:

> I suddenly remembered Allegra Gray's smooth apricot-coloured face rather too close to mine and wondered what it was that she used to get such a striking effect. There was a mirror on the counter and I caught sight of my own face, colourless and worried-looking, the eyes large and rather frightened the lips too pale. I did not feel that I could ever acquire a smooth apricot complexion but I could at least buy a new lipstick. (*EW* 130)

In comparison to Allegra, while confessing to the reader, Mildred finds herself colourless and plain. However, after buying a new lipstick, she tries to decrease the impact of her appearance on others. As Long observes, "she is the least presumptuous of narrators, admitting all of her weaknesses and inviting the reader to laugh at them and her" (58). On another occasion, Mildred also compares herself to other women in the shopping mall. While watching them shopping, eating, and drinking with their husbands, she regards herself as a lonely spinster whom nobody awaits for:

> Later I went into the restaurant to have tea, where the women, with an occasional man looking strangely out of place, seemed braced up, their faces newly done, their spirits revived by tea. Many had the satisfaction of having done a

> good day's shopping and would have something to gloat over when they got home. I had only my Hawaiian Fire and something not very interesting for supper. (*EW* 131)

The patriarchal society does not, by any means, value a woman who is not related to a man. The feeling of not being related to a man, therefore, afflicts her with the sense of self-deprecation. Comparing herself with married or engaged women further exacerbates her sense of self-understatement. Also, her sense of loneliness reflects her empathic condition in a society and culture wherein being a spinster is as equal to nonexistence. She can neither be a helpmate to a man, nor bring about any benefit to society. Her sense of self-deprecation in relation to her complexion and outfit is noticeable while she is getting ready to be present at Everard's house:

> I had no important jewels except for a good cameo brooch which had belonged to my grandmother, so I fastened this at the front of the little collar, brushed my hair back rather more severely than usual and looked altogether exactly the kind of person who would be able to correct proofs or make an index. (*EW* 248)

Her self-irony rescues her from the attacks and double oppressions of her society. By declaring, from the onset, that she is unattractive and mousy, she prevents critiques of the patriarchal culture and society.

Mildred is well aware that people do not want to see or talk to her to avoid embarrassment and for her own sake, but primarily for the free services she provides to them. In fact, people are able to gain advantage as a result of her being lonely and unrelated. When Everard arrives to see her, he surprises her in the middle of the street, situated in front of her office. At first, she thinks that he has come to see her, but soon realises his plan:

> I pondered over this remark for a while, asking myself what it could be going to lead up to, and then wondered why I had been so stupid as not to realise that he wanted to say some-

thing about Helena Napier. It was not for the pleasure of my company that Everard Bone had asked me out this evening – or rather not even asked me and given me the chance of appearing better dressed and without my string bag, but had waylaid me in the street. (*EW* 142)

When compared to Everard's behaviour, Mildred's reaction is even stranger. From habit, she deprecates herself and lowers herself to a status of being a mere mediator. She misreads Everard again when he takes her to his mother's house for dinner. Having returned from washing her hands and face upstairs, she states: "I was surprised to see that Everard was standing in the hall waiting for me, turning over a heap of old visiting cards that lay in a brass bowl on an antique chest" (*EW* 147).

Although Mildred offers her services to people, her sense of self-understatement fails her to suggest something to somebody or even remark on anything. When she writes a letter to Rocky upon Helena's request to help them reunite, she writes: "'You may think it very interfering, but it does seem to me...' What seemed to me? I wondered, listening to the rain which had suddenly become heavier, and why should he take any notice of what I said?" (*EW* 205) She is certain that nobody treats her with seriousness or cares about her opinions. However, she is utterly mistaken. Upon reading her letter, Rocky takes Helena home and they are able to reconcile. It would seems that Mildred's down-look on herself is due to her self-deception as well as her uncertainty about the result of her letter writing. She does not want to give false hopes to the reader. Mildred also self-deprecates while describing her meals. Her choice of food is clever, yet symbolic. While accompanying friends belonging to a higher status, she usually eats expensive, good food and drinks wine of good quality. However, when she is alone and sad, her choice of food symbolises her emotional state by usually preparing simple and unpretentious food for herself. She describes the food's plain quality and quantity. For example, when Rocky vacates the flat and his belongings are sent after his departure, she prepares a simple lunch in accordance to her mood:

> After I had seen the van go away I went upstairs to my flat to eat a melancholy lunch. A dried-up scrap of cheese, a few lettuce leaves for which I could not be bothered to make any dressing, a tomato and a piece of bread-and-butter, followed by a cup of coffee made with coffee essence. A real woman's meal, I thought, with no suggestion of brandy afterwards, even though there was still a drop left in the bottle. Alcohol would have made it even more of a mockery. (*EW* 176)

Mildred selects her meals voluntarily. Often, she eats meals that are of low quality while reporting them to the reader. Suggesting that she is eating a real woman's meal, Mildred implies that women generally eat simple foods and do not care about the quality of their meals much when compared to men. This is due to women's low expectations, and not necessarily their lesser needs. In this text, Mildred does in fact ridicule women by laughing at their habits and expectations through self-deprecation. Towards the end of the novel, when Mildred sees Everard crossing the street with another anthropologist from the Learned Society, she is annoyed and becomes jealous. Then, she decides to go to a public cafeteria to have lunch:

> Esther Clovis... hair like a dog, but a very capable person, respected and esteemed by Everard Bone, and, moreover, one who could make an index and correct proofs. I felt quite a shock at seeing them together, especially when I noticed Everard taking her arm. Of course they were crossing the road and any man with reasonably good manners might be expected to take a woman's arm in those circumstances, I reasoned within myself, but I still felt very low. I decided that I would go and have lunch in the great cafeteria where I sometimes went with Mrs. Bonner. It would encourage a suitable frame of mind, put me in mind of my own mortality and of that of all of us here below, if I could meditate on that line of patient people moving with their trays. (*EW* 240)

Mildred's ironic critique of Everard is related with their previous dialogue in relation to Esther Clovis. Everard describes Esther as being a very capable woman whom he holds in high esteem and respects. Mildred's surprise in seeing the two arm in arm originates from Everard's words about her since in his talk he did not suggest any romantic bond between himself and Esther. Mildred's decision to have a simple meal in a public cafeteria derives from her sense of being humiliated after seeing the two. She wrongly feels that she should punish herself after being betrayed by Everard although the reader is aware that she is not to blame in this case. However, since she is used to taking the blames and feeling guilty, she is ready to be punished for all her false imaginations as well as for the other people's deeds. She is, therefore, angry and embarrassed of her inaccurate perceptions about Everard: "I found myself wondering how I could have wanted so much to see him again, and I was embarrassed at the remembrance of my imaginings of him, alone and ill in his flat with nobody to look after him. Nothing more unlikely could possibly be imagined" (*EW* 241). She is angry with herself mainly because she is unable of coming out of the role of an excellent woman who always worries about other people's wellbeing. Although at this point she is playing the role of an excellent woman self-consciously, she is not satisfied with her role. Accordingly, she tries to escape from being an excellent woman but it is not so easy since she has internalized its values and manners. The only thing she can do is to ridicule her tendency ironically.

Mildred tends to feel guilty about matters over which she has little control. When someone asks her for a favour which she is unable to grant, her sense of guilt takes her to wild imaginings. For example, when Everard asks her to go to his house and cook his meat for the dinner, she refuses her since she is very tired. However, she begins to have regrets about having refused to help him, as she cannot refrain herself from feeling guilty:

> I had not wanted to see Everard Bone and the idea of having to cook his evening meal for him was more than I could bear at this moment. And yet the thought of him alone with his meat and his cookery book was unbearable too. He would turn to the section on meat. He would read that beef or mut-

ton should be cooked for so many minutes per pound and so many over. He would weigh the little joint, if he had scales. He would then puzzle over the heat of the oven, turning it on and standing over it, watching the thermometer go up .... I should have been nearly in tears at this point if I had not pulled myself together and reminded myself that Everard Bone was a very capable sort of person whose life was always very well arranged. He would be quite equal to cooking a joint. (*EW* 219-20)

Her inner feelings of guilt spring from the conventional image of the *serving spinster*, whom she has internalised as she fancies and imagines herself to be as one. Since any kind of selfishness or egoism is unpardonable for her, she thus feels guilty of having refused Everard's request to cook his meat. Although not approving of being people's handmaid, she is, nonetheless, frightened by the possibility of distorting her public image of being an excellent woman. This paradox leads to her anxious inner state.

Women humourists such as Barreca and Walker emphasise on the self-deprecatory, subtle, and gentle nature of women's humour. Likewise, Mildred's self-deprecatory manner originates from her particular condition in the society. Being a single woman, the society does not grant her any value in her single status, for she is neither a wife nor a mother, and thus no use to the patriarchal society. The most appropriate role that an unmarried woman like Mildred can have is being an *excellent woman*. Being acutely aware of this fact, Mildred acts as an excellent woman although she covertly revolts against it by deriding the image. Her critique of people related to powers of science and religion – anthropologists and clergymen – reverses the long-held beliefs and presuppositions about spinsters. Though manners and behaviour do not exhibit her dissatisfaction, her inner thoughts and speech reflect her discontentment and her distrust of the society. One strategy she strategically reveals is her dissatisfaction. By adopting the view of the patriarchal order, Mildred looks at herself with detachment and self-irony. In this way, she admits her lacks and shortcomings, such as being unattractive, unfashionable, or whatever the patriarchal culture ascribes to her. Mildred turns all upon herself. By confessing that she is not a really desirable woman, she succeeds in surviving and resisting the patriarchal order. Through the use of understatement, she takes upon herself the blames and accepts herself to be the guilty one in every situation although her inner thoughts are very different. Moreover, through such behaviour, on the one hand, she does not allow the patriarchal society's harsh critiques upon her since she has already accepted the blame that she is unworthy of finding a husband because she is not desirable enough. Additionally, she strengthens her position by placing herself at the position of the authoritarian oppressing system, thus resisting humiliation and ridicule.

3.1.2 Mildred's Double-Voiced Discourse

Double-voiced discourse is the most significant strategic method that Mildred applies in order to resist and survive within the patriarchal society in *EW*. Double text subverts the dominant discourse of the patriarchal society by ridiculing the order. Accordingly, Mildred is not a completely reliable narrator since she is obliged to act according to the codes of the dominating system. She has to survive in a society that does not recognise for her any social status as an unmarried woman. Long also confirms the unreliability of Mildred's narration observing that: "At various times Mildred is reluctant to admit her own feelings, and sometimes she is a duplicitous narrator" (52).The patriarchal order imposes some presuppositions upon her expecting her to tune her acts with the dominant communal beliefs and values. Mildred acts and talks as an obedient subject to the patriarchal order; however, her double-voiced discourse allows her to resist its laws and values.

The opening scene of the novel represents Mildred's double-voiced discourse. When Mr Mallet asks Mildred about the person who is moving in, he thinks that Mildred should know all about the people moving in since, being a lonely spinster, she is interested in people's affairs. However, Mildred does not provide any information for him and though she responds Mr Mallet as a typical spinster would, in her inner speech she questions Mr Mallet and the society's view of her as a spinster as primarily interested in other people's affairs rather than her own: "'Well, yes, one usually does,' I said, feeling rather annoyed at his presumption. 'It is rather difficult not to know such things.'" Her expression interweaves two discourses – the dominant male culture's discourse and the oppressed, female culture's discourse. Later on, Mildred ironically expresses the male culture's presuppositions of herself:

> I suppose an unmarried woman just over thirty, who lives alone and has no apparent ties, must expect to find herself involved or interested in other people's business, and if she is also a clergyman's daughter then one might really say that there is no hope for her. (*EW* 5)

Her real intention in saying so is to subvert the preconceptions and values existent in the dominating culture by questioning and criticizing them in her inner thoughts. Doan also emphasizes the double-voiced discourse of the narration:

> The irony here results from the tension that arises in the juxtaposition of the dutiful and subversive voice. ... this episode is paradigmatic of a narrative strategy that calls for the continuous, simultaneous sounding of two narrative voices. On the surface, the reader is presented with a narrative voice fully compliant with normal social expectations – a voice politely civil even when answering an impudent, audacious query. Yet, underneath this veneer of mild-mannered conformity, another voice speaks to challenge, even to ridicule, a social order that calls for the repression of unkind retorts. On this level, Mildred characterizes Mallett's remarks as roguish and pompous, but she internalizes her anger and irritation. These deeper feelings are revealed only to the reader. Most of Pym's characters are continually engaged in this quiet, civilized struggle which pits their individual needs against the larger set of social expectations. ("Text" 64)

A similar incident occurs when Mildred talks with Helena for the first time. Mildred is caught between her real feelings about Helena and her inner or conscience's voice:

> I decided that I did not like Mrs. Napier very much, and then began to reproach myself for the lack of Christian charity. But must we always like everybody? I asked myself. Perhaps not, but we must not pass judgment on them until we have known them a little longer than one hour. In fact, it was not our business to judge at all. I could hear Father Malory saying something of the kind in a sermon. (*EW* 10)

Due to the religious teachings of the dominant culture, she abstains from expressing her real feelings about Helena freely even to herself. The dominant order teaches her not to pass judgments on anybody, and not to detest anybody. It also prevents her from expressing her true feelings. Following that, she regrets having unkind thoughts about Helena when she remembers the Christian teachings and tries to correct her perceptions. She also does not express her feelings in different situations while having interaction with people. For instance, when Rocky makes compliments to a painter's drawing who lives near their house, Mildred, though she detests his drawings, does not comment: "Personally I thought them disgusting, but I made a noncommittal reply" (*EW* 31). Likewise she censors her true feelings and thoughts in similar situations. When Helena asks her view of Everard after she meets him, although she finds him dull and boring and impossible to speak, still Mildred describes him with positive adjectives: "'He seems very nice and he's certainly rather good-looking'" (*EW* 37). This is in opposition to her thoughts some days later, when she sees Everard in the church and gets upset:

> The preacher was forceful and interesting. His words seemed to knit us together, so that we really were like the early Christians, having all things in common. I tried to banish the feeling that I should prefer not to have all things in common with Everard Bone but it would keep coming back, almost as if he was to be in some way my Lenten penance, and I was quite upset to find myself near him as we crowded out of the church. (*EW* 51)

However, one can never learn of Mildred's true feelings for Everard. It is rather ironic that she finally marries Everard whom she detested once, and never gets to reveal her feelings to Rocky whom she likes. The only time Mildred talks about Rocky and expresses her feelings for him is when she is drunk. She confesses to William Caldicote, an uninteresting man, that she would have liked to marry Rocky: "I suppose it must have been the Nuits St. Georges or the spring day or the intimate atmosphere of the restaurant, but I heard myself to my horror, murmuring something about Rocky Napier being just the kind of person I should have liked for myself" (*EW* 68). This is the only time that she tells the truth although she regrets telling it afterwards since William reacts severely: "'But my dear Mildred, you mustn't marry,' he was saying indignantly. 'Life is disturbing enough as it is without these alarming suggestions. I always think of you as being so very balanced and sensible, such an excellent woman. I do hope you're not thinking of getting married?'" (*EW* 69) William employs the techniques of the suppressing patriarchal system and repeats to her the presuppositions of the order telling her not to expect too much and be in control of herself. He also praises her as being a sensible and reasonable person. Mildred hears all this but does not approve of it: "I suppose I should have felt pleased at this little compliment but I was somehow irritated. In any case, it was not much of a compliment, making me out to be an unpleasant inhuman sort of person. Was that how I appeared to others? I wondered" (*EW* 70). She is quite aware that William has described her as a mechanical, unfeeling being – just what the society expects and encourages her to be. Though she is annoyed by this description, she does not protest. Instead, she confines her thoughts to her inner speeches. However, by decoding the meaning of what William has said, she expresses both her thoughts and the dominant culture's view of her, thus undermining the dominant values.

In varied situations she prevents herself from entertaining any romantic thoughts about Rocky. Despite the fact that she loves him, she is fully aware that she cannot have any such relationship with him since he is a married man. Sometimes she thinks of him, but she later reminds herself of the impossibility of her:

But how was it possible to compare him with Rocky? All the same, I told myself sternly, it would not do to go on thinking about Rocky like this. Yesterday, with the unexpected spring weather and the wine at luncheon there had perhaps been some excuse; today there was none. (*EW* 80)

She also censors herself in very simple matters. When she goes to a restaurant with the Napiers and Everard, Rocky and Everard argue over the type of wine to drink. She thinks: "I began to think that it would really be much easier if we just had water, though I lacked the courage to suggest it" (*EW* 96). As on other occasions, she does not express what she thinks; rather, she ridicules men fussing over the choice of a bottle of wine. Another instance of Mildred's double-voiced discourse is shown when Allegra gives the news of her engagement with Julian. Although she dislikes Allegra and would like Julian to have married her rather than Allegra, she acts as if she is very happy by saying that they were suited to each other: "'Well, it seems a very good thing for both of you and I wish you every happiness,' I mumbled, not feeling capable of explaining any further gladness I did not really feel." Moreover, when Allegra asks her whether she sees any impediments in their marriage, Mildred replies: "'You and Julian will be admirably suited to each other,' I said more seriously" (*EW* 126). Though she disagrees with their marriage, she does not express her thoughts. When Allegra tells her that Julian is doubtful about Mildred's reaction to his marrying Allegra, although Mildred is upset, she replies: "'Oh, no, of course I don't mind,' I said. 'We have always been good friends, but there's never been any question of anything else, anything more than friendship'" (*EW* 127). Mildred herself knows that her words about Julian are not honest although she does not say so. She is aware that everybody had seen her as a possible wife for Julian; however, rejecting such a public expectation, she thinks:

> How stupid I had been not to see it like that, for it had not occurred to me that anyone might think I was in love with Julian. But there it was, the old obvious situation, presenta-

ble unmarried clergyman and woman interested in good works – had everyone seen it like that? Julian himself? Winifred? Sister Blatt? Mr. Mallett and Mr. Conybeare? Of course, I thought, trying to be completely honest with myself, there had been a time when I first met him when I had wondered whether there might ever be anything between us, but I had so soon realized that it was impossible that I had never given it another thought. (*EW* 127)

Mildred's narration in this part is evidently unreliable since she is being dishonest with herself. Although she had once thought of Julian as a possible husband, she refutes the idea that anybody else could have thought the same. Later on, she goes so far as to confess to Julian himself that she had never expected to marry him: "'I was never in love with you, if that's what you mean, I said, thinking it was time to be blunt. 'I never expected that you would marry me'" (*EW* 133). She is distressed at the thought that everyone would have expected her to marry Julian, and when she sees this as an impossibility, she tries to pretend that nothing in particular has existed from the beginning.

Mildred's double-voiced discourse is also at work when she is dealing with the anthropologists. She is suspicious and doubtful of them. To her, they are inhuman and mechanical. While they study the habits and behaviours of people in primitive tribes, they cannot understand their fellow human beings. She realises that nobody notices the professor's wife, asleep at the front row, in the seminar. When she goes to Esther Clovis's house for tea, she also realises that she and Helena talk to each other, and ignore her exactly as they had ignored the old woman:

> The conversation now turned into an exchange of views about various personalities whose names meant nothing to me. I am afraid Miss Clovis brought out little tit-bits of scandal about them and she and Helena seemed to be enjoying themselves very much. I began to wonder why I had been asked to tea as they made so little attempt to entertain me. (*EW* 176)

However, she does not protest, and gets involved in her imaginings about the anthropologists' manners, where she becomes an anthropologist who studies the anthropologists' behaviour in society. On the surface, she seems to be agreeing with the anthropologists, while she is, in fact, criticising their inconsiderateness and inhumane behaviour in her thoughts:

> The old woman nodding in her chair and falling asleep over her knitting. How she must have disliked those images, nasty malevolent-looking things, some with dusty unhygienic raffia manes. Perhaps they had even come between her and the man she had married. I wondered if she had had to have them in her drawing-room, though even if they had been relegated to his study they must have been a continual worry to her, especially at spring-cleaning time. (*EW* 177)

Although she seems to be a friend to the anthropologists, she always criticizes them in her inner speeches since she finds their manners rather inhuman and tough. Therefore, nobody in her society becomes aware of her thoughts and feelings about the anthropologists, since she never voices her thoughts aloud.

When Winifred leaves the vicarage, she comes to Mildred's flat hoping to live with her. Mildred, nevertheless, is afraid of this thought and dislikes sharing a home with her despite the fact that she likes her. When Winifred tells Mildred her plan, she is so surprised that she does not know what to say:

> For a moment I was too taken aback to say anything and I knew that I must think carefully before I answered. Easy excuses, such as the difficulty of finding a whole pair of clean sheets that didn't need mending, would not do here. I had to ask myself why it was that the thought of Winifred, of whom I was really very fond, sharing my home with me filled me with sinking apprehension. Perhaps it was because I realised that if I once took her in it would probably be for ever. There

could be no casting her off if my own circumstances should happen to change, if, for example, I ever thought of getting married myself. And at the idea of getting married myself I began to laugh, for it really did seem a little fantastic. (*EW* 207)

The main reason for her reluctance to live with Winifred is the thought that once she decides to live with Winifred, she would lose her choice of getting married, being forced to settle to the life of spinsterhood. A life with another spinster is, according to her, an obstacle/impediment to marriage. Although she does not confess it, not even in her inner thoughts, she obviously expects to get married despite her pretentions that marriage is a fantastic illusion. She is being dishonest with herself in saying that she does not know the reason why she does not wish to live with Winifred; and again when she says that she does not expect to marry, she is being dishonest with herself and her addressee too. Moreover, she hides all her thoughts from Winifred not telling her why she would not like to share her home with Winifred. At last, she finds the reason:

> The truth was, I thought, looking once more at the letter on my desk which could not now be finished tonight, that I was exhausted with bearing other people's burdens, or burthens as the nobler language of our great hymn-writers put it. Then, too, I had become selfish and set in my ways and would surely be a difficult person to live with. I could hardly add that the bed in my spare-room was hard or that Dora might want to come and stay with me. I must obviously make a gesture towards helping Winifred. (*EW* 207-08)

Mildred's stated reason seemingly is a cover for her more important, but concealed, reason – expecting to get married. However, she even does not express this to Winifred and instead, looks for a gesture to pretend that she is thinking of her, as she says: "'But of course you must stay for a night or two,' I said, 'at least until we see how things are going to turn out'" (*EW* 208). However, her intention is not to help her or any other person. She does not help her voluntarily. She is simply placed in a situation that leaves her no choice, other than giving help. Her relations with the Napiers, Everard, and many other people are much the same. She just pretends to be helpful and caring since that is what is expected of an *excellent woman*. For instance, she talks with Julian, hoping to sooth/comfort him after Allegra's departure. When he says that Allegra has gone to an unmarried friend's house, Mildred forgets all about Julian, and begins sympathising with the unmarried woman who is going to host Allegra:

> I lay back and closed my eyes, for I was very tired. I wondered if Mrs. Gray's friend was tired too. I imagined her in the tidy kitchen in her dressing-gown, just putting on the milk for her Ovaltine and being startled by the front door bell ringing and wondering who on earth it could be calling so late. And now she would have to sit up half the night, listening and condoling. (*EW* 210)

It is ironic that she sympathizes with the unmarried woman rather than with Julian or Winifred. She finds the friend's situation very similar to that of herself and ponders over it. However, she acts as if she is in great pain for what has happened to Julian and Winifred, but the reader is aware that she is only sorry for herself and thinks of avoiding the burden of other people.

The novel concludes with the scene of Everard's asking Mildred to do various jobs for him extending from proofreading to indexing. Although she accepts to do so, Mildred regards him with suspicion and in her inner speeches ironically searches for his real intentions. When Everard suggests that she can do various jobs in order not to get bored, she thinks:

> Yes, it would make a nice change,' I agreed. And before long I should be certain to find myself at his sink peeling potatoes and washing up; that would be a nice change when both proofreading and indexing began to pall. Was any man worth this burden? Probably not, but one shouldered it

bravely and cheerfully and in the end it might turn out to be not so heavy after all. (*EW* 256)

Her thoughts are contrary to what she expresses in words. She seems to be agreeing with Everard and his thoughts, however, her inner thoughts depict her dislike of him and the things she is obliged to do for him before being qualified to become his wife. Nevertheless, Mildred's desire to get married prevents her from negating him, and she readily accepts the burdens she has always meant to escape.

Mildred's double-voiced discourse is in line with her idea of pretending to be an excellent woman in a male-centred system that expects her to be so. She is obliged to act and talk in two different ways in order to be admirable and desirable for the patriarchal system. On the superficial level, she pretends to be the sensible spinster who voluntarily helps people and does whatever is expected of her. However, on a deeper level, she challenges and resists this order through her inner thoughts and speeches that express her real feelings and perceptions. She resists the dominating system through this voice although she manages to survive in the patriarchal society by adopting the voice of a complying spinster.

3.2 Themes and Motifs in the Construction of Humorous Plot

Motifs and themes play a vital role in the creation of a humorous plot in *EW*. Pym creates women's humour by interweaving the subversion of the images and stereotypes of women as well as the images of male characters. Pym's humour is also a tool of social criticism mainly done through undermining the institution of church and clergymen.

3.2.1 Subversion of the Stereotype of Excellent Woman

Mildred's voice ridicules the images and stereotypes of women through covertly revolting against the long-held beliefs and presuppositions regarding the stereotype *excellent woman*. The stereotype excellent woman is the image of the unrelated spinster who selflessly serves others. Without having any personal desires or wishes, she dedicates her entire life to the service of the others. Her services are taken for granted and she does not have a private life. She is always the responsible person in the church and parish affairs, jumble sales, tea parties, etc. and she is the one who always makes "cups of tea at moments of crisis" (*EW* 166). Ackley also stresses the humiliating role of the excellent woman throughout literature: "The prevailing images of spinsters for centuries in both British and American literature had been to denigrate them. Usually they were pitied, ridiculed or despised, seldom admired and even less frequently emulated" (26). According to Ackley, Pym's spinsters are suited to this image of the spinster since she

> reveals the way the spinster is firmly regarded by society as an unfortunate person. As the women that do volunteer work are often faithful churchgoers, and fuss over men, Pym's spinsters provide valuable support services; but as the odd women unable to secure husbands, they suffer reduced status in the social structure. (27)

Thus, Pym's spinsters are also the selfless servers who do not demand much because of their particular condition. On the one hand, they are expected to do all the good works and, on the other, society does not support them, and so they live in diminished conditions. Mildred is considered to be an excellent woman due to her unmarried status and her voluntary works in the parish and the church. Ackley suggests that she "is really the archetypal excellent woman, the spinster characterized by a self-deprecation and low self-esteem coupled with a self-sufficiency in handling crisis that make her a valuable, if secondary addition to society" (30). However, this portrays Mildred's life only on the surface level although Ackley proposes that Mildred is discontented with the role of excellent woman thrust upon her:

> On the surface, Mildred's life is quiet and uneventful, which often seems to imply a limited inner life as well. Mildred does, in fact, at first seem to conform to all the stereotyped notions about spinsters – their nosiness, their dullness, their settling out of necessary for less than a full life – especially as she is herself. The role of excellent woman is not at all

> pleasing to Mildred: she is dissatisfied with bearing the burden of "doing for" everyone else. (30)

Despite that, Walker argues that women's literature "has described myriad aspects of women's lives, employing familiar stereotypes about women for the purpose of mocking those stereotypes and showing their absurdity and even their danger" (*Very* 10). Similarly, Pym, through the employment of such stereotypes, portrays the absurd and subordinating view of the patriarchal culture in relation to them. Moreover, according to Walker,

> It is for this reason that women's humor so often seems to turn on and perpetuate traditional stereotypes of women: the gossipy spinster, the nagging wife, the inept housekeeper, the lovelorn woman, the dumb blonde. These are some of the roles in which women have been cast by men and male institutions, and as such they have, until quite recently, seemed fixed. (*Very* 11)

Pym depicts the stereotype spinster, not primarily to show their ineffectiveness, but mainly to display the shortcomings of the male-oriented culture in dealing with them. Walker also observes that: "What female humorists have done with these stereotypes, however, is to subvert them" (*Very* 11). By redefining the stereotype of the excellent woman, Pym likewise resists and undermines the dominant order through ridiculing the standards that the prevailing culture imposes on women. Furthermore, women's humour, in addition to challenging the standards prescribed for women, attacks the institutions and individuals who are in some way associated with the power structures.

The first paragraph of *EW* begins with Mildred being surprised at Mr Mallett's accusing words: "'AH, you ladies! Always on the spot when there's something happening!'" (*EW* 5) From the very beginning, Mildred is depicted as the meddlesome spinster whose sole occupation is to meddle in the others' affairs. Mildred is annoyed at his words and his tone, as it reminds her of the preconceived notions about spinsters: "'Well, yes, one usually does,' I said, feeling rather annoyed at his presumption." She then sums up the society's perception of the spinster:

> I suppose an unmarried woman just over thirty, who lives alone and has no apparent ties, must expect to find herself involved or interested in other people's business, and if she is also a clergyman's daughter then one might really say that there is no hope for her. (*EW* 5)

Mildred's thoughts also reflect society's perception of her as an unrelated spinster. Since she is not married and does not have a husband or children to care for, she is expected to be involved in the affairs of the others. Mildred reverses this presumption by reporting her thoughts. She undermines the presuppositions the society associates with the stereotype of the spinster, through questioning its fundamental beliefs and values. Helena too, like everybody else, expects Mildred's helps from the time she sees her. When Mildred tells her to let her know if she could do anything for her, taking it literally, Helena replies: "'Not at the moment, thank you,' she said, 'but there may be'" (*EW* 10). Mildred also ridicules herself for acquiring the habits of spinsters: "I hoped the Napiers were not going to keep late hours and have noisy parties. Perhaps I was getting spinsterish and 'set' in my ways, but I was irritated at having been woken" (*EW* 20). Moreover, the patriarchal society projects the image of the ideal woman, through the media. For instance, when Mildred turns on the wireless, she cannot find an appropriate programme for herself since all its programs are designed for married women: "I turned on the wireless to distract me. But it was a women's programme and they all sounded so married and splendid, their lives so full and yet so well organised, that I felt more than usually spinsterish and useless" (*EW* 28). The patriarchal society encourages women to get married and bear children. Not offering anything for their particular needs, it vehemently promotes their voluntary works and welcomes their sacrifices.

Mildred begins serving the Napiers even before Rocky comes home. When she finds Rocky's telegram, she tries to find Helena, who is not at home at the moment. Mildred conventionally thinks that a wife must be at home when her husband comes back from the war. Having failed in locating Helena, she herself welcomes and serves Rocky. Taking him to her own house, she serves him tea considering it to be her responsibility. Her beliefs originate from the society's perception of her as a lonely spinster, forever at service of those who need her. Helena and Rocky are truly happy to have Mildred as their neighbour since she does countless tasks for them from bringing them all the neighbourhood news to serving endless cups of tea. Helena expresses her satisfaction with Mildred by telling her: "'Oh, it is nice having you living above us,' said Helena surprisingly. 'Just think who we might have had, some dreary couple, or "business women" or a family with children, too awful'" (*EW* 56). However, Mildred is discontent about being primarily perceived as a helpmate.

One person who represents the society's view of spinsters to Mildred is William Caldicote. In their annual meeting, when he hears of Mildred's desire to get married, he immediately responds: "'But my dear Mildred, you mustn't marry,' he was saying indignantly. 'Life is disturbing enough as it is without these alarming suggestions. I always think of you as being so very balanced and sensible, such an excellent woman. I do hope you're not thinking of getting married?'" (*EW* 69) while on the one hand, society does not approve of women remaining unmarried, on the other hand, by calling them *excellent women*, it encourages them not to marry since it needs their free and voluntary services. When Helena goes away somewhere, the first thing that Rocky remembers is that Mildred will be available to give him tea or coffee:

> I was in the kitchen making some tea when there was a knock at the door and Rocky's head peeped round. 'Helena has gone to hear a paper about pygmies,' he said, 'and I'm all alone. May I come in?'... 'Are you going to give me some coffee?' 'Well, we were having tea,' I said, feeling a little ashamed, both of the tea and of myself for feeling ashamed of it, 'but I can easily make you some coffee.' (*EW* 106)

Another time, when Helena goes to a memorial service, again Rocky goes to Mildred to be served coffee: "'I'm all alone,' he said, 'and hoping that you will offer me some coffee.' 'Yes, of course,' I said, 'do come in and talk to me'" (*EW* 134). What Rocky needs is an excellent woman to serve him endless cups of tea and coffee. He finds this capacity in Mildred. However, Mildred also needs a companion to talk to and she finds Rocky a good companion for herself. Rocky confesses to Mildred his expectations from a wife. His ideal wife is an *excellent woman* who does everything she could for the sole comfort of her husband and children. Since Helena has not lived up to his expectations, he regrets having married her: "'You really must come and see our cottage now that the weather is nice. It needs a woman's hand there and Helena isn't really interested. Perhaps I should never have married her'" (*EW* 138). This implies that he expects Mildred to come to his country-house and clean and arrange it for him. However, Mildred does not do so. On another occasion, when Helena leaves Rocky after having a fight, Mildred goes to their apartment and finds everything in a mess. She asks Rocky over to her house to lunch and then washes and tidies their apartment like an excellent woman. Rocky tells her the reason for their fight was Helena's disorganized and messy way of life, in contrast to Rocky's expectations of an ideal wife: "'She couldn't even wash a lettuce properly,' he said, 'let alone prepare a salad like this'" (*EW* 156). Although Mildred disapproves of serving others, still it is the internalized image of an excellent woman that forces her to do so. After serving tea for Rocky and Julian, she goes downstairs and washes and tidies the kitchen:

> I felt resentful and bitter towards Helena and Rocky and even towards Julian, though I had to admit that nobody had compelled me to wash these dishes or to tidy this kitchen. It was the fussy spinster in me, the Martha, who could not comfortably sit and make conversation when she knew that yesterday's unwashed dishes were still in the sink. Martha's back must have ached too, I thought grimly, noticing that the plate rack needed scrubbing and the tea-cloths boiling. (*EW* 161)

She is acutely aware of the fact that she despises playing the *excellent woman*, however, as she confesses, there is something in her that makes her serve the others without any expectation. According to Tsangaris, "While Mildred is a spinster, she is not stereotypical. Mildred's powers of observation and her ability to create a fantasy, triggered from personal memories, make her into a kind of artist" (67). One day, Helena suddenly calls her and asks to collect and take her things to Ms Clovis: "I was wondering if you could pack a suitcase for me and meet her at Victoria Station under the clock?" (*EW* 162) As is her habit to help others, however tired she might be, Mildred accepts to do this favour for Helena. At the time of Rocky's departure, he again expects Mildred's selfless service. As he has arranged, the remover's men would come when she is at home: "'I imagine you will be here, won't you? I have asked the remover's men to come on Saturday morning so that you will be able to supervise them.'" However, she does not like to be regarded as an excellent serving woman:

> I wondered if he would suggest that we had tea together before he went, but he did not say anything and somehow I did not feel inclined to offer to make any. I suppose I did not want him to remember me as the kind of person who was always making cups of tea at moments of crisis. (*EW* 166)

Even after Rocky's departure, when Helena returns home, she is upset at seeing the things Rocky has taken with him, and asks Mildred to write to him in order to bring the furniture back: "Helena darted here and there in the flat, missing objects which she claimed as hers. 'Mildred, you'll have to write to him,' she declared, sitting down in the one armchair that was left." Helena blames Mildred for letting Rocky to take the furniture: "'Oh, you were always on his side!' she burst out" (*EW* 180). Mildred takes on the blame and writes Rocky a letter, asking him to send back the furniture – to which he refuses. Helena and Rocky continue taking undue advantage of Mildred until they completely empty the flat. Their treating Mildred as a mere helpmate goes so far that Mildred does not imagine herself a role other than a mediator and a soother:

> I began to think that if I went to see Rocky I might be able to bring them together again; I saw myself playing a rather no-

> ble part, stepping into the background when they were reunited and going quietly away to make a cup of tea or do some washing or ironing. (*EW* 185)

. She has internalized the role as a go-between, and ironically thinks of herself not as a friend but a mediator through whom people can reconcile and solve their problems. Her reaction to the expectations and presuppositions of the patriarchal culture, which considers her as an unrelated spinster, is considering herself not a friend but as a helpmate. However, Mildred becomes tired of dealing with people's problems and wishes to escape. She desires to go on a good holiday with Dora:

> I began to look forward to my holiday as never before. I felt that I needed to get away from all the problems – mostly other people's – with which I had been worried in the last few months. If I could look at them from a distance they might solve themselves. Helena would forget about the furniture, Allegra Gray would turn out to be the perfect wife for Julian, Winifred would marry or enter a religious community. (*EW* 186)

Even when she is on holiday, Mildred is not at ease. She accidently meets Helena who asks her to write to Rocky again, asking him to come and take her back to their house since she is bored in her mother's house: "'Oh, you can help much better than any vicar. Promise me that you will write to Rocky soon and tell him about me'" (*EW* 200). As always, Mildred does all she can to bring Helena and Rocky together and even succeeds. However, she regards herself with self-irony while dealing with the problems of the others. When Winifred takes a refuge in her, she "wondered irrelevantly if I was to be caught with a teapot in my hand on every dramatic occasion" (*EW* 205). She adopts the viewpoint of the patriarchal society and considers herself in the role of an excellent woman who resolves the problems of all who come to her seeking help. However, since she is dissatisfied playing such a role, she looks at herself with self-irony, criticising the role imposed upon her, but having no choice other than going on with it.

Nevertheless, Mildred's self-sacrifice does not accompany her in controversial situations. For instance, when both Allegra and Winifred ask her to share her house with Winifred, she refuses by arguing that it is more than she could bear since it would mean losing her independence and privacy. On another similar occasion, she refuses Everard's invitation for dinner since he expects her to cook his meat: "'I rang up to ask if you would come and have dinner with me in my flat this evening. I have got some meat to cook'" (*EW* 218). However, after refusing, she wonders how Everard would have managed to cook the meat, wishing that she had gone and cooked it herself. Some days later, she meets Everard and he again invites her to his flat. Mildred is happy since she can now cook the meat and atone for the past: "I promised that I would cook the meat and I felt better for having done so, for it seemed like a kind of atonement, a burden in a way and yet perhaps because of being a burden, a pleasure" (*EW* 241). As she has internalized the image of the *excellent woman*, she gets pleasure in self-effacingly bearing another's burden. Everard takes advantage of her tendency to serve others by asking her to help him with his scripts, despite her telling him that she does not understand anything about them: "'Oh, but I could show you,' he said eagerly; 'you'd soon learn. He got up and fetched a bundle of proof sheets and typescript from the desk. 'It's quite simple, really. All you have to do is to see that the proof agrees with the typescript'" (*EW* 254). Despite her protest, Everard is not satisfied and expects more: "'And perhaps you could help me with the index too? Reading proofs for a long stretch gets a little boring. The index would make a nice change for you'" (*EW* 255). The manner of his asking her to help him is indirect, and he pretends as if it is Mildred herself who enjoys working for him. However, Mildred notices this and ironically thinks that she is being used. She thinks about the possibility of being Everard's wife and is again disappointed, for she knows that her burdens would increase and she must do the housework in addition to his works. At the end, she thinks about her future, which does not look bright, especially when Everard reminds her of the wife of the Learned Society's President as being an older version of her:

> seeing myself once more in that room at the Learned Society where the old lady was sitting in a basket chair in the front row with her knitting. The lecture flowed over her head as she sat there, her needles clicking and then dropping from her hand as her head fell forward on to her breast. She was asleep, but it didn't matter. Nobody thought anything of it or even noticed when her head jerked up again and she looked about her with unseeing eyes, wondering for the moment where she was. After all, she was only the President's wife, and she always went to sleep anyway. (*EW* 255)

Mildred sees her future exactly as the woman in the seminar – marginalized, insignificant and unnoticed. As suggested, she remembers the woman clearly since nobody in the seminar seemed to care about her. They did not notice that she had slept in the middle of the seminar and then woke up. She was the unheeded person among the group of anthropologists whose main concern is to study the behaviour of man as a social being. Mildred empathizes with her since she is like her. She neither belongs to the group of anthropologists nor to any other group. She is the marginalized woman excluded from the rest of society. Although aware of her dim future with Everard, she decides to marry rather than remain single since she is aware of the benefits of marriage in the patriarchal culture. If she remains unmarried, people would continue taking advantage of her. So, of the two evil possibilities, she chooses Everard to take advantage of her. She thinks ironically, that she will finally have, what people call a full life:

> And then another picture came into my mind. Julian Malory, standing by the electric fire, wearing his speckled mackintosh, holding a couple of ping-pong bats and quoting a not very appropriate bit of Keats. He might need to be protected from the women who were going to live in his house. So, what with my duty there and the work I was going to do for Everard, it seemed as if I might be going to have what Helena called 'a full life' after all. (*EW* 256)

The life she visualises is not the kind of life she wishes for herself but a life that patriarchal order has defined for her. The *full life* that society expects her to lead is to get married, to be a helpmate to her husband in his jobs, to perform all household chores, and to participate in the parish and church affairs as well. That is the picture that the patriarchal society has drawn for an *excellent woman* such as Mildred Lathbury. Mildred has to bend to the patriarchal laws. Despite everything, she continues her subtle and covert subversion of the patriarchal order.

When Mildred sees Rocky for the last time, she asks him whether he found her letter interfering. In response, Rocky says something that reveals his idea of Mildred as a serving spinster: "'Of course not. I know how you love contriving things,' he smiled. 'Births, deaths, marriages and all the rest of it.'" Mildred ironically views herself from the viewpoint of the society: "perhaps I did love it as I always seemed to get involved in them, I thought with resignation; perhaps I really enjoyed other people's lives more than my own." Mildred represents the society's view of her as a comfortable unrelated spinster who does not have any family or personal matter to attend to. Thus, she should deal with other people's affairs – birth, death, marriage, etc. Through repeating such a viewpoint, Mildred ridicules and subverts it by telling that while she herself is unaware of her feelings it is the others who are more aware of them. Rocky, however emphasises her role as an excellent serving woman by telling that he hoped "you might suggest making a cup of tea. You know how you always make a cup of tea on 'occasion'. That's one of the things I remember most about you, and surely this is an "occasion?"" Mildred is nevertheless annoyed at hearing his description of her but decides that she cannot do anything about the stereotype: "So he did remember me like that after all – a woman who was always making cups of tea. Well, there was nothing to be done about it now but to make one" (*EW* 222). Later on, Helena also expresses Mildred's image as an excellent woman humiliatingly: "'You must look after poor Everard Bone,' said Helena. 'Oh, how he needs the love of a good woman!'" Everard (*EW* 235) Helena's description of her as a serving machine is mingled with humiliation since she herself was unable to give such kind of love to. Helena's humiliation and stereotyping of Mildred also presents itself when she asks Mildred what she is going to do after they leave: "'What will you do after we've gone?'" By asking such a question, Helena implies that Mildred does not have a life of her own and her main concern is to handle other people's business. Rocky corrects her saying: "Well, she had a life before we came,' Rocky reminded her. 'Very much so – what is known as a full life, with clergymen and jumble sales and church services and good works." However, his implication is the same as Helena's. According to him, Mildred is the excellent woman fully involved in people's lives. Helena responds that "I thought that was the kind of life led by women who didn't have a full life in the accepted sense.'" Although she is shown to be modern and unconventional, she reiterates the conventional patriarchal presuppositions and beliefs towards the stereotyped, prefabricated images of women, as represented in Mildred, the unrelated spinster. They discuss Mildred's future with the conclusion that she must get married.

Another character shown taking undue advantage of Mildred is Everard Bone, Helena's self-important colleague. Although he knows Mildred only through Helena, he expects her to perform his many odd jobs, including taking messages to Helena, proof-reading, and indexing his books. As time goes by, he comes to the conclusion that Mildred can be an excellent helpmate to him and asks her to come and meet his mother. Although he is fully aware that his mother is an eccentric, hard person to make conversation with, nonetheless, he expects Mildred to tolerate her and deal with the situation. Mildred, although resentful, bears with his mother's strange behaviour: "It occurred to me that I had been bearing the full burden of the evening, and at half-past nine I began to feel both tired and resentful and decided that I would go home" (*EW* 150). Everard praises Mildred's skill in dealing with his mother: "'A sensible person, with no axe to grind,' Everard was saying, almost to himself" (*EW* 151). This remark illustrates Everard's image of an excellent woman. Mildred, however, is not pleased with Everard's categorisation of her as being an excellent woman. On a later occasion, Everard confesses to Mildred that he wants to marry a suitable person. He speaks of marriage rationally and Mildred is surprised: "'Perhaps one shouldn't try to find people deliberately like that,' I suggested. 'I mean, not set out to look for somebody to marry as if you were going to buy a saucepan or a casserole'" (*EW* 189). When Everard repeats that he might choose a sensible and suitable person, Mildred ridicules his ideas by telling: "'Somebody who would help you in your work?' I suggested. 'Somebody with a knowledge of anthropology who could correct proofs and make an index, rather like Miss Clovis, perhaps?'" (*EW* 189). Mildred makes fun of him by deriding his description of the excellent woman. However, Mildred knows that *excellent women* – like herself – are not for marrying, but for taking care of other people's affairs and problem. Everard affirms these feelings by expressing his thoughts on an excellent woman, Esther Clovis: "'Of course I do respect and esteem Esther Clovis,' Everard went on" Mildred believes that respect and esteem are not natural feelings towards woman and retorts: 'Oh, respect and esteem – such dry bones!" (*EW* 190)

A woman's worth, socially speaking, is measured by her being married or single. As Mildred says: "after all, what had we done? We had not made particularly brilliant careers for ourselves, and, most important of all, we had neither of us married. That was really it. It was the ring on the left hand that people at the Old Girls' Reunion looked for" (*EW* 112). In Mildred's case, everybody had regarded Mildred as a suitable wife for Julian Malory. Mildred recognises her role as a suitable *excellent woman* for a vicar, when Julian and Allegra are engaged, and Allegra asks her whether she is annoyed. After Allegra's words, Mildred realises that everybody in the parish had considered her a suitable wife for Julian Malory:

> How stupid I had been not to see it like that, for it had not occurred to me that anyone might think I was in love with Julian. But there it was, the old obvious situation, presentable unmarried clergyman and woman interested in good works – had everyone seen it like that? Julian himself? Winifred? Sister Blatt? Mr. Mallett and Mr. Conybeare? (*EW* 127)

Winifred Malory, Julian's sister – who has sacrificed herself to take care of her brother, his parish and the church – is another female character in *EW* who has internalised the characteristics of the spinster. She is careless about her appearance and wears people's old clothes. She cannot even visualise herself, leading an isolated life away from her brother and the church:

> She was dressed, as usual, in an odd assortment of clothes, most of which had belonged to other people. It was well known that Winifred got most of her wardrobe from the garments sent to the parish jumble sales, for such money as she had was never spent on herself but on Good – one could almost say Lost – Causes, in which she was an unselfish and tireless worker. The time left over from these good works was given to 'making a home' for her brother, whom she adored, though she was completely undomesticated and went about it with more enthusiasm than skill. (*EW* 13)

Winifred's self-sacrificing nature is apparent in the way she selflessly helps Allegra Gray, their tenant who comes to live in the extra rooms of the vicarage. Allegra expects Mildred and Winifred's voluntary services. She even asks Mildred to come to help Winifred with the curtain, while she herself does not do anything in particular. Allegra also takes advantage of Mildred in another way. She asks Mildred to let Winifred to live with her after their marriage by saying that nothing could be better than two spinsters living together. Being shocked, Mildred turns down her request. Her rejecting to live the rest of her life with Winifred is a sign of her discontentment with her status as a spinster, and her will to change her condition. Dora Caldicote, Mildred's friend, is another such spinster who is quite well-set in her *spinster manners*. She is surprised at seeing Mildred's change of appearance and clothing, and expresses her disapproval by saying:

> Why, Mildred,' she exclaimed, 'what have you done to yourself? You look different," No compliments, of course; Dora was too old and honest a friend ever to flatter me, but she had the power of making me feel rather foolish, especially as I had not realised that she might find any difference in my appearance since the last time we met. I suppose I had taken

to using a little more make-up, my hair was more carefully arranged, my clothes a little less drab. (*EW* 100)

Dora has so internalised the society's imposed values that when she sees a change in Mildred's *spinster appearance*, instead of complimenting her, she tries to find faults: "'There's not much you can do when you're over thirty,' she went on complacently. 'You get too set in your ways, really. Besides, marriage isn't everything'" (*EW* 100). Dora thinks that Mildred has altered her appearance simply to get married. Dora's style of dressing is also spinsterish. She chooses to buy clothes with dull and unattractive colours. Despite Mildred's struggle, Dora refuses to wear a green dress for the occasion: "'Good Heavens, whatever would people at school say if I appeared in a dress that colour?' Dora exclaimed. 'I shouldn't know myself. No, I'll just ask for the brown in a larger size. It's just what I want'" (*EW* 102). Any change to Dora is unacceptable. In contrast to Mildred's suggestions to buy well-fitting and colourful dresses, she buys a larger size dress, simply to avoid looking elegant. On the contrary, she accuses Mildred of having changed so much: "They had the dress in a larger size which was now a little too large, but Dora seemed perfectly satisfied and bought it. 'I don't know what's the matter with you, Mildred,' she complained. 'You never used to bother much about clothes'" (*EW* 102). Mildred is not looking forward to living with Dora, and is disappointed and annoyed at even thinking of the future: "By the time we had got off the bus we were arguing quite openly. It was foolish and pointless but somehow we could not stop. I saw us in twenty or thirty years' time, perhaps living together, bickering about silly trifles. It was a depressing picture" (*EW* 105). The prospect of living with another spinster seems a kind of double labour for Mildred; she would rather remain a single spinster.

Stereotyping Mildred as an unrelated spinster is considered as a common practice in *EW*'s society. She is typecast as an *excellent woman* who, owing to her being single, is always voluntarily at the service of the others in order to solve their problems. She is shown interested in their affairs, rather than her own. However, Mildred's words and actions do not agree with this image of her as a selfless, serving spinster. Rather, she considers herself as an independent woman who values her privacy. Although curious about other's affairs, she does not meddle in their business, until they themselves seek her help. She is tired of endlessly serving the others, solving their problems and bearing their burdens. She does not approve of her role as the soothing excellent woman who is simply a refuge for those whose wives or fiancés have left them. Covertly, she subverts the stereotype of herself as an excellent woman. She ridicules and revises the presuppositions and values existent in the patriarchal culture by criticizing them in her inner thoughts and sharing them with the readers.

3.2.2 Subversion of Male Images

The image of the powerful Byronic hero is greatly undermined in *EW* by presenting the male characters as self-indulgent, idle and helpless figures who, though charming, are extremely superficial and shallow male characters. As Tsagaris observes: "Like some romantic writers, Pym sometimes shows her heroes needing a woman's help. In a way, showing male helplessness or ineptness in some situations is another way to deflate the Byronic hero." There is usually an *excellent woman* to take care of the male characters since they cannot do without such a woman: "In Pym's world, an excellent woman is the perfect candidate to nurse the hero, physically or emotionally. Unlike the romance heroine, though, the excellent woman does not necessarily win her wounded hero at the end" (69).

The three male characters in *EW* are all shown as in dire need of women who can support, help, and even pamper them – none of them can manage all alone. The first male character we are introduced to, is Julian Malory, the vicar of St. Mary's. Mildred is his, and also his sister Winifred's, best friend. Julian is a dependent man who needs the services of excellent women like Mildred and Winifred. For the sake of "her brother alone, whom she adored," Winifred has sacrificed herself for "'making a home' for her" (*EW* 13). Although a clergyman, he is unable do a single job without the help of these women. He even cannot paint the walls of the rooms in the vicarage: "wish I'd got the boys' club to do it,' said Julian. 'I'm afraid I'm no good at practical things. I always think it must be such a satisfying feeling, to do good work with one's hands. I'm sure I've preached about it often enough'" (*EW* 41). The contradiction between his teachings and preaching and his deeds, is a sign of his hypocrisy and indolence. Mildred recognizes this indolence in men and when Winifred tells Mildred of Julian's passivity in the face of Allegra's plots, she responds: "'This may sound a cynical thing to say, but don't you think men sometimes leave difficulties to be solved by other people or to solve themselves?'" (*EW* 206) Mildred's suggestion is in sharp contrast to the image of the independent and decisive romantic hero who conventionally sacrifices himself to resolve all challenges and obstacles.

The men Pym draws in *EW* passively let the problems solve themselves or rather to be solved by the others. Julian is so indolent and indecisive that he is unable to deal with his fiancé and his sister, both at the same time. When Allegra leaves him, he is so disappointed and helpless that does not know what to do. He hurries to Mildred's house where Winifred too has escaped from Allegra. Julian does not know what to say. Mildred recognizes that he is feeling lost; and Julian himself knows that they cannot do without Mildred: "'Thank you, Mildred,' he said, with a faint smile. 'You are very kind. I don't know what we'd do without you'" (*EW* 211). Some days later, Julian is so helpless that he even does not remember the affairs of church and says: "'What is it, Mildred?' he asked. 'The bazaar meeting? Good heavens, I'd forgotten all about it!'" (*EW* 229). His irresponsible behaviour shocks everybody since, being the vicar, he must manage everything. His indolence manifests itself when he cannot concentrate on the subject and, giving the entire responsibly to others, goes to a darts match with the boys: "'If you'll excuse me, I think I will go back.' He got up from the table and went off, leaving his tea unfinished" (*EW* 230). Although Julian is a clergyman, he is negligent, not caring about his duties, he expects the *excellent women* of the parish to handle his affairs.

In addition to Julian, Pym points at the indolent ways of the other churchwardens in handling any problems or burden. When asked by the women to help with the heavy teapot, they ignore their request: "Mr. Mallett and Mr. Conybeare, the churchwardens, and Mr. Gamble, the treasurer, looked up from their business, which they were conducting in a secret masculine way with many papers spread out before them, but made no move to help." The men are not the gallant heroes of the romance novels, but the indolent and unresponsive men with no desire to help the so-called *fair sex*. Moreover, they confess to the reversal of the roles: "'I see it is done now by the so-called weaker sex,' said Mr. Mallett. 'I think Miss Statham has got everything under control'" (*EW* 227). They are neither honest nor helpful, and Pym ridicules their lazy self-indulgent ways: "'Oh, yes, we leave it to you ladies to fight all that out,' said Mr. Mallett, recoiling in mock fear. 'We men will just do all the hard work, eh?'" (*EW* 232). Mildred too, in her inner thoughts, derides at their behaviour and words: "The men went on smoking and chatting while we gathered the cups together and struggled to fill the heavy urn between us. They belonged to the generation that does not think of helping with domestic tasks" (*EW* 233).

Rocky Napier is a self-important, self-dramatizing and indolent male character. Pym creates a male character who resembles the Byronic hero in appearance, but in reality lacks his characteristics completely. Though the women think of him as being charming and gallant, however, he turns out to be an extremely shallow person, forever seeking the support of a woman to attend to his odd jobs. He is dissatisfied with Helena since she is an undomesticated woman, shown fighting over trivial things such as washing, cooking, and cleaning which eventually results in her leaving him alone. He is incapable of performing his tasks single-handedly, and asks Mildred for help. Even when Helena goes to the Learned Society, he goes to Mildred to ask for tea or coffee. He also asks Mildred to help him move to the country-house and dramatizes his condition. For instance, when Helena leaves him, Mildred finds him helpless with the burnt saucepan on the stove: "'Oh, the saucepan,' Rocky said, passing his hand over his brow with a gesture of weariness that seemed to me rather theatrical. 'There have been other things to think about besides saucepans'" (*EW* 153). His self-dramatization is due to the fact that he himself has caused Helena's leaving over her messiness and inconsiderateness for the domestic trivialities. In this case, Tsagaris observes that "Pym's men are also somewhat peevish and inept. For example, Rocky Napier, that gallant paragon of Byronism, is upset with his wife for placing a hot saucepan on a good table" (69). On another occasion, he decides to move to his country-house. However, he does not do so silently: "Rocky behaved rather dramatically the next day, packing suitcases and going round his flat marking various articles of furniture and small objects which were to be sent after him to his cottage in the country" (*EW* 166). By playing the role of the charming but victimised male, he self-dramatizes through laying the entire blame on Helena, and subverting the image of the independent and courageous Byronic hero.

Everard Bond is another example of Pym's typical male character in *EW*. He is a self-indulgent bachelor who is seemingly independent and decisive, but actually in need of a woman to do his jobs. He too gradually takes advantage of Mildred's kind-heartedness by asking her to do things for him until finally asking her to be his wife. Helena is in love with him. Unlike the conventional heroes, who rescue the heroine from the chains of the victimizing husband, he rejects Helena when she comes to him, and sends her back home. Moreover, Everard asks Mildred to tell Helena that he does not love her and asks her to leave him alone; in fact, he escapes to a very distant city with a group of archaeologists to avoid seeing Helena when she leaves Rocky. His sense of self-importance does not let him admit his attraction towards Mildred, and every time he wants to see her, rather than calling her and making an appointment, he surprises her in front of her office. Moreover, not only he does not welcome her with a bright face, but he blames her for being late: "'Mildred – at last!' He turned round and faced me, but his voice betrayed the irritation of one who has been waiting for a long time rather than any pleasure at the sight of me. 'I thought you were never coming out. Don't people usually work till five?'" (*EW* 139) When Everard tells her about Helena, he seems quite confident of her love for him and when he asks her to help him deal with Helena's problem, she mocks him by replying: "'But men ought to be able to manage their own affairs,' I said. 'After all most of them don't seem to mind speaking frankly and making people unhappy. I don't see why you should'" (*EW* 145). Mildred undermines Everard's status by mentioning *realities* about himself and men in general. Mildred, on another occasion also subverts men's self-dramatization: "Men are not nearly so helpless and pathetic as we sometimes like to imagine them, and on the whole they run their lives better than we do ours" (*EW* 220). Everard wants to marry Mildred not because he is in love with her, but mainly for the sake of the things she can do for him. In addition to housework, Mildred can do his proofreading and indexing. When Mildred goes to his house, instead of conventionally proposing, he simply asks her to do his indexing and proofreading. Thus, he reverses the image of the romantic hero who sacrifices himself to reach his beloved. In fact, by proposing to Mildred that she can do his jobs, he intends to propose marriage to her. Mildred understands this and accepts it, although she is worried about its consequences. Therefore, unlike the romance heroes who are independent, decisive and self-sacrificing characters, being dependent on women and their services, all men in *EW* are lacking in self-assurance. However, Pym undermines the image of the romantic hero by creating male characters totally unlike the conventional romantic heroes. They are not the strong, self-sacrificing, honest and gallant lovers but shown to be helpless, dependent, hypocritical, self-indulgent men who are in need of the *excellent woman* to do their works. In her inner speeches, Mildred undermines not only the image of these individuals but also the system that has created them.

Through the use of her humour, on the one hand, Mildred resists the dominating patriarchal order and, on the other hand, she succeeds to survive within the patriarchal order. Mildred's humour at having been considered as an excellent woman takes many shapes. Through the employment of the rhetorical strategies such as understatement and self-deprecation, Mildred averts the dangers of the dominating patriarchal order, and armours herself through ridiculing the presuppositions. Alternately, her use of the thematic strategies such as double voiced discourse contribute to her survival in a society wherein being an *excellent woman* is considered as a self-contained value. Moreover, she applies it as a strategic technique to resist the ills of the patriarchal culture. Mildred revises the stereotype of the excellent woman and spinsters through ridiculing the values and presuppositions of the dominating order. Accordingly, through subverting the images associated primarily with the spinsters, Mildred undermines the patriarchal cultural values. Thus, Pym successfully creates male characters quite the reverse of the self-sufficient, gallant heroes one encounters in the romance novels. Her male characters are not the heroes of those novels, but indolent, egoistic men completely dependent on excellent women, like Mildred to help them live their lives.

4 *Jane and Prudence*: Unconventional Wife and Satisfied Spinster

> 'Let's go somewhere at the back, where we can have a good laugh,' said Edith.' (*STG* 174)

Pym's *JP* challenges conventionalised images of the housewife and spinster through two unconventional women, Jane and Prudence. Besides exposing false manners, behaviours and beliefs, Pym also subverts them. Courtship and marriage are among the chief values highlighted in *JP*. As Long observes, "Pym's concern with courtship in *Jane and Prudence* is ironic in the way it had been in *Some Tame Gazelle* and *Excellent Women*, in which the Victorian courtship novel is both evoked and parodied" (90). The conventional plot of courtship and marriage is undermined in this novel in that what "one finds, beneath its comic surfaces, is chiefly estrangement, the sense of the impossibility of the sexes to come to understanding or to enter confidently into a relationship of love and trust" (Long 90).

Jane's unconventional character has been discussed by many critics. Anatolle Boyard calls Jane

> 'The Woman Who Overflows Her Situation', filling this narrative with her presence: This woman, this archetype, this unsung heroine of the ordinary life, is always reaching for a further reference, always trying, in E. M. Forster's sense, to connect the low and the high, the near and the far, the everyday and the eternal. (Qtd. in Weld 97)

Prudence, however, according to Cooley, is capable of keeping her connection with the realities of the actual life or present context: "Prudence is not so much victim of literary phrases; rather, she has fallen under the sway of romantic narrative. Like Don Quixote and Emma Bovary, she is a great reader of love stories" (*Comic* 103). Pym's narrative essentially ridicules Jane's tendency to fantasise the reality and base it upon literary texts, as well as Prudence's tendency to romanticise the reality:

> In *Jane and Prudence* the two protagonists spend their lives in pursuit of the imaginary as it is defined by the books they have read. They represent not Don Quixote and Sancho Pan-

za, but two different sides of Don Quixote. Jane Cleveland can be thought of as representing the purely "literary" side of Don Quixote, Prudence as representing the "literary-amorous" side. (*Comic* 101)

Jane and Prudence, as a pair of friends, are seen attending a Reunion of Old Students at the beginning of the novel. Jane has been Prudence's tutor in Oxford and is now worried about her having remained unmarried in her twenty-ninth year. At the opening of the novel, Jane moves to a new parish in a village near London, with her clergyman husband Nicholas Cleveland. She has a fantastic bent of mind and some unrealistic thoughts. People in general consider her strange and unusual. She does not do any kind of housework and spends her time reading novels of the clergymen's households. Jane's fantasies and imaginings make her bring together Prudence and Fabian, a shallow widow in their parish.

Prudence lives in London and works in an office. She sees herself as a romantic heroine, as her main source of inspiration is reading romantic novels. Although she has a crush on her boss, she goes out with Fabian. A cruel husband to his deceased wife, Fabian is engaged to another woman, Jessie Morrow, in the end. In order to live out her romance, Prudence finds another young man to go out with, while Jane continues her task of looking for a suitable husband for Prudence.

4.1 Jane's Subversion of the Image of Conventional Clergyman's Wife

4.1.1 Jane's Creation of a Fantastic World

Jane Cleveland has a marked tendency towards imagining herself as the successful wife of a clergyman who does different tasks in the house and the parish and is a literary scholar. Her values and beliefs are derived from the literary texts she is reading. Her main weakness is not being able to distinguish between the literary world and the real one. Her mind creates unrealistic illusions of an imaginary world and a romantic marriage:

> When she and Nicholas were engaged, Jane had taken great pleasure in imagining herself as a clergyman's wife, starting

4 Jane and Prudence: *Unconventional Wife and Satisfied Spinster* 183

> with Trollope and working through the Victorian novelists to the present-day gallant, cheerful wives, who ran large houses and families on far too little money and sometimes wrote articles about it in the Church Times. (*JP* 6)

It seems that she does not like her real self, an inadequate clergyman's wife, because it falls short of the image that society imposes on her. However, she is disappointed as she comes face to face with the reality that she does not resemble any of the fictional characters she has been reading about. Moreover, in her particular community and condition, her literary and imaginative qualities are not encouraged. She is considered as strange for confusing literature and real life. Instead, society expects her to have what it considers an efficient housewife's qualities which she totally lacks:

> Jane's outspokenness and her fantastic turn of mind were not appreciated; other qualities which she did not possess and which seemed impossible to acquire were apparently necessary. And then, as the years passed and she realised that Flora was to be her only child, she was again conscious of failure, for her picture of herself as a clergyman's wife had included a large Victorian family like those in the novels of Miss Charlotte M. Yonge. (*JP* 7)

The values she upholds are not her own but dictated to her by the dominant culture. That is the main reason for her failure in her housework, in her literary studies, and in her role as a clergyman's wife. As Cooley states:

> her enthusiasm for the role of perfect clergyman's wife arose from the literary conception of the part, not the part itself. She is too bookish, too straightforward, too fantastical, too absent-minded, too impractical, and too lazy to be a successful clergyman's wife. She cannot manage either the domestic practicalities or the conversational diplomacies that are called for. She scarcely knows the location of the kitchen in her own house. (*Comic* 102)

Tsagaris asserts that "Outspokenness at the wrong times and rebellious thoughts are not Jane's only faults as a wife or 'excellent woman'" (77). Despite her desire to be a good wife and helpmate to Nicolas, Jane in fact lacks the qualities of a competent, organised housekeeper.

Jane's fantasies result in absurd and funny passages, because she

> has constructed an ongoing artificial world out of literary language and its web of associations. That world does not exactly contradict the real one, but goes in and out of parallel to it. Jane is a lover of phrases and is willing to sacrifice the event to the phrase, if the two don't quite fit. (*Comic* 103)

For instance, when she hears that the name of Prudence's beloved is Arthur, her mind takes her as far as possible to the literal and historical realms, to the Arthurs in literature: "She began to think of Arthurs famous in history and romance – the Knights of the Round Table of course sprang to mind immediately, but somehow it wasn't a favourite name in these days; there was a faded Victorian air about it" (*JP* 14). Her tendency to relate the simple things to books and literature surprises and amazes people. Her mind upsets her when she compares her life with what she reads in the books. In their first arrival to the village, she expects groups of people to welcome them; nonetheless, she is upset when she finds that nobody does so. Her husband Nicholas is a realistic man, wholly conscious of Jane's romantic and fantastic tendencies: "'That only happens in the works of your favourite novelist, said her husband indulgently, for his wife was a great novel reader, perhaps too much so for a vicar's wife'" (*JP* 15). Even according to mild Nicholas's view, who is supportive of Jane, her infatuation with literature prevents her from caring about real life. As Cooley observes, "Jane reads life by the light of the book, trying to force literary conceptions on an often recalcitrant reality" ("Barbara" 371). Pym's subversive language ridicules Jane's struggle to force abstract literary examples on reality. Jane's fantastic mind often offends Nicholas. Her imaginations make him impatient and he has to struggle to take her back to the real world.

4 Jane and Prudence: *Unconventional Wife and Satisfied Spinster* 185

Jane's deliberate inattention to housework is because she

> *never* learned to distinguish between the romance of her academic reading, acquired at Oxford, and the ordinariness of real life. Jane's daughter, Flora, is at times embarrassed by the 'vagueness' of her mother's mind, by the clothes she wears, and by the oddness of her comments. (Long 77)

Even when Jane finally goes to the kitchen to help prepare the food, her mind is haunted with the stories that Mrs. Glaze tells about the parishioners: "Mr. Mortlake and His Friends ... A Lion above the Bird ... but these are the titles of new novels still in their bright paper jackets, thought Jane with delight. And they are here in this parish, all this richness" (*JP* 21).

Jane's tendency to be engrossed mentally with fantasy rather than with domestic tasks makes her incapable of accomplishing the simplest household tasks. Habitually, she neglects domestic and ordinary affairs and her clothing. Other parishioners such as Miss Doggett and Fabian consider her way of dressing as dowdy and inconsiderate, which is how Jane subverts the image of the well-dressed, elegant clergyman wife. For instance, she writes to Prudence: "I still don't seem to have unpacked all my clothes and have just been burrowing in a trunk to find Nicholas a clean surplice! If only they could have made them of paper and just throw them away when they're dirty – or even of nylon – I dare say American clergymen do" (*JP* 50).

At one point, Jane confesses to her unsuitability: "'I've been such a failure as a clergyman's wife,' Jane lamented, 'but at least I don't drink; that's the only suitable thing about me'" (*JP* 91). Her confession is not to humiliate herself, but to defend and strengthen herself in the face of cultural beliefs and values associated with clergymen's wives.

Jane does not care much about the right conduct and manners as she gets bored of ordinary conversations. When Father Lomax visits the couple, she does not try to hide her tiredness (*JP* 24). Similarly, unlike conventional clergyman wives, Jane is not interested in decorating the church for Thanksgiving. She simply escapes when there is any such work to be done: (*JP* 30). Jane is aware of her inefficiency as a clergyman's wife: "'I'm afraid it's a fault in me and a great disadvantage for a clergyman's wife, not to be naturally gregarious" (*JP* 31). By her understatement and her confession of her inadequacy she does not in fact humiliate herself. Rather, she takes strength from the thought that intentionally resists her duties as a wife, thereby subverting the patriarchal order.

Jane's fantastic mind shows, for instance, when Mr Oliver, a bank clerk, comes to visit the couple. Jane's mind turns his dull job into something interesting: "'I always think of the medieval banking houses in Florence; great times those must have been'" (*JP* 71). Jane's habit of losing reality over ideal and romantic notions results in her appearing ridiculous and strange to people. This is the reason why she fails to create a satisfactory relationship with her family and the village people, since her standards are those of imaginary and literary ideals and all these people do not live up to her expectations. The narrative voice undermines and ridicules her inclination towards the fantastic and fictional realms. Her unrealistic attitude also prevents her from being a satisfactory wife and mother – as she herself is aware. For instance, when Nicholas asks her to take part in the Mother's Union Tea, she replies: "'I don't really feel so very much of a mother, having only one child, and you know how bad I am at presiding at meetings'" (*JP* 74). Having had only one child, she does not understand motherhood and takes advantage of every situation to remind people that she does not feel like a mother. In the train on their way to London, when Miss Doggett regrets to have missed the Mother's Union Tea, Jane replies: "'[...] I feel so unlike a mother when I am at these functions. I am so very undomesticated. They are all so splendid and efficient and have really quite wonderful ideas'" (*JP* 76). Her behaviour and attitude towards Flora do not resemble that of a real mother. It rather seems that in their relationship Flora is the mother and Jane the daughter. Flora does all the housework and her mother's strange behaviour embarrasses her before other people. She is always critical of Jane's dowdy way of clothing, her domestic incapability, and her fantastical notions.

Jane is not conscious of her daughter's views about her and considers herself quiet normal. Her only hope for Flora is to send her to Oxford and marry her to a nice and suitable man. Even while washing the dishes after a party, Jane's imagination draws her to her daughter and her boyfriend Paul,

4 Jane and Prudence: *Unconventional Wife and Satisfied Spinster*   187

as she fancies a bright future for Flora: "'Yes, she isn't like me. Somehow Paul isn't quite what I'd hoped for her. I know it's silly – but I'd hoped that Lord Edgar might fall in love with her – when they were at tutorials, you know.'" Her imaginations are so strong that she ignores the fact that the professor is not interested in women. Even when Prudence reminds her of it, Jane does not get disappointed, saying: "'I know, that's the point. I'd imagined Flora breaking through all that'" (*JP* 183). What is important for her are not the facts of the real world with all its restrictions, but the boundless imaginary world she has created. She does not allow anybody to destroy this imaginary world. Her unrealistic fantasies about people come up even when washing the dishes: "'Oh, Prudence,' she said, turning to her friend with a little dripping mop in her hand, 'you and Fabian must make a fine thing of your married life, and I know you will. You'll be a splendid hostess and such a help to him in everything'" (*JP* 183). However, the truth is that Fabian has not proposed to Prudence yet and when she says so, Jane unrealistically suggests:

> 'Why don't you ask him?' said Jane recklessly. 'Women are not in the same position as they were in Victorian times. They can do nearly everything that men can now. And they are getting so much bigger and taller and men are getting smaller, haven't you noticed?' (*JP* 184)

She is so much engrossed in her imaginary world that she forgets the actual circumstances of their life in a patriarchal society with its strict laws. As Prudence later on recognises, proposing to a man is totally unacceptable in such a society, and Jane's theorisations are mere imaginations.

Before meeting Dr Grampian, on whom Prudence has a crush, she imagines him as a Byronic figure merely because of his name. However, she is disappointed after meeting him: "I'd imagined a big, tall, dark man, a sort of Mr. Rochester" (*JP* 88). She bases her actions on romance without paying attention to or understanding people's real needs. This ends in her great mistake of bringing Fabian and Prudence together. Her decision to make a match between the two is merely led by the romance convention that the hero and the heroine must be handsome and shows no insight into their characters.

Jane's fantasy of being a scholar as well as a proper clergyman's wife makes her participate in literary societies from time to time to remind her of the notes she has collected in order to write a book on poetry. Her fantasy is not hindered by the reality that she is incapable of doing either:

> After supper Jane began rummaging in the drawer of her desk where her Oxford notebooks were kept, in which she had recorded many of her thoughts about the poet Cleveland. Creative work, that was the thing, if you could do that nothing else mattered. She sharpened pencils and filled her fountain-pen, then opened the books, looking forward with pleasurable anticipation to reading her notes. But when she began to read she saw that the ink had faded to a dull brownish colour. How long was it since she had added anything to them? she wondered despondently. It would be better if she started quite fresh and began reading the poems all over again. Then she remembered that her copy of the Poems on Several Occasions was upstairs and it seemed too much of an effort to go up and get it. How much could she remember without the book? A line came into her head. *Not one of all those ravenous hours, but thee devours* ... If only she were one of these busy, useful women, who were always knitting or sewing. Then perhaps it wouldn't matter about the ravenous hours. She sat for a long time among the faded ink of her notebooks, brooding, until Nicholas came in with their Ovaltine on a tray and it was time to go to bed. (*JP* 148)

Jane is frustrated by the attempt to produce valuable work as she is frustrated by housework. Despite her awareness of her shortcomings she continues her struggles. Her failure mainly derives from the fact that she herself does not have or is not aware of her own individual values and needs; rather, she sticks to the values imposed on her by patriarchal society, struggling to be an efficient wife and a capable scholar.

4 Jane and Prudence: *Unconventional Wife and Satisfied Spinster* 189

There is a great deal of gossip in the village about Jane's domestic failures. Men miss the days of their former vicar, and their extravagant style of life. They mock Cleveland's simple and humble life representing the dominant social view: "'Ah, it was very different in Canon Pritchard's time,' said Mr. Whiting on a note of lamentation which seemed excessive for the triviality of the subject. 'Even during the war years they had the big meal in the evening. It seems more in keeping'" (*JP* 150). Ironically, the parishioners praise extravagance, although the extravagant style life during the war years is inhuman and opposed to the Christian teachings. Moreover, they judge Jane unfairly by the values associated with an efficient housewife. Since Jane does not fill that position well enough, she is looked down upon and ignored: "'The dignity of the office,' said Mr. Mortlake. 'But then Mrs. Pritchard filled her position well. And she was a wonderful cook. I know that. They say Mrs. Cleveland hardly knows how to open a tin. It isn't fair on the vicar'" (*JP* 150).

In their meeting, Nicholas and other church council members behave as if Jane is an outsider who must not be trusted. They are annoyed when she tells her opinion, ignoring her afterwards. Similarly, Nicholas is ashamed of his wife's comments in the council meeting:

> Nicholas, who had thought it wiser to keep this matter of the magazine cover from his wife, smiled unhappily. She would never learn when not to speak, he thought, with rather less affectionate tolerance than usual. Not for the first time he began to consider that there was, after all, something to be said for the celibacy of the clergy. (*JP* 153)

Nicholas's intolerance in dealing with his wife's intellect is not primarily because of her being wise and exact, but because she does not shy away from disagreeing with others and fails to affirm their views as the other female members of the council do. They seem to be more conscious of their style of clothing than the discussions of the council:

> It seemed that there was a particular kind of hat worn by ladies attending Parochial Church Council meetings – a large

> beret of neutral-coloured felt pulled well down to one side. Both Mrs. Crampton and Mrs. Mayhew wore hats of this type, as did Miss Doggett, though hers was of a superior material, a kind of plush decorated with a large jewelled pin. Indeed, there seemed to be little for the ladies to do but observe each other's hats, for their voices were seldom heard. (*JP* 151)

Jane's attempts to change this superficiality are not welcome. She ridicules and undermines the out-dated views of the parish members and this finally results in her exclusion: "'Well, really,' Jane burst out, 'I never heard anything so ridiculous. Even if the covers looked alike, there could certainly be no confusion over the contents'" (*JP* 153). On a similar occasion, Jane one night accidently runs into a meeting of the male members of the parish and notices a disagreement among the members. She proposes to help them solve their problem, but as they do not consider their problem to pertain to the female sphere, they politely send her away (*JP* 129). Jane's fantastic mind, however, imagines them as characters in a drama:

> Really, thought Jane, it was like one of those rather tedious comic scenes in Shakespeare – Dogberry and Verges, perhaps – and therefore beyond her comprehension. She suddenly saw them all in Elizabethan costume and began to smile. 'Oh, well, I suppose I shouldn't interfere,' she said. 'We women can't always do as much as we think we can.' She had imagined herself mediating and bringing them together so that they all went off and settled their differences over a glass of beer. She turned to go, half hoping that they would call her back, but they watched her in silence, until Mr Oliver bade her good night and the others followed his example. (*JP* 130)

That women are not as capable as they think they are must not be considered as her honest opinion, since she knows she is more intelligent than most of the men. Rather, she reflects the opinion of patriarchal culture.

4 Jane and Prudence: Unconventional Wife and Satisfied Spinster

Ridiculing such a belief, she in fact subverts it by repeating it to the proponents of this view.

People who know Jane usually consider her an unusual woman and are ready to lay blame on her. When the former vicar and his wife come for a visit and Canon Prichard cannot find any soap other than animal soaps, he wrongly thinks that Jane has put it there: "'I think Cleveland is quite sound,' went on the Canon. 'None of this Modern Churchman's Union or any of that dangerous stuff ...' He hesitated, perhaps meditating on the soap animals and what they could signify'" (*JP* 170-71). However, the reader knows that it is in fact Nicholas who is fond of such things as animal soaps, while Jane considers Nicholas's behaviour childish.

As Nicholas admits, when he saw the Canon's motorcar in front of their house, he hid himself in the shed in order to avoid meeting them: "'I saw their car outside just as I was coming through the gate,' Nicholas admitted, 'so I slipped into the tool-shed till they'd gone. In any case, I had to see to my tobacco plants,' he added, looking a little ashamed" (*JP* 172). Thus, it is Nicholas who behaves like a child; however, people blame Jane's inefficiency as a housewife for his shortcomings.

Jane has internalised the image of the efficient housewife, which results in her feeling of guilt. But this also reverses values associated with her status. When she is in London, she tries to make amends for not being a capable wife: "She would go without tea, as a kind of penance for all the times she had failed as a vicar's wife" (*JP* 248-49). She undermines the values of good food and drink punishing herself, although that is exactly what society expects her to do.

Among the people who represent the view of established society of women is Fabian Driver. When they are out for dinner, Prudence tells him of her opinion about Jane's spoiling talent in the village: "'Yes; dear Jane. She is rather wonderful, and yet in a way she's missed something. Life hasn't turned out quite as she meant it to'" (*JP* 115). Naturally, Fabian does not understand her as he thinks that a woman does not need more than a family to serve in order to be happy: "'I mean, she leads a useful kind of life-work in the parish and that kind of thing,' he went on vaguely." According to patriarchal culture, this is the kind of work suitable for all women. His extreme reaction comes when Prudence tells him: "'But she's really no good at parish work – she's wasted in that kind of life. She has great gifts, you know. She could have written books.'" However, Fabian is opposed to women's writing books since he thinks that it destroys women's femininity and delicacy: "'I always think women who write books sound rather formidable'" (*JP* 115). Fabian, much like the dominating system, is in favour of women's being uneducated and feminine rather than wise and undesirable, since he is certain that when women get to know about the world, they would know more about men too, and their image of them would collapse.

Jane tends to mix common, everyday affairs with the ideals of romantic novels. She always is found comparing herself and her life with those of the vicar's wives as depicted in romantic novels. However, she falls short of them, because the values that she attempts to emulate are not her own. Likewise, she cannot fulfil her other fantasy – that of being a literary scholar. She attends literary circles and reads novels extensively, but is unable to produce anything herself. Her dreams do not turn into reality. Pym subverts patriarchal values and beliefs by embodying an unconventional clergyman's wife who does not care for housework and fashion.

4.1.2 Jane's Reversal of the Role of Serving Female

Jane is distinctly averse to playing the servile female role expected of her and she demonstrates this in words as well as deeds. She employs various strategies to portray men's expectations and their indolence that stems from being pampered by women. She is aware that women commonly consider men, like children, incapable of looking after themselves, and whenever she finds a chance, she reverses this and ridicules women's tendency to pamper men. This tendency is more clearly apparent in relation to single men like Fabian Driver. On one occasion, Jane ironically comments on men's dependence on women for providing them food: "And the clergy are always with us where meals are concerned" (*JP* 30). Jane uses her knowledge of texts such as scripture to ridicule women's willingness to serve men:

> She echoes the words of Jesus ("For ye have the poor always with you," Mt. 26:11) when she notes the clergyman's ex-

> pectation that women will reliably supply food. By using the rhetoric of the famous statement, Jane completely reverses the position of the privileged male clergy. They become instead "the poor," the neglected outsiders who constitute a dependable social problem, a reliable nuisance that deserves compassion but not moralistic obsession. (Little, *Experimental* 102)

Jane skilfully employs literary and scriptural narratives to undermine the presuppositions and values associated with women's concern about men's food and men's dependence on women for providing their food. Thus, she holds a critical light to the image of the serving woman and the indolent, self-important clergyman. Her refusal to prepare food for men also challenges the traditional order. Tsagaris observes that "Food for Jane is a way to express her unconscious contempt for cooking and housework. Food is also a way for Jane to criticize the role of woman in her society" (75). Ackley similarly states that: "The opinion that men's needs are superior to or more pressing than the needs of women is reiterated with the same sort of bemusement throughout the novels. Countless women perform domestic tasks and menial clerical labour for men. [...] men are fussed over at meals, given larger portions, and granted special treatment" (46).

At the meeting of the literary society, Jane notices even intellectual women writers and critics serving men and ironically criticises the fact: "'The last impression will have been good – one woman rendering homage to a poet and another mopping spilt coffee from the trousers of a critic. Things like that aren't as trivial as you might think'" (*JP* 135). Cooley suggests that Jane's domestic inefficiency is a type of rebellion itself:

> an unacknowledged rebellion against this state of affairs. She pretends to put men first, but in fact she often drifts off into a private world and leaves her wifely duties behind, so that her daughter and her housekeeper have to take care of meals and housekeeping, or Nicholas has to fend for himself. (*Comic* 116)

Thus, according to Cooley, she succeeds in subverting the patriarchal order "Without attacking the doctrine of male supremacy." Jane's disobedience and failure in domestic matters, therefore, is a voluntary rejection of patriarchal values and beliefs.

4.1.3 Jane's and Prudence's Use of Double-Voiced Discourse

As Doan points out, two different voices can be traced in *JP*: "the voice of the patriarchy and the voice challenging that authority" ("Pym's" 152). The double-voiced discourse used by Jane and Prudence undermines the discourse of patriarchy and helps them to express themselves indirectly. They use it to avoid openly challenging the dominant order. Jane's struggle to find a husband for Prudence is the result of her internalisation of patriarchal culture. Jane's voice in this case "functions as a mouthpiece for the social order, regarding her friend Prudence as an oddity and, occasionally, as an object of pity." Jane never speaks her mind or expresses her wish directly; rather, she employs the strategy of double-text in mentioning a suitable man for Prudence. In her letter to Prudence, she gently alludes to Fabian Driver:

> Jane was too wise to appear anything but casual in her tone as she mentioned this eligible widower. She knew that the pride of even young spinsters is a delicate thing and that Prudence was especially sensitive. There must be no hint that she was trying to 'bring them together'. (*JP* 82)

Prudence's response is an instance of double-voiced discourse, too. Prudence indirectly acquires information about Fabian:

> Yes – you said something about him eating the hearts of his victims,' said Prudence, equally casual. She realised that Jane might have some absurd idea in her mind about 'bringing them together', but determined not to let her see that she suspected or that she entertained any hopes herself. So they were both satisfied and neither was really deceived for a moment. The conversation went on smoothly – Jane revealed

that Fabian was good-looking and quite tall, about five foot eleven which was really tall enough for a man, and that he had a nice house. (*JP* 82)

Jane and Prudence thus communicate with one another through double-voiced discourse and are quite content in this way.

Another instance of double-voiced communication between the female characters is when Prudence's friend, Eleanor, herself a spinster, suggests to her to get married, because "'That would settle you'" (*JP* 227). Despite her emphasis on marriage in conversation with Prudence, it is apparent that she herself is completely satisfied with her own single status. On the surface, she pretends to regret not to have married and takes on the blame: "'Look at my awful stockings. I didn't have time to change after golf. I suppose I'll never get a man if I don't take more trouble with myself.'" However, while she talks about her life, there seems to be no place or time for a husband. She is happy with her condition: "she spoke comfortably and without regret, thinking of her flat in Westminster, so convenient for the Ministry, her week-end golf, concerts and theatres with women friends, in the best seats and with a good supper afterwards" (*JP* 227).

Eleanor's discourse functions at two levels: The superficial level hosts the discourse of patriarchal culture with its stress on the importance of marriage for women, while at a deeper level the patriarchal discourse is opposed and the advantages of being unmarried are emphasised. Though Eleanor talks and behaves as if she respects patriarchal values, her satisfaction with being unmarried and enjoying a rich lifestyle is felt.

Jane and Prudence mainly take recourse to double-voiced because they cannot openly express honestly views and desires in a patriarchal society. Their discourse, while seemingly endorsing the patriarchal order, subverts it at a deeper level.

4.2 Subversion of the Image of the Spinster and Prudence's Creation of a Romantic World

Although Prudence is an independent woman with a good job and an apartment of her own, she is urged by her friends and acquaintances to marry since by patriarchal standards she is at a critical age with only a few years left in which she might find a suitable match. Her words, deeds and views as recounted by the narrator's voice run counter to the conventional spinster image: "Prudence Bates was twenty-nine, an age that is often rather desperate for a woman who has not yet married. Jane Cleveland was forty-one, an age that may bring with it compensations unsuspected by the anxious woman of twenty-nine" (*JP* 6).

Contrary to patriarchal expectations, Prudence is satisfied with her role as a heroine of romantic plots and does not wish to marry. When at their reunion Miss Birkinshaw tells her that her career must be a compensation for not having married, she replies that she doesn't need compensation: "'I often think being married would be rather a nuisance. I've got a nice flat and am so used to living on my own I should hardly know what to do with a husband'" (*JP* 9). When Jane urges her to get married, her reasons seem ridiculous and not compelling: "Oh, but a husband was someone to tell one's silly jokes to, to carry suitcases and do the tipping at hotels, thought Jane, with a rush." Although educated and intelligent, Jane is a victim of a patriarchal culture that values marriage without deeper reason.

A spinster is generally regarded as a poor and apathetic person in service since she is without a family of her own. Nicholas, for instance, expresses this view when talking about Prudence with Jane: "'I've often wondered why she doesn't take up social work of some kind'" (*JP* 58). His views are similar to those of the patriarchal system's that expect contributions and services from the unmarried women. However, Jane ridicules his view: "'Now you are talking like a clergyman, or like Miss Birkinshaw, our old tutor […] You imagine Prue "fulfilling herself" by sitting on some committee to arrange amenities for the "poor."'"

Contrary to society's expectations, Prudence believes that it is marriage itself that ruins a woman. When she thinks about Jane and the works she could have accomplished had she not married, she feels her talents have been wasted:

> she seemed to have missed something in life; her research, her studies of obscure seventeenth-century poets, had all come to nothing, and here she was, trying, though not very hard, to be an efficient clergyman's wife, and with only very

moderate success. Compared with Jane's life, Prudence's seemed rich and full of promise. She had her work, her independence, her life in London and her love for Arthur Grampian. But to-morrow, if she wanted to, she could give it all up and fall in love with somebody else. (*JP* 93)

Although Jane as a wife and a mother considers herself more successful, Prudence, unrestrained by conventional values, is the only person who knows the reality of Jane's empty and wasted life.

Another character who runs counter to established spinster stereotypes is Jessie Morrow, Miss Doggett's companion. She is regarded as a naive, unattractive, and characterless woman until her engagement to Fabian. Fabian too does not think highly of her at first. When he sees her in their garden, he thinks: "he had noticed her even less than he had noticed his wife. Miss Doggett he knew, of course, but Miss Morrow had appeared always in her shadow, a thing without personality of her own, as neutral as her clothes" (*JP* 61). Thus, Jessie represents the typical selfless spinster whose duty is to serve and comfort other people. She serves Miss Doggett, a rich relation, and lives under her shadow.

Nonetheless, the same Jessie finally robs Fabian off the attractive Prudence. Though she appears quiet and naive, she has plans for Fabian and knows how to lure him. Unlike the characters who respect Fabian as "an inconsolable widower" (*JP* 63), she is aware of his imperfections and pretensions and mocks his Byronic image; as a result, "when he was with her he felt uncomfortable, as if she were laughing at him, or even as if she knew things about him that he didn't want known" (*JP* 62). Fabian believes that if he is better understood, his image will fall apart and he will lose his mysterious grandeur.

Jessie not only frees herself from the spinster stereotype, but also shatters Fabian's self-image. Her ridicule of the male image is not restricted to Fabian. For instance, she also makes fun of Miss Doggett's emphasis on men's need for more and better food than women. At times, Miss Doggett requires her companion's affirmation:

'I think a man needs a cooked breakfast, especially after an all-night sitting in the House. I can imagine Mr. Lyall needing a cooked breakfast then. Can't you, Jessie?' She turned to her companion and spoke rather sharply for, as Jane had noticed, Miss Morrow was smirking a little as if there were something funny being said. (*JP* 102).

Instead of affirming Miss Doggett expectation Jessie mocks her opinion: "'Men seem to need a lot of food at all times,' said Miss Morrow in a rough, casual tone."

Jessie also undermines the image of good wife when Mildred of *EW* is mentioned in the novel. She is described as a serving wife to her intellectual husband. Echoing the patriarchal view, Miss Doggett says: "'She [Mildred] helped him [Everard] a good deal in his work, I think. Mrs. Bonner says that she even learned to type so that she could type his manuscripts for him'" (*JP* 143). Miss Doggett considers this as the wife's responsibility towards her husband, while Jessie regards it as a technique to deceive the man: "'Oh, then he had to marry her,' said Miss Morrow sharply. 'That kind of devotion is worse than blackmail – a man has no escape from that.'" Jessie's mind, as opposed to Miss Doggett's and the conventional principle of duty, mainly functions with the principle of give and take. She establishes the same kind of relationship with Fabian. Through a deliberate change in behaviour, she reverses the image of an unattractive and unrelated spinster which society and even Fabian have imposed upon her. Visiting Fabian's house for the first time, she deliberately applies make-up and wears his deceased wife Constance's dress. When he asks her whether she would prefer a cup of tea or a hot drink, she surprises Fabian by asking for whisky. Jessie's quick reply contradicts his view of her as an old-fashioned, unattractive spinster: "'What did you imagine that I liked?' 'I don't know. I suppose I never thought.' 'You mean you never thought of me as a human being at all? As a person who could like anything?'" (*JP* 160). Jessie's words reflect not only Fabian's thoughts, but those of society at large. Her wisdom and knowledge of patriarchal society help her deal with her situation and she can surmise Fabian's views about her and women in general.

4 Jane and Prudence: *Unconventional Wife and Satisfied Spinster*   199

On the day of Fabian's garden party, Miss Doggett and Jessie talk about Fabian's lunch before going to the party. Miss Doggett stresses that he has had something light for lunch because of the party. She again emphasises the quality of a gentleman's food and is deeply concerned about its being adequate and nourishing. Aware of her views, Jessie replies: "'No, one could hardly give a man tinned salmon'" (*JP* 191), but she does not mean what she says. She merely undermines the importance society places on men's food ridiculing Miss Doggett's opinion.

Jessie's reversal of the patriarchal order goes as far as mocking Fabian's image in his presence. She imposes herself on him and forces him to break up with Prudence and marry her. While Fabian postpones taking any action and continues playing the role of an unfortunate widower, Jessie, unlike other women, ignores the projected image he has created for himself and decides to marry him: "'Now stop trying to look like Edward Lyall with his burden,' said Jessie sharply. 'Do you mean to tell me that you have said nothing at all to her?'" (*JP* 200). Jessie's behaviour with men, including Fabian, differs from that of other women. While other women pity Fabian and believe in his invented false image, Jessie sees through it and is aware that he is playing a role. She is also aware that the only reason he does not speak to Prudence about Jessie is that he does not want to lose her while at the same time keeping Jessie.

Jessie's real character is disclosed when Miss Doggett starts doubting her because of her frequent absences. One day when Jessie is on leave, Miss Doggett goes to her room and searches among her things:

> Jessie's room was without any definite character apart from that given to it by the miscellaneous pieces, unwanted in other rooms, with which it was furnished. In all the years that she had lived with Miss Doggett, Jessie had not succeeded in stamping it with her own personality. One would have imagined that a gentlewoman would have her 'things,' those objects – photographs, books, souvenirs collected on holiday – which can make a room furnished with other people's furniture into a kind of home. But Jessie seemed to have none of these [...] There were no books of devotion,

> not even a Bible or a prayer-book, which one might certainly expect a spinster to possess [...] it seemed almost as if Jessie had been at pains to suppress or conceal her personality. (*JP* 204)

Indeed, Jessie has been hiding her real personality all these years, because she is aware that she is not a conventional spinster who merely serves others, praises men, and desires or expects nothing from society.

Although not a religious person, Jessie publically attends church activities as a convention while she has a totally different private life and opinions. For example, she hides her affair with Fabian. Like the contents of her room, she conceals the realities of her actual life and character, because she is afraid of the judgments of other people. In this case, according to Doan, Pym's novels "become an opportunity to undermine traditional notions of the spinster and to create a positive self-identity. Pym presents spinsterhood as the embodiment or synthesis of all the better things life has to offer" ("Pym's" 54).

Jessie is not satisfied with her life as Miss Doggett's companion, and the common activities of spinsters do not give her any satisfaction. She expects more and finds her desired life in marrying Fabian. Prudence is also represented as living a full life and having her love affairs as well. These women thus run counter to the conventional spinster image. As Doan states, for them "Spinsterhood [...] is an alternative life-style which offers women an active role in society and allows them the opportunity to examine others critically" ("Pym's" 153).

While Jane tries to build a bridge between the world of novels and the real one, Prudence only uses novels as an escape from reality, both during and after her failed love affairs. As Cooley suggests, "Imagination of a literary kind has led her far more deeply astray than Jane; she scarcely even thinks of ordinary happiness" (*Comic* 104). Prudence employs romances in novels as her guideline for her life, looking upon herself as the heroine of a romantic novel with an unhappy ending. She defines one book she reads as "a love affair in the fullest sense of the word and sparing no detail, but all in a very intellectual sort of way and there were a good many quotations from Donne" (*JP* 51). Her attempt to live in accordance with romantic

4 Jane and Prudence: Unconventional Wife and Satisfied Spinster 201

novels prevents her from getting married or setting up a lasting love relationship.

Prudence's desire to construct a romantic plot is far greater than her interest to live it to its full extent. She does not really fall in love, but only plays the role of a romantic heroine who gets disappointed in every love affair. She does not start an affair with the intention of getting married, but with the thought that it will end someday. She thinks that if the outcome of an affair is marriage, it will lose its romance. When Prudence has an affair with her colleague Geoffrey Manifold, she tells Jane: "Everything would be spoilt if anything came of it [...] That's almost the best thing about it'" (*JP* 246). Prudence quotes from Marvell to support this: "'Therefore the Love which us doth join/ But Fate so enviously debars, /Is the Conjunction of the Mind, / And Opposition of the Stars'" (*JP* 247).

Both Jane and Prudence are in some ways duped by imagination and romance so that their relation with the real world and people is restricted and in this way they both become static characters:

> One of the most curious aspects of Jane Cleveland and Prudence Bates is that they seem never to have outgrown Oxford. Jane still clings to her memories of the romance of learning, research and writing experienced in her undergraduate years; and Prudence pursues love affairs that are merely an endless replaying of the ones she had known during Oxford's golden autumns. Meanwhile the world has altered around them, contracted, grown niggling and small, making the idea of romance to which they cling seem unreal. Rather than being characters who are capable of expansion, they are figures entrapped within their own isolation. (Long 85)

Prudence's way of coping with reality differs from Jane's. She finds the world of romantic novels so much to her liking that she arranges her life accordingly. She so deeply identifies herself with the romantic heroine that she is unable to actually fall in love and continue a normal relationship with a man. She considers all men as a medium to attain the ideal of being a heroine in an unending romantic fiction. Her emphasis on the importance of literary quotations and their application to her life are so heavy that she loses her suitors one by one. In fact, she does not care about getting married; rather, she is in love with the image of herself as a romantic partner in a relationship that, as the reader knows, is doomed to fail from the beginning. She does not expect much from her various affairs and is happy and satisfied when an affair comes to an end, because she believes that is the fate of star-crossed lovers, as in romantic novels.

4.3 Subversion of the Male Image by Exposure of Men's Indolence and Self-Indulgence

Pym portrays male characters as indolent, egoistic and comic characters who lack self-knowledge. The most important indolent male personage in *JP* is the pretentious widower Fabian Driver. In the first part of the novel, Jessie describes his character to Jane, because Jane is surprised to find a large-framed photograph of Fabian on his deceased wife's grave. Jessie says:

> 'We thought at first that the photograph was put there temporarily until he could get a stone put up, but he seems to have come to the conclusion that he need not go to that expense after all. People are used to seeing it there now. I believe that does sometimes happen. Her death came as a great shock to him – he had almost forgotten her existence.' (*JP* 29)

Jessie's ironic comment that the photograph on his wife's tomb spares him buying a gravestone displays Fabian's selfishness. Moreover, he victimises his wife both in her life and after. Although he did not care for her, he still continues to impose his ideas upon her after her death. His actions expose his self-image and egoistic character as Jessie confirms his pretension: "'He is one for the grand gesture and has no time for niggling details'" (*JP* 30). Fabian does not even work, instead he spends his days in total indolence since his wife has provided him with enough property and money: "'Oh, there is some business in the City which belonged to his father-in-law. Whatever it is, it doesn't seem to require his attendance every day of the week. He is often here, apparently doing nothing.'"

4 Jane and Prudence: *Unconventional Wife and Satisfied Spinster*   203

Fabian's pretension is also reversed by the narrative voice according to which he always pretends to be an "inconsolable widower" (*JP* 30) and enjoys people's pity for him. He always self-dramatises and, at one point, pretends to Jane that he has taken care of himself after his wife's death by doing all the house work. When Jane asks how he manages to do all that alone, he replies: "'One manages [...] one has to, of course'" (*JP* 35). Jane feels sorry for him, but is aware that Fabian awakens such pity intentionally: "The use of the third person seemed to add pathos, which was perhaps just what he intended, Jane thought." Still, Jane is greatly affected by Fabian: "He is going back to cook a solitary lunch, [...] or perhaps it will just be beer and bread and cheese, a man's meal and the better for being eaten alone." Jane primarily analyses Fabian on the basis of the false information he gives himself. Later on, however, Mrs. Glaze informs her that Fabian has a perfect cook who does his housework.

The female characters in the novel usually serve men, while the male characters pretend they are helpless. Jane's daughter Flora, falling in love with Mr Oliver, pities him, thinking that he is too weak and thin and she must feed him. When Jane and Nicholas go to a café to have dinner, Jane assumes again that since Mr Oliver lives alone, he does not eat proper food: "He certainly looked very pale reading the Lessons on Sunday evenings, but perhaps that was just a trick of the lighting" (*JP* 57). A little while later, Jane is taught better when the waitress brings him roast chicken while all they have are beans and eggs.

Fabian's self-pity – "I'm a lonely person" (*JP* 106) – also affects Prudence when they meet for the first time. Prudence, ready sympathise, becomes sentimental: "She looked up at his face and found his profile pleasing. Poor, lonely Fabian ... She began to wonder if he would kiss her outside the vicarage gate." However, her expectations are all in vain since "There is no Mr. Knightley for Prudence, no masculine figure of solid worth and judgment to guide the heroine, no male who is both father-like and lover-like, the embodiment of masculine authority, stability, and reliability" (Cooley, *Comic* 112).

Fabian again plays the role of inconsolable widower when he asks Miss Doggett and Jessie to come and collect Constance's clothes and other belongings for a jumble sale. He sits languidly, appearing to mourn, but cares neither about Constance nor her things, not even the book she gave him as a present. His only concern, as Jessie is aware, is to keep-up his self-image, as when he is sitting in a public house looking at himself in a large mirror (*JP* 59). When he talks to Jessie in the garden, it emerges that he did not know Constance and her likes and dislikes well: "'Alas, no. Constance was so fond of quinces!' […] Constance was so fond of quinces! thought Miss Morrow scornfully. As if Fabian had known or cared what Constance was fond of – why, Miss Doggett had several times offered her quinces and she had always refused them!" (*JP* 62). Fabian's knowledge about his deceased wife does not go beyond some general information based on his own point of view. His self-indulgence is apparent in the following passage:

> She had been pretty when he had married her and had brought him a comfortable amount of money as well as a great deal of love. He had been unprepared for her death and outraged by it, for it had happened suddenly, without a long illness to prepare him, when he had been deeply involved in one of the little romantic affairs which he seemed to need, either to bolster up his self-respect or for some more obvious reason. The shock of it all had upset him considerably, and although there had been several women eager to console him, he had abandoned all his former loves, fancying himself more in the role of an inconsolable widower than as a lover. Indeed, it was now almost a year since he had thought of anybody but himself. But now he felt that he might start again. Constance would not have wished him to live alone, he felt. She had even invited his loves to the house for week-ends […] they would be talking a little awkwardly, as two women sharing the same man generally do; there would inevitably be some lack of spontaneity and frankness. (*JP* 63)

Even when Constance was dying Fabian was involved in one of his love affairs. Her unexpected death shocked and even angered him. The surprise was so great because her death was the only thing in her life over which he had no control. Fabian is also unable to understand why Constance really invited his mistresses to their house. He thinks that she approved of his affairs, while the true reason was that she wanted him to remain home so she would not be alone. His only concern was the upkeep of his image; he did not care about his wife until she finally died of misery and loneliness.

Fabian's desire to maintain his self-image is so strong that he even competes with the member of parliament Edward Lyall about who comes to parties later. When Jane asks about the reason, Jessie replies: "'A good entrance. He has to time his appearance carefully – it mustn't be too soon after the arrival of Edward Lyall, otherwise he wouldn't be noticed'" (*JP* 103).

Male indolence and self-indulgence are also depicted in further scenes. For instance, Fabian's garden party is an ideal opportunity for men to pretend that they are exhausted. Every one of them describes his daily work in detail, presenting his job as an unbearable burden. Lyall, who has inherited his seat in parliament from his father and grandfather, self-dramatises thus: "'It is so deliciously restful here. I can't think how long it is since I sat lazily in a garden, and it's really one of my favourite ways of spending time'" (*JP* 194). Other men assist and encourage him to talk about his burden so that they can also go on about theirs. Actually living in a peaceful house with a garden in a village, and only occasionally going to the city for business, Fabian exaggerates the demands on him: "'Yes, one does find it a great relief just to be able to relax in a garden [...]. I find the bustle of the City quite intolerable'" (*JP* 195). Asked about his work, he pretentiously replies: "'Oh, it is quite unspeakably dull. [...] I suppose it is the dullness of it all that makes me feel so exhausted.'" Nicholas, being in the right place, also pretends to be tired as a clergyman.

Jane ridicules such self-indulgence: "'Perhaps it would be better if we all sat in silence. If the men find life so exhausting, our chatter might disturb them.'" Still, men continue to describe their burden: "Fabian and Edward seemed to be trying to outdo each other in weariness, and even Nicholas was making some attempt to compete, detailing the number of services he had to take on Sundays and the many houses he had to visit during the week" (*JP* 195). The novel concludes with a shattering breakdown of Fabian's self-image, as he gets entangled with Jessie, which ends his marriage. This marriage can be considered as a symbol of his imprisonment, since

Jessie, unlike his deceased wife, will not approve of his affairs. When Jane asks him whether he has forgotten Prudence, Pym ridicules his self-dramatising:

> 'I – forget? My dear Jane ...' He put one hand up to his brow with a characteristic gesture, while his other hand seemed to wander along the slatted wooden shelves of the conservatory, with the flower-pots full of old used earth and dried-up bulbs with withered leaves, until it came to rest on what felt like a piece of statuary. He looked down in surprise at feeling his hand touch stone, and started at seeing the headless body of a dwarf which had once stood in the rockery in the front garden. (*JP* 243-44)

The headless dwarf symbolises Fabian's lost self-image. Due to his newly-gained awsarenes Fabian cannot be the same self-indulgent man anymore. To affirm this, Miss Doggett asks him to escort her and Jessie back home. After their departure, Jane comments: "'Rather a sad little procession [...]. Fabian being led away captive by the women'" (*JP* 244). Pym subverts the image of the self-absorbed, egoist Fabian by marrying him to Jessie and, metaphorically, to the dominating Miss Doggett.

What Jane takes to be her life-values are in fact the internalised values of patriarchal culture, not her own. Accordingly she is unable to adapt herself to them. Her most significant flaw is to confound the literary and the real world. Her inclination towards imaginary worlds is an obstacle to dealing with realities. As a result, she is unable to communicate properly with the members of her family. Her obsession with romantic plots also results in her mistake of bringing Prudence and Fabian together. Her participation in literary societies and her reading of novels do not lead her to produce literary works herself. Pym undermines the conventional housewife image portraying a woman who is neither efficient in housework nor successful in her scholarly research. Unlike other women, Jane does not pamper men serving them and she ridicules women who do so. Women in *JP* perform unending, thankless jobs for men. However, Jane undermines the opinion

4 Jane and Prudence: Unconventional Wife and Satisfied Spinster

of women who consider men's needs as more important than female ones and whose only concern is the quality of food for men.

The discourse of the dominating culture functions as a cover for the subverting double-voiced discourse of Jane and Prudence. Patriarchal discourse urges Prudence to get married, while the subversive discourse encourages her to remain single. While Jane confounds the romantic world of novels with the real world, Prudence escapes from the real world by taking refuge in the romantic world portrayed in novels. Prudence is happy in her current position of imagining herself as a heroine in an incessant romantic novel. Although she will soon be beyond what is considered to be a marriageable age, she does not seriously contemplate marriage since she has a comfortable life, enough money, and her affairs. Thus, she subverts the image of the spinster as a hapless, poor and indolent woman whose chief concern is to be of service to others.

Another unconventional spinster is Jessie Morrow, who, before marrying Fabian, is considered an unattractive, naive and selfless person. However, her decision to marry Fabian and to be Prudence's rival reveals her true character. She wants to alter her situation since she is not satisfied with playing the role of an obedient companion to the dominating Miss Doggett. She thus undermines the image of a spinster without desires of her own to marry Fabian without showing any consideration towards the conventions of society.

Similarly, through portraying pretentious and self-indulgent male characters, the narrative voice also ridicules and subverts the conventional male image. Male characters in *JP* usually pretend to be helpless and lonely individuals with numerous unbearable burdens to shoulder. However, they are revealed to be indolent and self-indulgent, having no rewarding work, while the entire burden of the household is borne by women who have to look after men and sympathise with them. The character who best reflects male indolence, pretence and self-indulgence is Fabian Driver, whose self-constructed image Pym shatters through Jessie's ridicule.

Conclusion

Women's humour in this study is considered as a specific category of women's writing. This is in accordance with feminist theorists such as Showalter, and Gilbert and Gubar, who grant women's writing a specific status. Similarly, theorists of women's humour such as Walker, Gillooly, and Barecca argue that women's humour can be considered as a distinct type of humour different from that of the dominant male culture.

The strikingly original and appealing humour in Pym's novels may be considered among the most significant examples of this. Humour in Pym's narratives function differently from the conventional types of humour which is part of the tenets of English Literature. Referred as women's humour, this type of humour mainly functions through rhetorical (linguistic) and thematic strategies in Pym's *STG*, *EW* and *JP*. By highlighting this and applying the theories proposed by women's humour theorists, the present study tried to show how Pym's humour derides and thereby challenges the dominant or patriarchal culture's preconceived images of women. Having been based on the established male standards, which do not take into account the peculiar features of women's lives and experiences, women's humour theorists consider the traditional humour theories as inadequate to read women's humour.

Pym's humorous discourse is directed at undermining the established conventions of the patriarchal world. She ridicules the dominant order by questioning its presuppositions and values. By focusing on the images of the conventional spinster, and the ideal housewife and the excellent woman, Pym questions male standards by covertly deriding the values and images associated with women. She applies some strategies in *STG* in order to dismantle the existing dominant culture. Furthermore, the conventional romantic love plot in *STG* is subverted through the reversal of the gender-based roles – older women falling in love with young men – and also through giving significance to the insignificant, trivial details, such as the curate's combinations shown under the trousers. In order to undermine the conventional image of the woman, as presented in romantic love plots, Pym succeeds in creating intelligent, self-sufficient, and independent middle-aged spinsters.

Spinsters in Pym's novels are represented as the intelligent lovers, while men are shown as being silly, inefficient and indolent characters – very different from the traditional lovers in the romantic novels. Women are shown as proposing marriage to men. Harriet's and Belinda's marriage proposals reverse the conventional proposal scenes of romantic novels since there is no lover and the beloved, neither is there the desire to get married. Marriage is a mere act of calculation and profit-seeking. The Bede sisters too, in *STG* undermine the love plot and reverse the happy ending by rejecting marriage proposals and living together as spinsters. Pym, further subverts the romantic plot by introducing and focusing on domestic triviality. She also employs double-voiced discourse in order to resist and survive in the dominant patriarchal culture. Belinda Bede's usage of double-text discourses are employed, at a superficial level, to help her survive within the society; at a deeper level, however, they are targeted at undermining and challenging the patriarchal order. Belinda's acts of disobedience are detectable in her discourse.

STG presents the absurdities and limitations of the patriarchal culture. The narrator makes a connection with the female characters through the application of sympathetic humour, thus, the narrator does not ridicule or humiliate Belinda. The Bede sisters' extremely protective feelings and sympathy towards one another enables the two middle-aged spinsters survive and resist the dominant order. The narrative voice too, in *STG*, through humour, questioningly mocks the long-held values, presuppositions, images and stereotypes of women. The humorous discourse of the narrative about the character of Belinda, considered as an ideal woman, undermines the stereotype of the angel in the house through the light-hearted ridicule of her services and her staunch belief in etiquette.

By choosing spinsters as her heroines, Pym does not reproduce the presupposed beliefs and stereotypes in the patriarchal culture, but reverses them by portraying their absurdity. Moreover, she also derides women's internalization of the images ascribed to them. In addition, she also reverses the image of the strong, dependable, and responsible male characters through a portrayal of their indolence, self-dramatization and pretension. Pym undermines the presupposed images of the spinsters and bachelors by portraying strong, independent, and self-sufficient female spinsters and self-important, indolent, and pretentious bachelors. Moreover, by highlighting women's difference from men in relating to the power structures such as the institution of church, Pym undermines the socio-cultural structures of the society. For example, Pym criticizes the institution of Church by presenting indolent and materialistic clergymen in the character of Henry Hoccleve. She thus manages to subvert the authority and the power they represent by highlighting their absurdities and hypocrisies.

The narrator in EW ridicules the social perception of Mildred as the perfect prototype of the excellent woman. By highlighting Mildred's understatement and self-deprecation in *EW*, the roles and functions of rhetorical strategies in the construction of women's humour are examined in this study. Mildred employs the strategic use of understatement, not to humiliate or deride her status as a spinster, but as a weapon to protect and strengthen herself by resisting the oppressions of the patriarchal structure. On the one hand, she refuses to actually comply with the laws of the patriarchal society through self-deprecation and, on the other hand, she covertly revolts against the existent injustices of the dominating culture. Mildred's self-deprecatory manner originates from her particular condition in the society. Because of being neither a wife nor a mother, she is not looked upon as a productive element in the patriarchal society. Her unmarried status, consequently, results in the society's ignoring and oppressing her. The most suitable role for her in the society is playing the role of an excellent woman. Through acting as an excellent woman, however, she covertly resists the dominant culture by ridiculing and undermining the values associated with the image of the excellent women. The strategy of self-deprecation helps Mildred adopt the view of the patriarchal culture wherein she may look at herself with a sense of detachment and self-irony. She survives and resists the patriarchal order by admitting that she is not a desirable woman. Thus, she takes the blame upon herself in conflicting situations. Her dissatisfaction is portrayed mainly through her inner thoughts and speeches, which do not confirm to her outward behaviour. Therefore, Mildred, on the one hand, prevents the patriarchal society's critique and assessment of her by taking-on and accepting the accusation of being unmarried and, on the other, by fortifying her status through placing herself at the position of the patriarchal system and resisting its humiliation and ridicule. Additionally, Mildred's strategic employment of the double-voiced discourse in *EW* is another effective way to deal with the patriarchal society. Mildred makes use of the double text to act according to the established patriarchal codes, and to simultaneously undermine the culture that does not grant her a status due to her being an unmarried woman. On the surface, Mildred pretends to be a selfless spinster who voluntarily helps people and acts in accordance to their expectations. However, on a deeper level, she challenges and resists this order through her inner thoughts and speeches by inwardly expressing her actual feelings and perceptions. In her inner perceptions, the dominant patriarchal discourse is ridiculed and the dominant order reversed. She resists the dominating system through this voice and yet manages to survive the onslaught of the patriarchal society by consciously adopting the voice of a complying, servile spinster. Everyone casts Mildred as the excellent woman who, owing to her single status, is expected to be forever at the service of others, to attend to their needs, solve their problems, and ignore her own wishes or desires. However, the excellent woman is shown ridiculed by Mildred's resisting voice. Although stereotyping Mildred as an unrelated spinster is considered as a common practice in the represented fictional society in EW, however, her words and actions do not conform to her image as a selfless and serving spinster. Rather than being a nosy and idle spinster, Mildred considers herself an independent individual who values her privacy and does not relish serving and helping others as expected by society. Thus, she ridicules and revises the stereotype of the excellent woman of the patriarchal culture through an inner analysis of the values and beliefs. EW, similarly undermines the image of the independent hero of romantic novels by portraying dependent, helpless, and egoistic male characters who are quite the opposites of the typical male characters, who are utterly superficial and shallow though being attractive and handsome, who depend on women to do their jobs. Everard and Rocky are ridiculed through representing their pretentions, self-dramatizations and hypocrisy.

Pym's JP subverts the conventional stereotype of the housewife and the spinster mainly by focusing on the conversation between Jane and Prudence, as the discourse of two unconventional women. Jane, the unconventional wife of a clergyman, reverses the image through creating a fantastic

4 Jane and Prudence: Unconventional Wife and Satisfied Spinster

and imaginary world in which nobody is allowed to enter, except herself. This results in her remaining disconnected from the real world of real people. She is incapable of making a distinction between the real and the imaginary world. Jane's immersion in literature makes her imagine herself to be a successful wife of a clergyman managing a large household, as well as being a productive literary scholar. However, she is neither efficient in housework nor in literary scholarship. She is incapable of making a distinction between the real and the imaginary world. Because of the values and ideals she holds, she struggles to reach that which are not of her own, since they belong to the ideals and values of the dominant order. Thus, Jane's tendency towards fantasy and romance is subverted through the ridicule of the narration.

Moreover, Jane' another strategy to undermine the dominant order is to deliberately avoid serving and attending men as well as ridiculing the notion that needs of men are of greater importance than those of women. Additionally, Jane and Prudence employ the strategy of the double-voiced strategy discourse to express their real thoughts indirectly so as not to be considered as an open challenge and revolution to the dominating order. Though they seemingly appear to be obedient to the dominant order, in their inner thoughts they undermine the patriarchal value structure by challenging its authority. Likewise, Prudence, like Jane, lives in an imaginary world slightly different from that of her sister Jane. She looks upon romance novels as to provide her guidelines and arranges all her love affairs according to them. She does not establish a real relationship with anybody, rather she merely takes joy in imagining herself as the heroine of a romantic novel. Her belief that all the lovers are invariably destined to separate, and that there is no happy ending to love, makes her relationships with men unrealistic. Moreover, her lifestyle undermines the presupposed image of the spinster. Her independent and contented way of living appears strange to her acquaintances who find it contrary to the conventions and values of the society, and thus, force her to get married. However, she is quite happy in living an independent life with her numerous love affairs which keep her occupied. The narrative voice, along with Prudence's thoughts, undermines the patriarchal notion that a spinster leads an unhappy, lonely life. She reverses the image of the spinster as a hapless and indolent woman whose main responsibility is to be forever in service to others. Jessie Morrow's actions also subvert the ideas associated with the conventional notion of the spinster. Jessie's unconventional ways to first seduce, and then marry Fabian, also reverse the conventional perception of the spinster. She is transformed from a characterless spinster into a determined and respectful married woman, thus subverting the prototype of the embarrassed and passive spinster. Similarly, Pym undermines the images of the strong, independent male characters by portraying lethargic self-indulgent male characters such as Fabian Driver. The narrative voice constantly undermines Fabian's and other male character's tendency to self-dramatize.

Thus, women's humour in Pym's fiction functions through both the rhetorical and thematic strategies. Unlike conventional humour, it neither humiliates nor ridicules the woman; on the contrary, it creates a sympathetic bond with the heroine and among the female characters and portrays their victimization by the patriarchal culture. In this way, Pym's narratives undermine the dominant culture. Moreover, her humour shatters the images and stereotypes such as the spinster and the Byronic hero through undermining the values and presuppositions associated with them. Through understatement and self-deprecation, the female characters do not humiliate themselves; rather, they fortify their position by becoming the oppressors rather than being the oppressed – thus avoiding further oppression. In addition, the female characters reverse the dominant order through the employment of the double-voiced discourse. This strategy, without threatening or endangering the dominant order, pushes through reforms within that order. They also reverse the romantic love plot by focusing on trivia, creating significant out of the insignificant, and making gossip function as a shaping force of the narrative. Thus, Pym's humour deliberately functions through questioning preconceived images, stereotypes, beliefs, and values in a patriarchal culture.

Works Cited

Ackley, Katherine Anne. *The Novels of Barbara Pym*. New York: Garland, 1989.

Barreca, Regina. Introduction. *Last Laughs: Perspectives on Women and Comedy*. Ed. Regina Barreca. Philadelphia, PA: Gordon and Breach, 1988. 1-21.

___. *The Penguin Book of Women's Humor*. New York: Penguin, 1996.

___. *They Used to Call me Snow White – But I Drifted: Women's Strategic Use of Humor*. New York: Penguin, 1992.

___. *Untamed and Unabashed: Essays on Women and Humor in British Literature*. Detroit: Wayne State University Press, 1993.

Benet, Diana. *Something to Love*. Columbia, MO: University of Missouri Press, 1986.

Bennett, Barbara. *Comic Visions, Female Voices: Contemporary Women Novelists and Southern Humor*. Baton Rouge: Louisiana State University Press, 1998.

Bentley, Nick, Alice Ferrebe, and Nick Bubble, eds. *The 1950s: A Decade of Modern British Fiction*. London: Bloomsbury Academic, 2018.

Berg, Temma F. "Suppressing the language of Wo(Man): The Dream as a Common Language." *Engendering the Word: Feminist Essays in Psychosexual Poetics*. Ed. Temma F. Berg. Urbana: University of Illinois Press, 1989.

Bilger, Audrey. *Laughing Feminism: Subversive Comedy in Frances Burney, Maria Edgeworth, and Jane Austen*. Detroit, MI: Wayne State University Press, 1998.

Bunkers, Suzanne L. "Why Are These Women Laughing? The Powers and Politics of Women's Humor." *The Humor Prism in 20th Century America*. Ed. Joseph Boskin. New York: Wayne State University Press, 1997. 159-71.

Caliskan, Sevda. "Is There Such A Thing as Women's Humor?" *American Studies International* 33.2 (1995): 49-59.

Cixous, Hélène. "The Laugh of Medusa." *The Norton Anthology of Theory and Criticism*. Ed. Vincent B. Leitch. New York: W. W. Norton, 2012. 2035-56.

Cixous, Hélène, and Catherine Clément. *The Newly Born Woman*. Trans. Betsy Wing, Minnesota: University of Minnesota Press, 1987.
Colebrook, Claire. *Irony*. New York: Routledge, 2004.
Copper, Jilly. Introduction. *Jane and Prudence*. By Barbara Pym. Virago Modern Classic Book 312. New Ed Edition. Kindle Edition. 2011.
Cooley, Mason. "Barbara Pym." *British Writers, Supplement II: Kingsley Amis to J. R .R. Tolkien*. Ed. George Stade. Charles Scribner's Sons, New York: 1992. 363-85.
___. *The Comic Art of Barbara Pym*. New York: AMS, 1990.
Cotsell, Michael. *Barbara Pym*. Modern Novelists. New York: St. Martin's, 1989.
Curlee, Judith. "'One Said a Jealous Wife was Like': The Constructions of Wives and Husbands in Seventieth-Century English Jests." *Performing Gender and Comedy: Theories, Texts and Contexts*. Ed. Shannon Eileen Hengen. Amsterdam: Gordon and Breach, 1998. 35-46.
Doan, Laura L. "Pym's Singular Interest: The Self as Spinster." *Old Maids to Radical Spinsters: Unmarried Women in the Twentieth-Century Novel*. Ed. Laura L. Doan. Illinois: University of Illinois Press, 1991. 139-54.
___. "Text and the Single Man: The Bachelor in Pym's Dual-Voiced Narrative." *Independent Women: The Function of Gender in the Novels of Barbara Pym*. Ed. Janice Rossen. Sussex: Harvester, 1988. 63-81.
Donato, Deborah. *Reading Barbara Pym*. Rosemont, Massachusetts: 2005.
Dresner, Zita. "Domestic Comic Writers." *Women's Comic Visions*. Ed. June Sochen. New York: Wayne State University Press, 1991. 93-114.
Fernald, E. Anne. *Virginia Woolf: Feminism and the Reader*. New York: Palgrave Macmillan, 2006.
Finney, Gail. "Unity in Difference? An Introduction." *Look Who's Laughing: Gender and Comedy*. Ed. Gail Finney. Amsterdam: Gordon and Breach, 1994, 1-13.
Franzini, L.R. "Feminism and Women's Sense of Humor." *Sex Roles* 1.11-12 (1996): 811-19. <https://doi.org/10.1007/BF01544094>. Accessed 8 Feb. 2015.

Gagnier, Regenia. "Between Women: A Cross-Class Analysis of Status and Anarchic Humor." *Last Laughs: Perspectives on Women and Comedy.* Ed. Regina Barreca. London: Gordon and Breach, 1988. 135-47.

Gilbert, Sandra M. and Susan Gubar. *The Madwoman in the Attic: The Woman Writer and the Nineteenth-Century Literary Imagination.* 2nd ed. New Haven: Yale University Press. 1980.

___. "Sexual Linguistics: Gender, Language, Sexuality." *New Literary History* 16.3 (1985): 515-43.

Gillooly, Eileen. *Smile of Discontent: Humor, Gender, and Nineteenth-Century British Fiction.* Chicago: University of Chicago Press, 1999.

___. "Women and Humor." *Feminist Studies* 17.3 (1991): 473-91.

Lakoff, Robin. "Language and Woman's Place." *Language in Society* 2.1 (1973): 45-80.

Lang, Candace. *Irony/Humor: Critical Paradigms.* Baltimore: Johns Hopkins University Press, 1987.

Little, Judy. *Comedy and the Woman Writer.* Nebraska: University of Nebraska Press, 1983.

___. *The Experimental Self: Dialogic Subjectivity in Woolf, Pym and Brooke-Rose.* Carbondale and Edwardsville: Southern Illinois University Press, 1996.

___. "Humoring the Sentence: Women's Dialogic Comedy." *Women's Comic Vision.* Ed. June Sochen. Detroit: Wayne State University Press, 1991. 19-31.

Long, Robert Emmet. *Barbara Pym.* New York: Ungar, 1986.

Mackay, Marina. "World War II, the Welfare State, and Postwar 'Humanism.'" *The Cambridge Companion to the Twentieth-Century English Novel.* Ed. Robert L. Caserio, New York: Cambridge University Press, 2009. 146-62.

Moi, Toril. *Sexual/Textual Politics: Feminist Literary Theory.* London and New York: Routledge, 1985.

Naranjo-Huebl, Linda. "From Peek-a-boo to Sarcasm; Women's Humor as a Means of Both Connection and Resistance." *FNSA Journal* 1.4 (1995): 343-72.

Nilsen, Alleen Pace and Don L. F. Nilsen. "Literature and Humour." *The Primer of Humor Research*. Ed. Victor Raskin. De Gruyter, New York: 2008. 243-80.

Parsons, Debora. *Theorists of the Modernist Novel: James Joyce, Dorothy Richardson, Virginia Woolf.* New York: Routledge. 2007.

Pershing, Linda. "There's a Joker in the Menstrual Hut: A Performance Analysis of Comedian Kate Clinton." *Women's Comic Visions*. Ed. June Sochen. Detroit: Wayne State University Press, 1991. 93-235.

Pym, Barbara. *Excellent Women*. Quality Paperback Book Club, London: 1984.

___. *Jane and Prudence*. Hertfordshire: Granada, 1981.

___. *Some Tame Gazelle*. London: Harper & Row, 1984.

Raz, Orna. *Social Dimensions in the Novels of Barbara Pym, 1949-1963: The Writer as Hidden Observer*. New York: Edwin Mellen Press, 2007.

Rossen, Janice. *Independent Women: The Function of Gender in the Novels of Barbara Pym*. New York: St Martin's, 1988.

Sanborn, Kate. *The Wit of Women*. New York: Funk & Wagnalls, 1895.

Smith, Alexander McCall. "Barbara Pym's Excellent Women: 'One of the 20th century's most amusing novels.'" *Guardian International Edition*. 5 Apr. 2008. <https://www.theguardian.com/books/2008/apr/05/features reviews.guardianreview30>. Accessed 11 Dec. 2020.

Showalter, Elaine. "Feminist Criticism in the Wilderness." *Critical Inquiry* 8.2 (Winter 1981): 179-205. <https://www.jstor.org/stable/1343159>. Accessed 25 Jan. 2020.

___. *A Literature of Their Own: British Women Novelists from Brontë to Lessing*. London: Virago, 1982.

Sochen, June. *Women's Comic Visions*. Michigan: Wayne State University Press, 1991.

Stimpson, Catherine R. "Forward." *Smile of Discontent: Humor, Gender, and Nineteenth-Century British Fiction*. Ed. Eileen Gillooly. Chicago: University of Chicago Press, 1999. ix-xi.

Stott, Andrew. *Comedy*. New York: Routledge, 2005.

Tsagaris, Ellen M. *The Subversion of Romance in the Novels of Barbara Pym*. Bowling Green: Bowling Green State University Popular Press, 1988.

Walker, Nancy A. *The Disobedient Writer: Woman and Narrative Tradition*. Austin: University of Texas Press, 1995.

___. *Feminist Alternatives: Irony and Fantasy in the Contemporary Novel by Women*. Mississippi: University of Mississippi Press, 1990.

___. *A Very Serious Thing: Women's Humor and American Culture*. Minnesota: University of Minnesota Press, 1988.

___. "Wit, Sentimentality and the Image of Women in the Nineteenth Century." *American Studies* 22.2 (Fall 1981): 5-22. <https://www.jstor.org/stable/40641651>. Accessed 22 May 2014.

Weld, Annette. *Barbara Pym and the Novel of Manners*. New York: Macmillan, 1992.

Woolf, Virginia. *The Death of the Moth and Other Essays*. A Project Gutenberg Australia eBook. 2012. <http://gutenberg.net.au/ebooks12/1203811h.html.>. Accessed 14 Sep. 2017.

___. *A Room of One's Own*. New York: Brace & World, 1957.

Wyatt-Brown, Ann M. *Barbara Pym: A Critical Biography*. Columbia: University of Missouri Press, 1992.

STUDIES IN ENGLISH LITERATURES

Edited by Koray Melikoğlu
ISSN 1614-4651

1   *Özden Sözalan*
       The Staged Encounter
       Contemporary Feminism and Women's Drama
       2nd, revised edition
       ISBN 3-89821-367-6

2   *Paul Fox (ed.)*
       Decadences
       Morality and Aesthetics in British Literature
       2nd, revised and expanded edition
       ISBN 3-89821-573-3

3   *Daniel M. Shea*
       James Joyce and the Mythology of Modernism
       ISBN 3-89821-574-1

4   *Paul Fox and Koray Melikoğlu (eds.)*
       Formal Investigations
       Aesthetic Style in Late-Victorian and Edwardian Detective Fiction
       2nd, revised and expanded edition
       ISBN 978-3-89821-593-0

5   *David Ellis*
       Writing Home
       Black Writing in Britain Since the War
       ISBN 978-3-89821-591-6

6   *Wei H. Kao*
       The Formation of an Irish Literary Canon in the Mid-Twentieth Century
       ISBN 978-3-89821-545-9

7   *Bianca Del Villano*
       Ghostly Alterities
       Spectrality and Contemporary Literatures in English
       2nd, revised editon
       ISBN 978-3-89821-714-9

8   *Melanie Ann Hanson*
       Decapitation and Disgorgement
       The Female Body's Text in Early Modern English Drama and Poetry
       ISDN 978-3-89821-605-5

9   *Shafquat Towheed (ed.)*
       New Readings in the Literature of British India, c.1780-1947
       ISBN 978-3-89821-673-9

10   *Paola Baseotto*
       "Disdeining life, desiring leaue to die"
       Spenser and the Psychology of Despair
       ISBN 978-3-89821-567-1

11   Annie Gagiano
Dealing with Evils
Essays on Writing from Africa
2nd, revised and expanded edition
ISBN 978-3-89821-867-2

12   Thomas F. Halloran
James Joyce: Developing Irish Identity
A Study of the Development of Postcolonial Irish Identity in the Novels of James Joyce
ISBN 978-3-89821-571-8

13   Pablo Armellino
Ob-scene Spaces in Australian Narrative
An Account of the Socio-topographic Construction of Space in Australian Literature
ISBN 978-3-89821-873-3

14   Lance Weldy
Seeking a Felicitous Space on the Frontier
The Progression of the Modern American Woman in O. E. Rölvaag, Laura Ingalls Wilder, and Willa Cather
ISBN 978-3-89821-535-0

15   Rana Tekcan
Too Far For Comfort
A Study on Biographical Distance
2nd, revised and expanded edition
ISBN 978-3-89821-995-2

16   Paola Brusasco
Writing Within/Without/About Sri Lanka
Discourses of Cartography, History and Translation in Selected Works by Michael Ondaatje and Carl Muller
ISBN 978-3-8382-0075-0

17   Zeynep Z. Atayurt
Excess and Embodiment in Contemporary Women's Writing
ISBN 978-3-89821-978-5

18   Gianluca Delfino
Time, History, and Philosophy in the Works of Wilson Harris
2nd, revised and expanded edition
ISBN 978-3-8382-0265-5

19   Taner Can
Magical Realism in Postcolonial British Fiction: History, Nation, and Narration
ISBN 978-3-8382-0724-7

20   Maria Festa
History and Race in Caryl Phillips's *The Nature of Blood*
ISBN 978-3-8382-1433-7

21   Naghmeh Varghaiyan
The Rhetoric of Women's Humour in Barbara Pym's Fiction
ISBN 978-3-8382-1503-7

***ibidem**.eu*